THE SMART KITCHEN

How to Create a Comfortable, Safe, Energy-Efficient, and Environment-Friendly Workspace

David Goldbeck

Line Drawings by Merle Cosgrove

Ceres Press
Woodstock, New York

Published by Ceres Press
          PO Box 87, Dept. SK-B
          Woodstock, New York 12498

Cover illustrations: Sherlie DeLong (top left), Julius Blackwelder
(top right), Joseph Bracchita (bottom left), Nicholas J. Geragi, Jr., (bottom right)
Book illustrations: Merle Cosgrove and Gilles Malkine

Printing 10 9 8 7 6 5 4 3 2 1
Second Edition

Library of Congress Catalog Card Number: 85-71838
Goldbeck, David
ISBN: 0-9606138-7-0

DISCLAIMER
   All the designs and recommendations in this book are intended
to be installed or approved by reputable designers, builders, fabri-
cators, or service personnel who warrant their products and work,
which should be done in accordance with building codes. Neither
Ceres Press nor David Goldbeck is responsible for any damages,
losses or injuries incurred as a result of any of the material contained in this book.

Library of Congress Cataloging-in-Publication Data
Goldbeck, David
          The Smart Kitchen - 2nd ed. Ceres Press, 1994, 1989
          144 p. : ill.
     ISBN 0-9606138-7-0 : $15.95 Paper
     1. HOME ECONOMICS-HOUSE AND HOME. 2. KITCHENS.
     I. Cosgrove, Merle, illustrator. II. Title.

Other books by David Goldbeck
(with Nikki Goldbeck):
     The Goldbeck's Guide to Good Food
     American Wholefoods Cuisine
     The Dieter's Companion
     The Good Breakfast Book
     The Supermarket Handbook

Printed on recycled paper.

Printed in Canada

For Nikki

ABOUT THIS BOOK

The Smart Kitchen was written with many different audiences in mind. Primarily it is directed to those who are creating a kitchen or improving an existing one. It contains ideas and information that will be helpful to owners, renters, remodelers, and builders. Additionally, professional designers and decorators, as well as anyone involved with energy, safety, the environment, or those with special physical needs, will find points of interest.

Though some concepts in *The Smart Kitchen* may be expensive to fulfill, others may cost nothing at all. Some will even pay for themselves.

In the introduction I describe the rationale and history of the *Demonstration Kitchen*, which was the genesis of this book. Parts I, II and III are its essence, providing the information needed to improve, design, and build a smart kitchen. Many chapters end with a

section entitled "Environmental Choices," encompassing recommendations for people with product sensitivities or allergies, and for those wishing to create an environmentally friendly space. Part IV, on planning, brings all the material together and includes such aids as templates and graph paper. This part also contains a table of "Smart Kitchen Maintenance" to help keep the workplace safe and sound.

"Selected Resources," at the back of the book, is a compendium of products, publications, and organizations in the U.S., Canada, and England mentioned in the text or otherwise of interest. This is followed by an extensive bibliography for those who wish to do additional research.

Where the pronoun *we* appears, it refers to myself (the author) and Nikki Goldbeck, my wife and collaborator on the design project.

ACKNOWLEDGEMENTS

The Smart Kitchen and the Demonstration Kitchen Project could not have been completed without the assistance and support of many talented, generous, and wonderful people. To begin with, there is Nikki Goldbeck, my wife, collaborator, and chief inspiration. In addition, there are many others whose names and contributions should be recorded: Stephen Robin, master builder, who turned all our ideas into beautiful, functional realities; architect Jeffrey Milstein; designer Alan Dubinsky; electrical expert Eldad Benary; and designer Larry Garrick—all of whom added important advice and expertise. Experts, strangers all, who provided me with invaluable technical advice include: Richard Karg, ventilation expert; Bruce Small, engineer and environmental expert; Dr. Thad Godish, air quality expert, Ball State University; Howard Geller, John Morrill and Peter Miller, American Council for an Energy-Efficient Economy; Brian Lowey, acoustics expert; Dr. Arthur Rosenfeld, Director, Center for Building Science, Lawrence Berkeley Laboratory; Dr. Richard Sextro, air quality expert, Lawrence Berkeley Laboratory; Peter duPont, co-founder of *Home Energy*; B. Leslie Hart, editor and publisher *Kitchen & Bath Business*; Nicholas Geragi, C.K.D.; and Dr. Louis G. Porter, engineering research psychologist.

I wish to thank those who worked on the manuscript of *The Smart Kitchen*: Nikki Goldbeck; Adrienne Becker; Rebecca Daniels; Daniel (Tamil) Bauch, engineer, inventor, and technical editor; Allan Edmands, editor; Alan McKnight, art director; Merle Cosgrove, illustrator; and Judy Fishetti, research librarian. A special thanks to the Kaypro Corporation for supporting the Demonstration Kitchen project by providing the computer that much of the project's work (including this book) was done on.

Those who built the kitchen are listed below, but I cannot give enough praise to Stephen Robin, who contributed his considerable expertise as a builder, designer, and mechanic and without whom the Demonstration Kitchen project would not have been possible. In addition, the fine carpenters: Greg Bennett, Mike Alewood, Samvid (David Glick), Ron Hahn, Colin Waterous, Stewart Austin, Dick Morrill, Paul Henderson, Peter Gundell, and Paul Petrov. Thanks also to Bruce and Justin Tuchman for their voluntary assistance.

All of the electrical work was done by Charlie Lombardo, the plumbing by George Lombardo, Russ Ouwerkerk and Bob McNally, of Heckeroth Plumbing. Structural steel was provided by Bernie McCabe, Kevin McCabe, Tom Rice, and Wayne MacDonald, of Universal AKT Industries. Decorative stainless steel work from Ken St. John, tiling by Dan Nelson, painting by Deborah Bell, neon by Ray Lang, and the etched glass panels by Gene Mallard.

A special mention is due David Rodale, whose interest spurred the early participation of Rodale Press and helped guarantee the success of the Demonstration Kitchen project. His untimely death was a personal sorrow as well as the loss of a wonderful human being who was making a difference.

David Goldbeck
Woodstock, NY

CONTENTS

INTRODUCTION

It's time to take a fresh look at how our kitchens are designed and equipped.

Kitchens are not friendly enough. Although they are often interestingly designed and beautifully decorated, this design and decor too frequently is without regard to comfort and practicality. Hard floors, fixed counter heights, inadequate ventilation, bumped heads from cabinet doors, and annoying noise levels are enough to drive even the most dedicated cook from this workspace.

Kitchens should be designed with regard to people's differing physical capabilities and needs. The diverse ages, heights, strengths, and mobility of current users, as well as future cooks, should be considered in order to provide "universal access."

Likewise, appliances and fixtures could be more sympathetic to culinary tasks. The microwave oven, the newest and fastest-growing addition to the modern kitchen, needs to be looked at more carefully, in terms of both safety and cuisine. Sinks with no forgiveness to dropped dishes, ineffective air quality equipment, inaccessible storage, and unresponsive cooktops are other examples of standard features that are no friend of the cook.

Kitchens are not safe enough. In fact, they are the most dangerous room in the house. Dennis Smith, author of the *Fire Safety Book*, says that more fires start in the kitchen than in any room other than the living room, and 16 percent of all fatal fires start there. According to a 1983 study by the American Association of Poison Control Centers, 64 percent of all poison victims are children under six years of age, and more than two thirds of all poisonings are from nondrug substances, such as kitchen supplies. The extent to which electric shocks occur in the kitchen and elsewhere has prompted the Association of Home Appliance Manufacturers and the Underwriters Laboratory to take action in the form of public education campaigns.

Kitchens are also the source of a substantial amount of wasted energy. Largely because of poorly designed appliances, particularly refrigerators, kitchens in the United States, according to the American Association for an Energy Efficient Economy, utilize a whopping 20–25 percent of household energy. This massive waste of resources is directly responsible for the costly construction of otherwise unnecessary power plants, and it is indirectly responsible for poor air quality, global warming, and other environmental problems. Although the U.S. government has mandated major appliance efficiency standards, these only eliminate the worst offenders. Truly effective action is left in the hands of consumers and builders; the public can have an enormous impact by shopping for energy efficiency.

Ironically, kitchens are often unhealthy spaces. Cooking gases are known to create a form of air pollution that can sicken members of the household, but this is often not attended to. Even the materials used in kitchen construction can cause adverse health reactions.

Proper lighting may nurture the health of the occupants by adding to their exposure of natural light as well as decreasing accidents in the kitchen and saving energy.

Kitchens are not involved enough with food itself: More food production could easily be integrated into their design. Baking, canning, seed sprouting, and food dehydrating and the like are all easier when the kitchen is set up to accommodate these activities.

There must also be a more active concern for the recycling of kitchen-generated wastes to conserve resources and cut down on the accumulation of solid waste. As with food production, recycling and the composting of food wastes can be facilitated by attention being paid to these needs in kitchen design.

It was these concerns and more that inspired the Demonstration Kitchen, which was built in 1984. Having observed the contemporary cooking scene for more than a decade, I was interested to see not only whether some of the negative factors I saw could be removed, but also whether more effective kitchen design could be developed.

The plan for the Demonstration Kitchen was this: Examine the commonly used materials, appliances, and design standards to see where genuine improvements could be made to make the kitchen more "user-friendly," and then build the kitchen. This book is an outgrowth of that project.

My goal has been (and still is) to stimulate new thought and design in this area. So you can imagine my surprise when I learned that I was, to some extent, following in the footsteps of a movement that had begun in the 1920s in Frankfurt, Germany, my ancestral home. Indeed, the Bauhaus movement that had its roots there was one of the unusual and diverse forces that shaped kitchens as we know them today. Other notable influences, in addition to the kitchen industry itself, include the work of Catherine Beecher (sister of Harriet Beecher Stowe), who revolutionized kitchen design in the 1870s; Cornell University, Purdue University, the University of Illinois, and Lillian Gilbreth, all responsible for basic research in kitchen standards; and the inspirations of Frank Lloyd Wright.

Up until Catherine Beecher's time the kitchen in North America was usually a dark room at the back of the house with a table and dresser for worktop, sink, hand pump, and wood stove. Not exactly a congenial place. But as the number of domestic servants in the home decreased, the kitchen became more humane and the work sequence organized in accordance with some of Beecher's ideas. By the mid-1930s streamlined kitchens appeared, again as a result of Catherine Beecher's earlier concepts. By the 1940s kitchens were being sold in sets. This was made possible by an agreement in 1945 among the twenty-five leading gas appliance makers and eight cabinet manufacturers to standardize kitchen fixtures: Counters were to be 25½ inches deep to accommodate appliances and 36 inches high for "women" of "average" stature.

There have been trends in kitchen design since the 1940s, but mostly superficial; the white kitchens of the 1950s did become the colorful kitchens of the 60s and 70s. (Too often the big question in the kitchen industry is what color will be the next rage.) Where there have been improvements in contemporary kitchens, they have been mostly in the area of small appliances. The blender, food processor, convection oven, and toaster/oven are examples of appliances that more than pay for themselves by simplifying the preparation of fresh foods without a loss of quality (contrary to microwav-

ing). The only comparable innovation in major appliances are stove-top grills.

My interest in kitchen design has another motive: I'm concerned about the direction our eating habits are going and what this means in terms of personal and global health. I believe that one of the reasons for the declining interest in cooking is that our kitchens have not kept up with changes in life-style. This is one of the reasons for the success of the microwave oven: At least they reflect, for better or for worse, that people are beginning to view the preparation of food in a different light. If real cooking is to survive, kitchen design and appliances must be improved. Unless we adapt this workspace to contemporary needs, we will abdicate to mass producers one of the true pleasures of life and one of our most important sources of health: fresh food. We will be condemned to a "boil 'n bag" and "slit 'n serve" future.

I have spent the last seventeen years writing and lecturing in the area of food and nutrition with Nikki Goldbeck. As I see it, our contribution has been to help remove some of the impediments that keep people from eating well in today's world. *The Smart Kitchen* is another extension of this work. The kitchen can be friend or foe to the cook; an inhospitable workspace, like poor ingredients and badly tested cookbooks, is just another stumbling block.

I was very pleased to see one kitchen cabinet manufacturer refer, not so long ago, to "nutrition centers." This purpose is often forgotten by those in the kitchen industry who, whether they realize it or not, play a vital role in our health and well-being. The industry must seize the opportunity now to develop new designs, fixtures, and appliances that make the kitchen an inviting playground. Unless we build convenience into our kitchens, rather than buying it from the food processing industry, kitchens, and all the joy that they bring, may one day be lost.

DO YOU HAVE A SMART KITCHEN OR AN IDEA FOR ONE?

If you are aware of a kitchen that has "smart" features, let us know. We're interested in any workable ideas or products that relate to safety, energy efficiency, comfort, product sensitivities, environmental issues, or productivity. Drawings, photos, samples are all welcome. Send to SMART KITCHEN IDEAS, Ceres Press, PO Box 87, Woodstock, NY 12498.

Part I
HUMAN COMFORT AND SAFETY

Human comfort has always been an essential part of kitchen design. Most of what is done in this regard, though, seems somewhat narrow, generally focusing on saving steps and keeping things in easy reach, and softening corners for safety— important considerations but not the only ones. Not nearly enough attention is paid to ergonomics, or "human engineering"—that is, organizing the design of the physical working conditions in regard to the capacities and needs of the worker. Safety, air quality, thermal comfort, and acoustics are related to comfort, yet they do not receive enough attention from builders and designers.

In consideration of the cook's physical well-being, this part explores kitchen counters, cabinets, lighting, acoustics, floor material, as well as the opportunity to sit while working. The presence of high heat and fire, electricity, sharp implements, powerful appliances, and toxic cleaning substances bring together elements that make the kitchen the most dangerous room in the house. These concerns as well as new ones about the dangers of certain building materials often used in kitchen construction will be dealt with here too.

The part concludes with a short chapter on personal computers and other electric kitchen aids. PCs have the capacity to bring a new level of comfort and health by easing menu planning, providing recipe analysis, and even giving nutritional advice.

Chapter 1:
KITCHEN COUNTERS

COUNTER HEIGHT

The standardization of counter heights, first done in the 1940s, though it helped the marketability of kitchen sets, is actually one of the most vexing problems in the kitchen. On the one hand, it is quite evident that the flow of activity is made easier when appliances and countertops are all on the same level. On the other hand, this uniformity underlies the discomforts of many people who are not of "standard height." It also ignores the fact that certain tasks are better done at a lower elevation, or what is often referred to as "top-of-the-thigh height." According to Cornell University's publication *Functional Kitchens*, such tasks as shelling peas, mixing, beating, chopping, kneading bread, and rolling pie crust are better done at about 6 to 7 inches *below* standard counter height. Studies also suggest that sinks should be 2 inches higher than comfortable counter height in order to minimize uncomfortable bending. Additionally, standard counters put stress on children and the physically disadvantaged.

You can determine *your* ideal counter height by measuring the distance of your bent elbow from the floor. The usual standardization, however, allows only for the ideal height of the "average" cook. The *average* bent-elbow height for a woman is 35 inches, for a man 39 inches. Thus, the universal compromise of 36-inch high countertops, skewed toward the average woman. (For standard kitchen dimensions, see Part IV.) Many thoughtful designers have noted the problem of standardization. *The Cornell Kitchen* (1952) listed a number of "important guides to better kitchen design" that "home management specialists" have developed. For example, "counters should be made so that they are adjustable to the different heights of the *women* who use them" (emphasis mine). This standardization problem was addressed once again as recently as 1985 in the trade magazine *Kitchen and Bath* by an expert who saw the need for different counter heights "to accommodate the taller *male* cook in the family" (emphasis mine). Times certainly have changed, but the need hasn't. According to the experts at Cornell, "even 5 minutes holding poor posture is uncomfortable."

Of course, future problems may be created when an untypically tall or short person has kitchen counters custom-built to his or her height. And who can blame such cooks for making themselves comfortable? No one but the next user.

In Europe, kitchen cabinets and counters, often considered furniture rather than a standard feature to be passed on to the next inhabitant, are removable; they typically can be hung at any height. This system is not utilized in the United States, although the 1952 Cornell Kitchen featured cabinets that not only could be hung at different heights but could be moved and even made freestanding (that is, hung from their own stands). These base cabinets could be adjusted from 32 to 38 inches. Unfortunately, no detailed plans are available, but this is what they looked like:

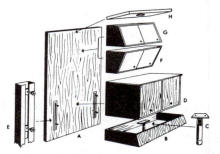

YOU CAN TAKE THIS KITCHEN WITH YOU! Plywood panels (A) are free-standing, as movable as furniture. Work surfaces are adjustable: Cabinet base (B) attaches to panel; cabinet (D) is joined to panel with sliding steel supports (E), rests on leg (C) that can be raised or lowered with wrench. Slanted cupboards (F and G) have narrow shelves at top and bottom; and valance (H) contains lighting for unit.

ADJUSTABLE WALL CABINET FROM THE CORNELL KITCHEN (1952)

More Than One Counter Height

Any sensitively designed kitchen built today should have counters at varying heights. Every kitchen should have a desk-height counter and if possible two other counter heights for standing workers. Those heights are dependent on whether the kitchen is being designed to accommodate two cooks or one. (Extremes should be avoided, though, which may make the kitchen troublesome to future users.)

With multilevel counters, if you need to butt a counter into a corner, make sure it's the higher one, or you will end up with an unreachable space. Also, the higher counter should contain the sink, since sinks with a bottom surface 2 inches higher than usual are easier on the back. (See also the section "Sink Seating" in Chapter 3.)

An Adjustable Counter

For the Demonstration Kitchen I was interested in designing a new counter that would provide flexibility—a counter capable of being raised and lowered at any time to provide infinite "universal access." The adjustable counter that we eventually built is 25 inches long and can be raised or lowered electronically at the push of a button. This is obviously an unusual approach, done for experimental purposes, but it's actually not that difficult to copy or adapt. (Cabinetmakers who make built-in bars and TV sets that can be raised and lowered will understand the mechanism.)

The counter moves up and down on bearings that ride on rails. The drive mechanism is a small actuator. (Actuators are the same small motors that we are accustomed to seeing on hospital beds, dental chairs, and so on.) Although the actuator sold for about $225 in 1984, and the price of the four bearings (called *pillow blocks*) and two rails was about $300, the money was well spent. (For a less expensive source of actuators, consult surplus catalogs. One catalog I examined at the time listed one for $50. See "Selected Resources".)

The counter was installed where there are no below-the-counter cabinets, making it possible to operate it without interfering with anything underneath. It is positioned over the garbage/recycling area; by moving the garbage can, opening the bifold doors, and lowering the counter, you create a desk/countertop surface where you can sit down and work. This option is especially useful for people in wheelchairs, the elderly, and those of large or small stature.

Even a sink can be built into the adjustable counter if you use flexible hoses instead of rigid pipes.

(By the way Nikki, at first skeptical about the practicality of the adjustable counter, loves to lower it for baking.)

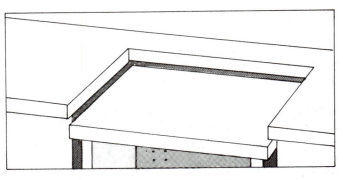

Adjustable Counter: Lowered Position

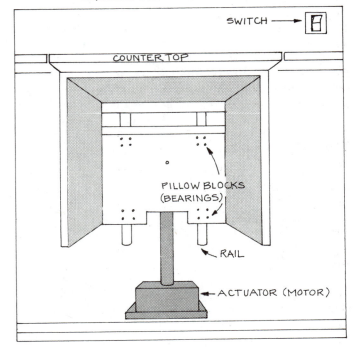

Adjustable Counter: Front View

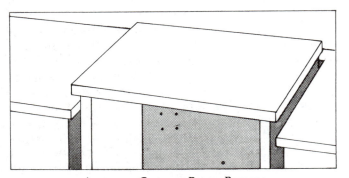

Adjustable Counter: Raised Position

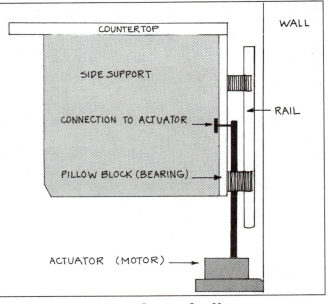

Adjustable Counter: Side View

Although I highly recommend industrial bearings and shafts, there are other ways to get similar stability and movement. Rods or pipes within pipes that are lubricated might do the job. An automotive scissors jack could serve as a drive mechanism.

You can make much longer sections of counter adjustable than I did, but you must always expect to lose at least the top drawer space.

Hydraulic lift tables, which are complete working adjustable tables on wheels, may be the simplest approach of all. I have seen them only in industrial catalogs, but apparently all you need to do is remove the wheels and build the table into the counter span. Or, even easier, use it as an island. (See "Selected Resources.")

It goes without saying that unusual equipment like this should always be built and designed with safety in mind, particularly childrens'. A key operated switch, for example, would limit inappropriate use.

The Skid

Generations of children have used the kitchen stool to elevate them so they could help in the kitchen or reach the cookie jar. The floor skid, a raised platform usually made of wood, is the least expensive way to similarly accommodate people for whom standard counter height is too great or to provide a lower work surface for specific tasks when needed. It's probably the only option for renters. The skid is typically seen in commercial kitchens, where it offers a safe surface to stand on and allows spilled food to fall between the slats to the floor beneath. In the residential kitchen a skid can be built into a lower cabinet kick so that it can easily be pulled out by hand or foot. (The kick is the indentation where the floor meets the base cabinet, which allows you to stand close to it without kicking it.) If this design is not possible, store the skid somewhere else, even vertically. Kitchen supply stores may be a source of skids, but they are easy to knock together yourself.

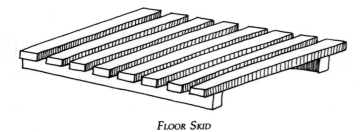

Floor Skid

The Countertop Skid

Taller people who are uncomfortable in the kitchen might want to consider a "countertop skid" to build up the height of a particular counter. The simplest approach is to stack cutting boards to a comfortable level.

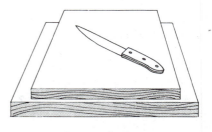

Countertop Skids

Counter Depth

The standard counter depth is 25 inches. This offers ample space at the rear of the counter for small appliances, such as the blender or food processor, canisters of foods you use frequently, or even recessed cubby holes (or "garages," as they are often called) between wall studs so that supplies or cooking utensils are out of the way yet in easy reach.

But you may wish to disregard this 25-inch standard for various reasons. For example, when kitchen space is at a premium, 18 or 19 inches will actually provide sufficient workspace and still house ample storage in the cabinets below. In the Demonstration Kitchen, on one 4-foot-long run, this narrower dimension made two adjacent counters more accessible. But you must make certain that your overhead cabinets allow for adequate headroom. Hang the cabinets at least 20 inches above the countertop and at least 30 inches above the sink. Or you can install narrower overhead cabinets or even open shelves. For the Demonstration Kitchen we created more space over this narrow counter by mounting an 11-inch-deep open shelf at normal cabinet height and installing more conventional overhead cabinets 30 inches above the counter.

You may also want a counter deeper than 25 inches. Designer and architect Richard Crowther suggests that the added storage gained from 30-inch deep counters is an effective way to minimize the need for and use of overhead cabinets. (Wall cabinets can then be hung lower and made shallower.)

A 36-inch-deep counter is ideal for bread making and pastry rolling; this is an option those fortunate to have ample kitchen space may want to consider. But since people with a short reach find outlets or items housed at the rear of such a counter inconvenient, you should not make all your counters 36 inches deep.

An island or peninsula (see the next section), where eating, homework, or chatting with the cook takes place, can also be deeper than the standard. And when two cooks work at opposite sides of the counter, you may want a depth of 42 inches.

The Peninsula/Island, or "Kitchen Magnet"

One design element that has been wisely emphasized in modern kitchens is the kitchen peninsula, or "bar." (A variation is the freestanding island.)

Extending perpendicularly from a wall or another counter, these counters provide additional workspace and, more important, are "kitchen magnets." Place a few stools on the less active side, and the cook will never lack company. (Add a 4-to-8 inch overhang here to provide leg room.) Of course, the counter is an ideal place to serve informal meals.

The peninsula or island can also bring two sides of a kitchen closer by helping to connect them. And they can slow down the traffic when there are many doors in the kitchen.

Selecting Countertop Material

There are many countertop materials you can use, but there is no perfect one. The least advantageous material, in my opinion, is ceramic tile. I am mystified by the popularity of countertop tiles among kitchen builders and home owners. Think about it: The kitchen counter is a workspace for wet, perishable materials. To construct a surface that has not only hundreds of cracks (grout lines), but cracks filled with a substance prone to stain and flake, seems almost perverse.

In many cases the grout lines are not minimal but are made ⅛ to ¼ inch wide as a detail. Usually, these lines are slightly recessed, creating avenues that require extra maintenance and that are subject to unattractive water, liquid, and food discoloration. Even after the best tiling job, grout has fissures that can wear away, especially around sinks. Food deposited in these crevices can create potentially unhealthy conditions. Of course, grout lines can be very thin and can even be sealed, but why not go for a smooth surface with as few interruptions as possible in the first place?

Kitchen work surfaces are often used for vigorous tasks. Using a cleaver on a tiled surface can have a disastrous outcome. I realize that most people do not work directly on countertops but on cutting boards, but even using a cutting board set on a tile countertop is undesirable. Damaging impact can be transmitted to the countertop. And a glass or dish accidentally dropped on this hard surface has little chance of surviving. "Anything but ceramic tile on countertops" is my motto (although I love them on walls).

Wood

Wood is a countertop material that is favored by many because it offers a solid surface, yet its resilience makes it comfortable to work on. Wood is a durable, inexpensive, attractive material that can be repaired, refinished, or resurfaced when needed. Since wood can easily be shaped, sharp edges and square counter corners can be softened to minimize bumps and

---

The Foot/Footstool

One of the universal problems in any kitchen, especially if you're under 5 feet 5 inches, is not being able to reach overhead items. In most cases it is solved with a commercial stepladder or footstool. In general, I have no argument with these products, provided they are stable. But I want to share with you a pleasant experience I've had with a homemade stool.

A number of years ago a friend gave Nikki and me a holiday gift, a consummate do-it-yourself project, which turned out to be one of the best tools we have had in the kitchen: a wooden footstool made of four pieces of pine held together by six screws. Its light weight and design make it easy to move with one foot and thus the name *foot/footstool*. We have found this is a great convenience in the kitchen; one always seems to have loaded hands when the stool is needed.

To keep the stool out of the way, yet always in reach, we built an open "nest" for it under one of the kitchen sinks. (See illustration, Part IV.) You simply have to extend your foot into the opening,

hook it onto the small strips of wood on the underside of the stool (the toe catch), and slide it out. The addition of nylon glides make for effortless, scratch-free movement.

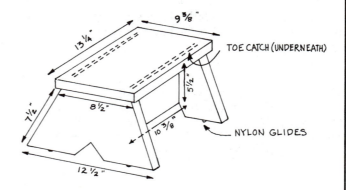

Foot/Footstool.

Four pieces of wood make a simple multi-use tool. Sit on it, stand on it, or use it like a bar rail. Move it around with your foot for hand-free use. Another stool that works as well is the kind usually seen in libraries. It rolls but will not move once it's stepped on.

bruises. The most appropriate woods are such hardwoods as maple, oak, and cherry. Tight-grained maple has long been considered the best because it absorbs less food substances than does other wood.

Hardwood countertops are made of boards, planks, or strips glued together. When the strips are narrow, it's called butcher block. Many lumberyards carry factory-made butcher block, as well as premade wood countertops. Oak flooring, although somewhat open-grained, is also sometimes used for countertops because it is inexpensive and joins tightly with a tongue and groove. But countertops of any hardwood can be made by a woodworker with a jointer and planer. In the Demonstration Kitchen I chose oak planks for one counter, since they were readily available and gave an interesting pastry-board look.

Unless you buy a prefinished countertop, the wood must be treated to make it less absorbent and to reduce staining. There are a number of different ways to finish or seal wood, ranging from such hard finishes such as polyurethane to penetrating oils. Since hard plastic urethane-type finishes contain substances that are toxic when ingested, they seem inappropriate for a food preparation area, where surface scratching is inevitable. Thus I prefer an oil finish that can be renewed as it wears. Mineral oil is traditionally used to seal wood counters, but it tends to "gunk up" or rise to the surface again later. Though linseed oil is another popular wood finish, the toxicity of the refined finishing variety disqualifies it for a food surface. Many people mistakenly choose food-grade oils, but they are subject to rancidity.

One good choice is FDA-approved tung oil, a natural oil from the tung tree that is easy to apply, is practically odorless, and—when rubbed sparingly in several layers—leaves a silklike finish with no residue. Of particular interest is the Livos Company's complete line of wood finishes made without toxic chemicals.

Oil finishes are not, however, impervious, especially when new. Any iron object—such as a carbon steel knife, cast iron pot, or metal can—left wet on the counter even for a few minutes may leave a mark. Beet and grape juices, wine, and curry seasonings can stain, too. But reoiling can build up quite a protective coating. One expert recommends scrubbing the counter periodically with scouring powder (I prefer coarse salt) and reoiling. Severe stains can be removed by using fine sandpaper or steel wool first.

One reason I like wood is that as it ages, darkens, and shows some wear and damage, it becomes a work surface with "character," which you can use with impunity. On the other hand, wood countertops tend to discolor unattractively around sinks due to water accumulation. Thus, you might wish to use a more impervious material around the sink, such as plastic or stainless steel (never tile).

Plastic Laminates

Plastic laminates are usually referred to as Formica™, although this is only the trade name for one particular brand among many. Plastic laminate comes in many different colors and is a very popular countertop and cabinet surfacing material. It can provide an almost seamless surface, it is easy to wipe clean, and it is somewhat heat resistant. Laminates have a reputation for scratching quite easily, though, and they show wear rather early, which keeps it from being the material of choice for countertops. On the other hand, it is excellent for cabinet fronts, doors, drawers, and so on, since it is a very durable material on vertical planes.

Newer laminates, such as Solicore™ and Colorcore™ are colored throughout, unlike previous laminates, which are just colored on the surface. This should mean that scratches do not show as much, making them a more attractive countertop material.

Stainless Steel

Stainless steel has the advantages of being totally heat resistant, seamless, and hygienic. It is expensive, though; it tends to be noisy unless it's well backed, and it cannot be cut on directly. Backing with hardwood will minimize dents and help absorb sound. It is excellent around sinks, as drainboards, and on surfaces next to the stove for setting hot pots. Only high-quality stainless steel should be used, at least 22 gauge if unsupported.

Water, oil, and food show up readily on stainless steel and though it can be cleaned immaculately, unless it is dried immediately, it will spot. It can also be scratched if not treated properly, so it is best to use a cleaner made expressly for stainless steel. A wonderful biodegradable soap, Murphy's Oil Soap™, which

---

PROTECTING AGAINST FOOD POISONING

The U.S. Department of Agriculture estimated in 1977 that half of American families commit at least one major mistake in food handling. Cross-contamination, whereby microorganisms in raw animal products come in contact with vegetables or other foods that are eaten raw or lightly cooked, is the most common error. It is the most common cause of food poisoning at this time. Therefore, you should always reserve a separate, movable surface for cutting raw meat, fish, and poultry. Not only the preparation site but all utensils and hands that have made contact with the uncooked flesh should be washed in hot soapy (preferably lightly chlorinated) water before other foods come in contact with them.

seems to clean just about anything, also does a good job on stainless steel. Steel wool should never be used unless it is *stainless* steel wool. After cleansing, you might want to cover the counter with a very thin film of oil to protect it.

Stainless steel develops a patina from daily use, scratching, and age.

Solid Plastic Countertop Materials

At one time there was only one solid plastic countertop material: Corian™, made by du Pont. Today there are a number of manufacturers of similar acrylic products as well as newer polyester resins such as Avonite.™ They are considered by many to be the ultimate in countertops. They are expensive, but the price may be offset by the fact that they are rich-looking, sanitary, durable, and highly heat resistant—although most cannot, according to the manufacturers, be used as a hot plate. Note that the acrylics have some restrictions in their use such as humid environments but are available in more colors.

Another advantage is that although some acrylics, such as Corian™, can scratch, the scratches can be removed with fine sandpaper. Since the surface is nonporous, blood, coffee, curry, and even grape juice will not stain. Hygiene can be maintained with any conventional scouring powder. The Demonstration Kitchen contains two sinks and gets a lot of use, so I decided to invest in this material to see if it would live up to its reputation. It has.

A new entry in the area, Tuff Top™, is said by its manufacturer to be more heat and scratch resistant than other solid plastic countertop materials.

Note that although these products can generally be worked like wood—that is, corners rounded, routed, and so forth—it requires a professional installation, especially if a sink is to be inserted. Because it is extremely heavy and brittle, lack of attention during installation can cost hundreds of dollars. If you intend to do any cutting or routing of the Corian™, a good mask and ventilation are essential.

Marble

This stone, which has a reputation for being cool to the touch, is excellent for pastry, and every serious baker should have one marble work surface for this purpose. Its second great asset is that it is very heat resistant. Unfortunately, it is also porous, and grape juice, wine, and so on will stain readily. Soap will cause dulling. Two coats of sealer should be applied initially, and it should be resealed regularly. This is why even those who can afford marble shy away from its extensive use. One marbleman strongly suggested to me that only light-colored marble be used because it will not hide unsanitary food deposits.

Slate

Slate is a countertop material that does not get much attention. It is a hard-wearing, nonporous stone that can be cut to any specifications, including cutouts for the sink. It is available fairly smooth (honed) or more natural (natural cleft) and should be maintenance-free. It comes in grays, greens, purple, black, and red. Slate is considerably less expensive than marble. Check local tile and stone dealers or those in the resource directory of this book.

Granite

Granite is reputed to be an impervious material, but it's expensive. You probably wouldn't want to do a whole kitchen in granite, but you might want to use it in a baking area. One magazine suggested tombstone makers as a source of bargains for odds and ends of granite.

Inserts

An inexpensive way to have varied workspaces is with countertop inserts. Instead of constructing an entire counter of expensive material, you can inset a small piece. Marble, stainless steel, and heat-resistant glass ceramic boards (especially made for this purpose) are the most common inserts. Often the insert is placed near the stove for an extra heat-resistant surface. Cool, smooth inserts can also be used for baking.

REPRESENTATIVE COUNTERTOP COSTS (APPROXIMATE)	
Butcher block	$18–24 per running foot
Plastic laminates	$22–28 per running foot
Stainless steel	Call fabricator for estimate
Solid plastic (acrylic)	$85–125* per running foot
Solid plastic (polyester)	$125–175* per running foot
Marble (solid)	$150–200 per running foot
Granite (solid)	$150–200 per running foot
Marble (composite)	$15–30 per running foot

*Dependent on edge treatment.

ENVIRONMENTAL CHOICES

Stone, stainless steel, and solid plastic are the best choices for counters. Plastic laminates can be used, but make sure the glue does not contain formaldehyde and the best underlayment is used and properly sealed if necessary (see "Environmental Choices" in Chapter 2). Unsealed wood is inappropriate for counters; use a nontoxic sealer. Note that wood may allow mold growth, which may bother those who are mold sensitive.

Chapter 2:
CABINETS

The advertisement in the kitchen trade magazine read: "What to Look for in a Cabinet." The illustration below it was of a cupboard filled with money! Kitchen cabinets are an excellent source of income to the kitchen industry and a major expense when building. Since cabinets can cost a lot of money, up to hundreds of dollars a running foot, it is incumbent upon consumers to know something about them.

TYPES OF CABINETS AND BUYING TIPS

Stock cabinets are preassembled units that are produced in certain standardized configurations and motifs. The drawback to buying stock cabinets is that they come in a limited number of colors and styles and there is no opportunity to vary the basic module. One advantage is quick delivery. They come in lengths from 12-inches to 48-inches, in 3-inch increments.

Special-order cabinets are also factory-made, but to the buyer's specifications. Special-order cabinets offer a wide range in styles and other design options; delivery time is six weeks or more.

Custom-made cabinets built to your specifications by a cabinetmaker are costly, but they offer maximum flexibility.

One money-saving strategy is to buy as many stock or special-order cabinets as possible for your project and have custom cabinets fill in where you need something unique. A good cabinetmaker should be able to make them all match.

To save on cabinetry, buyers should know what they want. This may sound obvious, but part of what you pay a cabinetmaker or cabinet salesperson for is their time. So if you have stock or special-order cabinets "specked out" to exact model numbers, or if you have workable plans for a cabinetmaker, you can save 15 to 20 percent or more.

Also if you are aware of standard cabinet sizes in the planning stage, you may be able to incorporate more stock items. Some layouts may also be considerably cheaper simply because of how companies price their cabinets.

Learning how cabinet costs are estimated can save you money. There can, for example, be "hidden" add-ons. Prices are usually based on the running foot, but how about an island or peninsula? Is the figure based only on the length, or is it doubled when the unit is deeper than normal and therefore considered two counters back to back? How much extra will you pay for three or four finished sides?

How are measurements made? If the outside—that is, the wall side—of cabinets is being measured, you may be paying twice for corners. The answers can be worth hundreds of dollars. One solution is to compare complete prices not price per foot.

Installation and service are often overlooked when cabinets are purchased. You may be buying the cabinets of your dreams, but they must also be level and plumb and properly secured. Improper installation will show up, particularly in how well doors and drawers work over time. If there is a problem, will the company make good? Referrals are always your most reliable source of information about competence and reliability.

Refacing

One of the least expensive ways to save on cabinets is to reuse old ones. There are many companies that will rejuvenate old cabinets by resurfacing old doors and drawer fronts or replacing the old ones. In the Demonstration Kitchen we put new fronts on some cabinets as well as building new ones. The savings were considerable.

CONSTRUCTION

Many people are not aware that there are many different grades of cabinet construction. This section will help demystify cabinets so that you can get what you want at the best price.

Think of a cabinet as no more than a box with doors or drawers. As such, one can see that the box itself is aesthetically not very important, but it does provide the foundation for the cabinet so it must be structurally sound. Doors and drawer fronts, on the other hand, must be not only durable but attractive as well.

The Cabinet Box

Cabinet boxes can be made from numerous materials, including hardwood, plywood, fiberboard, particleboard, and metal. Although hardwood is desirable in other construction, here it is expensive and may present problems; it can shrink and warp over long expanses. That is why plywood or some other processed wood product is commonly employed. Plywood is a very sturdy material, but it and lesser-quality fiberboard or particleboard, used in cabinet construction (as well as paneling, and hardwood veneer) are "materials in crisis" because of their unfortunate health aspects. (See "Environmental Choices" at the end of the chapter.)

Face-frame cabinets, the most traditional types of construction, are considered the strongest. These cabinets, as their name describes, are built with a 1-inch frame around the front edges. The disadvantage is evident: The frame interferes somewhat with access.

Frameless, or European-style, cabinets are increasingly popular. These cabinets have a modern look about them, and they do not have that annoying frame barrier. For strength, however, frameless cabinets should ideally be built out of a little thicker material than their face-framed counterparts.

How the cabinet is joined also determines its strength. The joints—that is, where the horizontal and vertical come together—must be strong. The whole box should look and feel stable. The best joints are dadoed (one piece set into the adjoining piece). Also, joints that are supported by blocks are stronger than those that are not. Screw joints are classic, but staples are fine as long as the surfaces they connect are glued as well. Alignment is another good test of quality construction. Are the corners square? How well do drawers and doors work?

Narrow cabinets are stronger, but broader ones are less expensive (fewer sides, and so on). Proper material thickness varies with the length of the unsupported span and the amount of load the span needs to hold. With that in mind, note these minimum dimensions:

Face-frame: Box, ½ inch; backing, ¼ inch. Much thicker dimensions may not add much strength if made well. Also suitable for upper cabinets if "hanging strip" used.

Frameless: Box, ½–¾ inch; backing, ½ inch. Minimum also for upper cabinet.

Minimum Thickness of Cabinet Shelves (in Inches)	
Length of Span	Thickness (in Inches)
10–25	½
26–35	⅝
36–47	¾
48–71	1

Note: These figures apply for normal loads of dishes and utensils.

Doors

Doors can be made of solid wood, wood covered with laminate, or -in the case of metal cabinets—metal. Many doors are made like picture frames with a panel insert. The panel may be made from any of the above materials or any decorative material including plastic and glass. It is most important that doors and drawer fronts be made of resilient material and that their finish is washable.

Wood

Wood is a near-perfect material, particularly for doors. It is durable, rich-looking, easy to care for and repair, and easy to shape. It also provides some sound-deadening qualities. Warping is a real possibility but can be minimized if your cabinetmaker uses well dried wood and takes extra care in construction, and if you control the ambient humidity in your kitchen. Hardwood is more durable, softwood less expensive.

Suitable finishes generally include paint, plastic laminate, varnish, urethane, and other moisture-resisting wood finishes. I mistakenly chose lacquer for the Demonstration Kitchen. Lacquer is often recommended for its attractive surface. I discovered too late, however, that lacquer chips. (Fortunately, it does touch up easily.) Varnishes and paints are less expensive and more durable.

Be certain that your cabinetmaker is not using "poisonous" paint, such as automotive lacquer. These paints contain lead and are prohibited for residential application, yet one cabinetmaker I spoke to used them, since they chip less.

Plastic laminate is easy to clean, and durable, but it can chip, scratch, or stain, and it is hard to repair. There are many different qualities of laminates, so choose carefully.

Paint, varnish, and laminates are my choices for cabinet doors and drawers fronts.

Glass

Glass is often used in overhead cabinet doors inside a wood frame. The decorative effect of glass attracts many to it. However, if you are not a tidy housekeeper, the fact that you can see through it may make it an eyesore, not an attraction. Frosting minimizes the view.

Glass requires careful cleaning, and if you are the type of person who likes to slam doors, select another material.

Plastic

While not common as a panel insert, plastic can give a similar effect to glass and is more resistant to handling. A colored plastic can mask disorder within.

METAL

Metal is highly durable, but depending on quality, it may dent or scratch. Painted metal can also chip and possibly rust. It is hard to modify metal cabinets, put up hangers inside, and so on.

Hardware

Quality of the hardware is worth the price, particularly for drawer slides and hinges. Inexpensively made drawers ride directly on wood or plastic guides, whereas good ones slide on double metal tracking with nylon and ball-bearing rollers. Full-extension slides provide about 6 inches more drawer access. "European hinges" have a lot going for them: They are self-closing and easily adjustable. Plastic clips instead of metal hardware are a sign of intermediate or moderate quality. Avoid handles with sharp edges and dangerous protrusions. If childproofing is a consideration, look for handles that might easily be barred or locked. (See also Chapter 8.)

Shelves

Shelves must be easy to clean. Many shelves today are available with a plastic laminate finish, which is highly desirable. If the shelf material is not washable, you should cover it with a laminated, washable contact paper.

Shelves should be well made, thick, removable, and adjustable. Long spans should be supported in the middle to prevent sagging. For overhead shelving, consider clear plastic.

I used plastic (plexiglass) in the Demonstration Kitchen, since the ability to see through shelving makes it so much easier to locate items, particularly on higher shelves. Plastic thick enough to span spaces without mid support is very expensive. However, you could use even ¼-inch plastic (as indicated below), if you plan ahead, and include four-sided bracing (that is, bracing consisting of the three sides of the cabinet plus a support across the front of the shelf).

The following table indicates the proper plexiglass thickness needed depending on the span, type of construction, and weight it is intended to support.

PLEXIGLASS SHELVES: THICKNESS REQUIREMENTS (IN INCHES)								
Self Size		Required Plexiglass Thickness Load per ft. of shelf width					Dead Load Deflection*	
Width	Maximum Depth	35 lb.	25 lb.	15 lb.	10 lb.	5 lb	Short Term	Long Term
Two Edges Supported								
24	9	.750	.625	.625	.500	.500	—	⅟₃₂
30	12	.875	.750	.625	.625	.500	⅟₁₆	³⁄₃₂
36	15	1.000	.875	.750	.750	.625	⅟₁₆	⅛
42	18	1.000	1.000	.875	.750	.750	³⁄₃₂	⁵⁄₃₂
48	24	1.125	1.000	.875	.875	.750	⅛	¼
Three Edges Supported								
24	9	.500	.500	.375	.312	.250	Max. long	
30	12	.625	.500	.500	.375	.312	term de-	
36	15	.625	.625	.500	.500	.375	flection, 1%	
42	18	.875	.750	.625	.625	.500	of shelf	
48	24	.750	.750	.625	.500	.500	*width*, at 77° or less	
Four Edges Supported								
24	9	.250	.250	.187	.187	.125	Max. long	
30	12	.312	.250	.250	.187	.187	term de-	
36	15	.312	.312	.250	.250	.187	flection, 1%	
42	18	.312	.312	.250	.250	.187	of shelf	
48	24	.500	.375	.312	.312	.250	*depth*, at 77° or less	

Notes:
* Expected sag unloaded.
  35 lbs. per foot = full book load.
Courtesy: Rohm and Haas Company

Other Features

One of the most seductive things about kitchen cabinets today is the many fittings available for them. Cookbook holders, pull-out shelves, breadboxes, cutlery dividers, breadboards, spice racks, towel bars, and pull-out garbage cans can add dramatically to storage space and comfort.

NKCA Seal

The National Kitchen Cabinet Association (NKCA) certifies cabinets that meet their performance standards. If you are uncertain about quality, look for the NKCA seal.

Lower Cabinet Storage

I have found that the area below the counter, commonly fitted with cabinets, is often better taken up with drawers. In addition to the small utensil drawers universally positioned here, oversize drawers on heavy-duty rollers serve well for everyday dishware and frequently used cookware, which may be hard to reach overhead, especially when members of the household with short reaches wish to assume more responsibility for serving themselves. Moreover, removing a stack of heavy dishes or a cast iron pot from a knee-bend position is kinder to the back and eliminates the potential danger of the load falling on you. Drawers are particularly suited to deep counters: Even the items in the back are easily reached.

At the very least try to place sliding shelves in lower cabinets. Fortunately, there are numerous wire racks, slides, baskets, revolving shelves, and other "cabinet aids" available to make much of this easy. Any cabinetmaker will have this information, as will hardware stores and lumberyards.

Vertical slots, like those Nikki designed into the Ideal Cooker (see Chapter 11), are very handy for storing baking sheets, racks, muffin tins, pizza pans, shallow casseroles, and oversize platters. (These slots should be made wide enough for a vacuum cleaner nozzle.)

Open shelves, even in lower cabinets, are advantageous for easy access to such regularly used items as

Knife Rack

Wire Roll-out Lid Rack
(for 14-1⁄2" opening)

Cookbook Rack

Wire Roll-out Lid Rack
(for 20-1⁄2" opening)

Wire Roll-out Tray
(for 20-1⁄2" opening)

Revolving Spice Rack

Wire Roll-out Tray
(for 14-1⁄2" opening)

Towel Rack

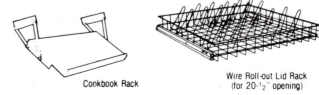

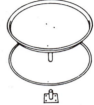

12" Door Mounted Shelves

Undersink Roll-out
Storage Tray

Some of the Cabinet Aids Available.
Courtesy: Outwater Hardware Corp.

cutting boards, favorite pots, casseroles, or the salad spinner. Open shelves are best reserved for utensils used frequently enough to keep them clean. With vessels and items stored vertically, dust accumulation is minimized.

Skip the Lazy Susan

Lazy Susans are often offered as a space-utilizing device for corners, but the advantages of these revolving shelves is often illusory. If you calculate the capacity of the lazy Susan and compare that with the usable drawer or shelf space available in a corner cabinet, which the lazy Susan is intended to replace, you may find that you have paid a lot for very little added shelf space. These turntables are expensive to buy and install. Also, usually only two lazy Susans are installed in a space that might have accommodated three or even four levels of drawers or shelves, which means you get a lot less storage space at greater cost.

Note that in many cases you can utilize the dead space by accessing it from the room behind it or if the cabinet runs along an outside wall, you can use the dead space for a compost system. (See "Composting" in Chapter 14.)

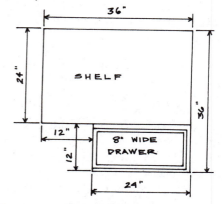

Construction Technique D: Drawer and Shelf

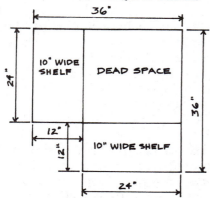

Construction Technique A: Lazy Susan

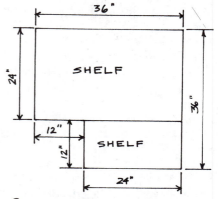

Construction Technique E: All Shelves

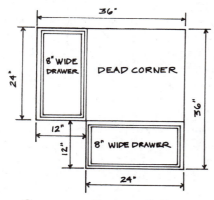

Construction Technique B: Drawers

COMPARISONS OF CONSTRUCTION TECHNIQUES FOR CORNER CABINETS (CALCULATIONS BASED ON 36' × 24' CORNER CABINET AND LAZY SUSAN WITH 14-INCH RADIUS AND 80% AVAILABLE SURFACE.)

Construction	Square Footage Available per Level	Cost
A) Lazy Susan	3.4	High
B) All drawers (dead corner lost)	2.4	Moderate
C) All shelves (dead corner lost)	3.0	Low
D) Shelf into dead space plus drawer in small cabinet	6.3	Low
E) Shelf into dead space and in small cabinet	6.7	Low

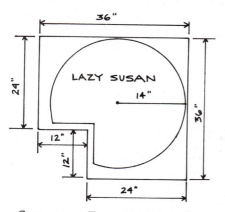

Construction Technique C: Shelves

Towel Hangers

Cloth towels hung at hand level from countertops are a small thing but a great convenience. The best spots for them are near sinks and work stations. The Demonstration Kitchen has towels hanging at the cooker and at each sink. Kitchen and bar supply stores sell clips especially made for this purpose.

OVERHEAD CABINETS AND AVOIDING BUMPED HEADS

Overhead cabinets interfere with head space, have shelves that can be hard to reach, and are too often the cause of head injuries from doors left ajar. I would love to ban them from the kitchen, especially above work areas, but in most cases space considerations mandate their presence.

Many of the kitchen plans developed in the past by the U.S. Department of Agriculture and by Cornell University addressed some of these problems. Unfortunately, to my knowledge, these concepts were never extensively utilized. It may have been because of the aesthetics; but though the execution was not particularly attractive, the plans did make some interesting points. In *The Cornell Kitchen* (1952), for example, the overhead cabinets were designed so that both the bottom and top shelves were narrower than the middle, presumably opening up headroom above the counter and making items on the top shelves more accessible. Drawings show that the cabinets also had doors that slid horizontally. A project in 1963, the Beltsville Energy Saving Kitchen, modified this design so that cabinets were narrow only at the bottom, flaring out as they got higher (5½ inches at bottom to 9½ inches at top). The cabinets were equipped with accordian-type doors that could be left open during use. These ideas were very progressive and deserved attention, but they did not catch on. Possibly it was because they specified unpopular materials (pegboard) and designs (accordian doors) as well as the fact that they were promoted primarily to farm families.

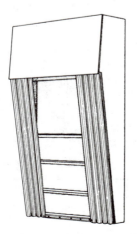

OVERHEAD CABINET: BELTSVILLE ENERGY SAVING KITCHEN (1963)

Although I was not aware of these earlier projects when the Demonstration Kitchen was in the planning stage, I was conscious of the problems they addressed and decided to put a different perspective on the use and purpose of overhead cabinets.

I resolved that there would be no danger of cabinet door contusions in the Demonstration Kitchen. Thus, you will not find any overhead doors that are side-hinged. The majority of doors slide from side to side on tracks. These doors are safe, provide wide access to the interiors, and can be left wide open without risk when working at the counters below. (Note that sliding doors at shoulder level are easy to slide, but those at higher levels require more upper body strength.)

As an added feature, we graphically numbered each cabinet door— in this case, numbers 1 through 6—to eliminate one irritating problem: directing kitchen helpers to the proper cabinet. The question "Where's the salad bowl?" can now be answered "In number four" rather than "the first cabinet to the right of the ————." I incorporated the numbers by etching them into the pattern of glass panels (designed with glass artist Gene Mallard), but any numbering or lettering system will do. An application of colors or graphics could be equally functional and add their own elements of style.

There are other ways to hang doors to eliminate the bumped-head syndrome, and we utilized two of them in the Demonstration Kitchen. An inexpensive approach is to hinge the door upward, a technique we utilized for the cabinet over the refrigerator. (The door can be kept in an open position with a "lid stay.") Another solution we took advantage of is pocket doors— cabinet doors that slide into vertical pockets at the sides of the cabinet rather than extending into the headroom of the work area. Note that these types of hinges are relatively expensive and you do sacrifice 2½ inches on either side of the cabinet. These or similar hinges also enable doors to disappear into the tops of the cabinets, but if these cabinets are up high, it may be difficult to reach the doors to close them. All of these modes allow the doors to remain safely open during kitchen use, which can be quite a convenience.

Of course, permanently open shelves (shelves without doors) are the simplest solution to the safety problem and afford maximum accessibility. They are especially practical in active kitchens but serve well for frequently used items in any kitchen. Open shelves do demand a certain level of neatness, and unless the items they hold are used regularly, they can be dust collectors.

Most of the overhead cabinets in the Demonstration Kitchen are not used for storage of often-used or heavy items in order to minimize reaching. Instead, large drawers beneath the counter contain most of our everyday cups and glasses, while a single chest-high open shelf below cabinets 1 through 4 hold oft-used dishes.

An additional feature of the open shelf is that the absence of doors allows the shelf to be narrower than a conventional cabinet. This improves headroom at counters, giving workers less of a closed-in feeling.

WAIST-HIGH STORAGE

Environmental designer Richard Crowther suggests that as much storage as possible be at waist height. This minimizes strains obtained from dishes, utensils and the like stored overhead. By coupling this with 30-inch-deep counters, you can minimize overhead storage.

THE OPEN PANTRY (ADVERTISING PAYS)

Surveys of popular food habits reveal that most of us tend to eat what we have on hand. In other words, we are more apt to use food we have than to go out and get something we may desire. For this reason we have always emphasized the idea of a well-stocked whole-foods pantry, as well as displaying these foods to encourage their consumption. Anyone in food retailing knows that visible shelf space is the key to success.

In the Demonstration Kitchen we built a bookshelf-type unit with several narrow shelves (about 6 inches deep) to hold jars of food, particularly snack items. There you will find a variety of dried fruits, nuts, wholegrain crackers, pretzels, popcorn, and similar nonperishable treats and staples. The display is very appetizing, and friends, whether adult or child, have no hesitation about opening a jar and sampling its contents. Children are much less likely to ask for candy when they see this attractive display.

ENVIRONMENTAL CHOICES

Formaldehyde is used in the fabrication of many materials that are extensively used in cabinet construction—including such pressed-wood products as decorative paneling, hardwood plywood, particleboard, and fiberboard. Moreover, formaldehyde emissions are worse in hot and humid conditions, making the kitchen particularly vulnerable. In experiments with laboratory animals, formaldehyde vapors have been shown to cause cancer. Many scientists believe exposure to formaldehyde increases the risk of cancer for humans as well. Because of this serious health hazard the U.S. government has set standards for formaldehyde emissions within mobile homes. Some states don't believe these standards are strong enough and are taking action on their own to limit formaldehyde "outgassing."

Even if formaldehyde gas doesn't kill you, it may make you sick. Exposure to formaldehyde can cause eye, nose, throat, and skin irritations as well as nausea, headaches, nosebleeds, shortness of breath, and asthmalike symptoms. People with respiratory problems or allergies often have a more serious reaction to formaldehyde, although some people with no previous history develop symptoms after exposure to it.

Reactions to formaldehyde may be temporary and may be relieved by leaving the source of exposure, or they may become chronic, like a sensitized allergy. People who become sensitized to formaldehyde often experience a severe reaction when they come in contact with even small amounts of it in such products as newspapers, perfumes, or telephones.

To address this problem:

- Consider having your cabinets constructed of solid wood.
- Consider metal cabinets.
- Have cabinets constructed of plywood made with *phenol formaldehyde* rather than with *urea formaldehyde*, since the phenol form is much less of a health hazard.
- *Solar Age* Magazine also recommends exterior composition boards or exterior sheathing board such as waferboard. When in doubt, always check with the manufacturer.
- Make sure also that no formaldehyde-containing glues are used.
- Stock cabinets can be allowed to outgas before installation for about three months at another location. The same can be done with any materials to be used in custom work. This will reduce outgassing by about 50 percent according to Dr. Thad Godish of Ball State University.
- Sealing in the formaldehyde is a strategy that works well with plywood and similar products. Polyurethane will seal in most of the fumes, according to Anthony V. Nero, co-leader of the Building, Ventilation and Indoor Quality Program at the Lawrence Berkeley Laboratory, University of California. Some companies make low-tox products that should seal in as much as 80 percent of the gases. (See Selected Resources.)
- Researchers at Oak Ridge Laboratories working on formaldehyde emissions counsel that unless a wood finish is visibly thick and is an effective vapor barrier, it probably has little effect on emissions. You may want to keep this in mind when buying new cabinets or sealing the gas in.
- Where cabinets have already been installed, good ventilation will reduce outgassing by 20–30 percent according to Dr. Godish. Sealing joints will also help.

Chapter 3:

SINKS

Stainless steel sinks are "state of the art," and I have a definite preference for them. Porcelain and ceramic sinks are just too hard; any dish or glass that slips from your fingers has almost no chance of surviving. Stainless steel, on the other hand, has a bit of resiliance, giving dropped items a second chance. So even though they don't come in as large a range of "decorator colors," stainless steel sinks should be the first choice in the kitchen.

THE TWO-SINK KITCHEN

The Demonstration Kitchen has two sinks: one for food preparation and one reserved for dishes, pots, and cleanup. This may appear extravagant, but since it makes food preparation so much easier, it is a worthwhile indulgence. If there is someone on hand to help, two sinks mean plenty of space for two workers. And if you must work alone, having two sinks allows you to save the dishes for washing at a convenient time without tying up a food preparation site. Thus, having two sinks is a concession to human comfort that encourages the use of fresh foods, particularly produce, by eliminating the need to keep the sink free of dirty utensils.

Sinks are available with one, two, or three bowls, in a variety of dimensions. A food preparation sink rarely needs more than one bowl unless there is no drainboard or adjacent counter. A dishwashing/utility sink, however, should have at least two bowls. And if you have a three-bowl sink, you can conserve water while you wash the dishes by "ponding" the water. That is, you can fill each sink with increasingly cleaner water—soapy water, rinse water, and then final rinse. Where there is only one sink, a triple-bowl model is advisable, especially if there is more than one cook. A double-bowl sink is mandatory.

Sinks rarely need to be deeper than 6 to 8 inches, especially when an automatic dishwasher is present; bowls deeper than this result in uncomfortable bending. An important feature is a sink broad enough to allow large frying pans, roasting dishes, and baking sheets to lie flat while soaking, something not possible in most models. For the Demonstration Kitchen we used a well-designed double-bowl model manufactured by Moen. While fitting a 24-inch counter, one side of this sink can accommodate an 18-inch vessel set to soak, since the faucet and controls are cleverly offset.

We used another intriguing, recently developed Moen product: their "rising faucet." This faucet can be raised as much as 6 inches above the normal position, allowing plenty of room for a large pot to fit under the faucet. (Formerly a deeper sink would be needed.) I have also found that tall people appreciate the faucet in the elevated position for dishwashing. Although no hose is provided with this faucet, in its risen position the rotating head can spray virtually every corner of the sink. This is a single-handle faucet, which allows you to flip the water on and off without constantly adjusting separate controls, saving energy and water. The single-lever faucet is also well suited to those who have trouble gripping a conventional faucet; you control it by flipping the single lever side to side and up and down. When this feature is needed, also look into so-called "elbow faucets," which are oversize single-lever faucets.

The requirements for a food preparation sink are different from the utility sink. Here a small bowl may suffice, particularly if coupled with an area for just-washed produce to drain. This frees the sink for continuous use without monopolizing the nearby counters. There are not many American manufacturers of small, single-bowl sinks with built-in drainboards, but several European imports incorporate this feature. To provide maximum access, in this sink we used a bar-type faucet. The high arch of this design, often preferred by professionals, provides more space to work under. The attached hose does an excellent job of cleaning the sink, drainboard, and adjacent compost entry. By the way, carrying filled pots of water to and from the stove can be difficult for many, as well as a hazard. An extremely long sink hose is a good idea and may be available from some faucet makers.

DRINKING FOUNTAIN/CARBONATED WATER TAP

Many faucet manufacturers make drinking fountains and soda water dispensers that can be installed in the kitchen sink. Add one and watch adults and children alike enjoy its low-calorie convenience. As an added attraction there will be fewer bottles to recycle.

ENERGY-SAVING INSTALLATION

It is highly advisable to insulate hot water pipes. You will be rewarded not only with lower fuel bills but with more responsive hot water faucets and a better-functioning dishwasher. Pipe insulation is easy to install and pays for itself in only a few months time.

SINK STORAGE

The space directly beneath the sink, taken up internally by the bowl, is lost to conventional drawer space. But this does not mean it has to be wasted. By hinging the sink's front piece, or *breather plate*, to the cabinet beneath the sink and installing *false-front trays*, especially made for this purpose, you now have a handy spot to keep scouring pads, vegetable and dish scrubbing brushes, a bar of soap, and other useful small sink items. Also, as you will see in the next section, you can modify one of the sink cabinet doors to allow seating at the sink.

SINK SEATING

An area of comfort rarely addressed in kitchen design, which I experimented with in the Demonstration Kitchen, is the ability to sit while working. There are many people, particularly the elderly, who would welcome being able to relax while working at the sink. One well-known kitchen consultant, Ellen Cheever, wrote that "sensitive planners" should consider "a spot for the tired cook to sit down while peeling potatoes." The interesting thing is that it only takes very slight modification of the under-sink cabinet to make this feature available.

If you open the door under the sink cabinet in almost every kitchen and pull up a chair, your knees will strike the breather plate, the piece across the front of the cabinet. You would also have no room for your feet. To circumvent this problem, I attached the breather plate to the door beneath the sink so that when the door is opened, the attached plate swings out too. This one simple modification gives much more knee room. If you deepen the "kick" below (where your toes fit under the counter), you can provide even more comfort. In the Demonstration Kitchen, the nest for the foot/footstool (see Chapter 1) provides this extra footroom. Either an adjustable office chair or an architectural stool works for sitting here.

This design also allows the stool to be used like a bar rail to relieve back strain when standing.

SPLASHBOARDS AND WALLS

The walls above counters and cooking appliances—and, of course, sinks—require a washable surface.

SINK SYSTEM PROVIDES DIFFERENT COMFORT MODES
Here the design permits sink seating.

Many materials will work, which makes this area well suited to interior design preferences. Suitable splashboard materials include tile (with a thin grout line), laminates, and even stone.

Make sure that the top of the sink splashboard is well sealed. This will prevent mold growth as well as deterioration of the wall itself. Silicone rubber-based caulk provides an excellent seal. Use the back of a plastic spoon to smooth out the caulk and masking tape (which should be removed after one hour) to keep the line neat.

ENVIRONMENTAL CHOICES

It's no joke that water purity is a serious concern. (See Chapter 13.) But even if the water entering your home is acceptable, it may become contaminated from the lead in the solder used to join the water line's copper pipe (plastic is rarely used.) This is especially true if the water is very acidic, alkaline, soft, or hot.

SINK SYSTEM PROVIDES DIFFERENT COMFORT MODES
The design provides opportunity to relieve back strain.

Since June 19,1988, the Federal government has required that solder and flux be lead free. Before this legislation, solder was typically 50 percent lead. There is no known tolerance for lead.

In preexisting situations you should have your water tested, blood tested and/or have a plumber examine the joints for lead solder. Also, since plumbing in older homes tends to acquire a protective coating (especially if there is calcium carbonate in the water), you can have your pipes examined for this, too; the coating will help shield the lead. But if lead is present the plumbing connections should be redone.

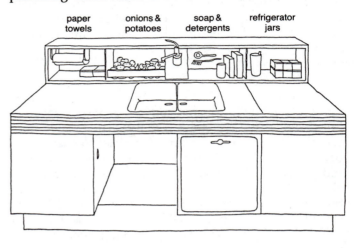

SINK CENTER: CORNELL KITCHEN (1952)

Many pre-WWII homes may also have lead water supply lines. If the water line is lead it will have some or all of these characteristics: grey in color, not magnetic, scratches easily, no threads at shut-off valve or meter, and bends when coming out of floor or wall rather than using straight pipes or an elbow fitting. This must be replaced.

Other options include a proper filter. Reverse osmosis or distillation units are the most appropriate, according to the Water Quality Association. (See Chapter 13.)

If there is cause for concern and none of the above is possible, water used for drinking and food preparation should be run from the cold faucet for at least three minutes particularly after sitting for long periods (such as overnight) and should not be used by pregnant women or for baby food or formula. Hot water from lead contaminated water lines should never be used for cooking or drinking.

The foregoing applies to anywhere there is drinking water, such as the bathroom tap.

Chapter 4:
LIGHTING AND THERMAL COMFORT

Kitchens require two kinds of lighting—area lighting and task lighting. Area lighting provides an inviting atmosphere, brightens traffic paths between work areas, allows you to see into cabinets and corners not illuminated by task lights, enhances productivity, and protects against accidents. Task lighting concentrates light at specific locales, such as the countertop, sink, or cooker. Insufficient lighting, lights incorrectly positioned, and lack of lighting flexibility are common kitchen design errors.

There are also two kinds of lighting with respect to source: natural lighting and artificial lighting. The first part of this chapter deals with natural light, which for practical purposes is area light. Artificial area and task lighting is discussed in the second part. (Subsequent parts focus on room color, thermal comfort, and environmental concerns.)

And since there is a growing understanding about the relationship between natural light and health, I think it appropriate that the place where we get so much of our sustenance and spend so much of our time also provide an "oasis of light."

Additionally, although we tend to think of electric lighting costs in term of pennies, it actually accounts for 25 percent of U.S. electricity use, according to the Lawrence Berkeley Laboratory. Although 95 percent of that amount is for non-residential applications, consumers can select energy-efficient lighting technology and make a step toward cutting both personal and national energy consumption if they chose to.

THE NEED FOR NATURAL LIGHTING

It is known that we need ultraviolet light for our bodies to synthesize vitamin D, which in turn is necessary for calcium absorption. Lack of calcium causes rickets and other bone-related problems, such as osteoporosis. Dr. Michael Hollick of Tufts University Nutrition Center postulated in 1985 that the lack of natural light may have created a "hidden epidemic" of vitamin D deficiency. Ordinary window glass, air pollution, long winters indoors, and the like reduce our exposure to natural light.

Experts disagree on minimum exposure needed; some say that fifteen minutes of natural light on hands and face is all that is required, others two hours or

more. All agree on one thing: we need "some" natural light to stay healthy.

Research done at the Massachusetts Institute of Technology (MIT) and the National Institute of Mental Health has revealed that there may be other important relationships between light and health. Dr. Richard J. Wurtman of MIT and other scientists investigating responses to light believe that people who spend most of their days indoors illuminated by lights that are a poor substitute for the brightness and spectrum of the sun could suffer untoward effects from inadequate light exposure. In experimental animals, prolonged exposure to ordinary indoor lighting has been linked to reproductive abnormalities and enhanced susceptibility to cancer. Preliminary studies in people have suggested such problems as increased fatigue, decreased performance, diminished immunological defenses, reduced physical fitness, and possibly impaired fertility associated with living under incandescent or cool-white fluorescent lights.

This is a significant consideration to keep in mind in total residential design, but since it is estimated that we spend as much as 50 percent of our time in the kitchen and since the kitchen should embody a healthy environment, natural lighting is doubly important there. This is even more important in regions with long winters and for people who tend to spend much of their time indoors.

Windows

In planning a new home or modifying an existing home, paying attention to the placement of windows can yield large benefits in comfort and beauty by providing good ventilation and ample natural lighting (Note that windows provide "natural light" but not true "full-spectrum" light. For "natural full-spectrum light," special window glazing is needed.) Windows can also be the cause of incurable problems. So let's spot some major pitfalls and then move on to the basics of good window choice and placement.

- Avoid putting windows near or over a stove. The possibility of curtains catching fire will be a hazard even if you use blinds or other noninflammable window covering, since someone else may come along and add the inflammable décor later on.

- Westward-facing and, in the southern states, southward-facing windows can cause nasty overheating problems if they are not properly shaded. (See "Thermal Comfort" later in this chapter.)
- Operable windows that will be used for ventilation should be placed away from desks and bulletin boards so that an occasional strong breeze will not cause chaos.
- Windows placed so that they can cross-ventilate are a big plus in term of indoor comfort and air quality.
- Overhangs outside windows will prevent wind-driven rain from wetting down critical areas indoors. If no overhang is present and the window will be left open and unattended, it should be located where an occasional deluge will do no harm, such as over a sink.

The sink is a favorite location for a window. A window there is handy for a plant shelf (easy to water), it provides refreshing and entertaining views while you're washing dishes, and it's a good source of natural lighting in an area that gets a lot of use. Other heavily used areas, such as food preparation counters and desks, will also benefit from windows.

Windows are multifunctional; they provide not only ventilation but also view, emergency exits, and—of course—light. Since the kitchen is the room occupied most of the waking time at home, it is a good idea to include a window with a view of the approach to your home and the play areas of children. This saves steps and adds to the feeling of security. Take advantage of any pleasant views that exist; they do not necessarily have to be panoramic— a garden, hedge, rosebush, or tree can offer an interesting picture. Windows that are intended mainly for viewing should be at eye level and fairly small. If you need both standing and sitting view, use a tall, narrow, vertical window.

Windows also provide emergency fire exits; every room with no exterior door should have one window that is the proper size and in the proper location for a timely retreat in case of emergency.

Most windows that are intended primarily for lighting, as opposed to viewing or exiting, should be high on the wall and wide. A nice diffuse light will bounce off a light-colored and reflective ceiling. However, north-facing windows (which, in the Northern Hemisphere, do not get direct sunlight) should be lower down, closer to the work area, and larger.

Since windows have many functions, there are many types to choose from. I suggest that you look for quality units and avoid "bargains." Reputation usually is the best guide, and reliable builders are your best source of information. Wood-framed units are suitable but may require periodic painting. Vinyl-clad wood offers "no maintenance" features. Vinyl-framed units can also be of good quality; be sure of what you are buying, though, since there are a lot of poor-quality vinyl windows being made. *Casement* and *hopper* types will give the tightest seals if you are energy conscious; however, sliding and double-hung windows may be more convenient. Crank-operated windows are handy in such locations as over the sink or counters, since you don't have to reach as far to operate them. *Fixed-glazing* (windows that do not open) is less expensive and should be used where you want light and views but do not need ventilation or emergency exits.

Don't be afraid to move, remove, or replace a window that's not right. The additional cost will be a small percentage of your remodeling bill, and the benefits can be significant. See "Thermal Comfort" later in this chapter for more information on shading and the comfort aspect of windows.

Where more natural light is desired, you can have some of the glass in a window or skylight replaced with glazing that doesn't block ultraviolet light.

The Skylight

The use of skylights to bring light, air, and even solar heat to the home dates back to prehistory and has been reestablished as an architectural feature during the last decade. While skylights have been defamed by some energy-conscious designers as frivolous energy hogs, this is a unfair criticism. Properly placed and operated, these "windows in the roof" can bring in heat in winter, vent in summer, and supply free, healthy light year round.

For area lighting in the Demonstration Kitchen I started with a skylight, which immediately made a dramatic difference in the room. Just this one step changed the kitchen from a cold, dark box to a sun-bathed space.

Selecting and Situating a Skylight

In cooler, cloudy climates you should try to place the skylight so that it looks to the south and west. Nighttime insulation (see "Thermal Comfort") and triple-layer construction should be considered, especially if the skylight must face north. In warmer climates north- and east-facing skylights are preferred.

Shading is a must for south- and west-facing skylights in hot climates, and it is highly desirable in cool climates. The best shading device is a big tree that casts its shadow over the skylight and blocks one half or more of the direct sun, particularly the afternoon sun. Exterior-mounted shades or awnings that block a percentage of the direct sunlight are also good; some skylight manufacturers supply these. An interior shading device is not always very useful; although it shades the floor area, the heat has already entered the room and must somehow be dissipated. However, if the shading device's upper side is highly reflective (silvered or shiny white), and if you open the skylight, it can be effective.

Skylights can add greatly to the ventilation scheme if

- They are placed high enough to prevent heat buildup.
- They are no fuss to operate.
- They seal tightly. (Look for air leakage rating test reports in the sales literature; .07 cubic feet per minute per foot of perimeter is the maximum allowable, and .03 is desirable.)

Other features to look for are

- **Insulated curbs.** The curb (frame) is a real heat conductor if it is not insulated.
- **Condensation gutters.** These are located on the inside of the frame and catch condensation in winter and hold it until it evaporates, thus preventing drips.
- **Flashing** seals the curb to the roof. Have your builder approve of the flashing if you are in doubt. This is your assurance against leaks.
- **Domed glazing** stays cleaner because of slope, but not everyone likes the bubble look.
- **Plastic glazing** is safer than glass, although laminated safety glass is good, and tempered glass is okay.
- **Easy installation.** Some units can be installed from within the house. This eliminates climbing on and doing possible damage to the roof (or to yourself).

The Paeco skylight chosen for the Demonstration Kitchen has dual glazing and double-wall-insulated construction. This skylight also has a shade screen for shielding out the sun's rays when it is too hot and a storm panel for extra insulation when the weather is frigid. The window portion can easily be unhinged and removed, which makes installation much easier.

The skylight shaft in the Demonstration Kitchen is painted white (any bright color will do) with a semigloss paint to maximize the amount of light reflected into the room. (Dark colors and flat paint absorb light.)

I wanted the skylight to provide for something else I found was often ignored in the kitchen: the ability to grow food. To accomplish this I installed plastic shelves and a pulley system for plants. (For more details, see Chapter 15.)

Artificial Lighting

At this writing about 6 percent of residential energy is used to provide artificial lighting. This translates into $40 to $75 a year per household. While not a for-

midable amount at present, according to *Electrical World*, a trade publication for electric utilities, we can expect a 2 percent increase in electric rates per year. This figure may be even higher in the Northeast. This translates approximately into a 33 percent increase by the year 2000. Since incandescent bulbs turn 80 to 90 percent of their power into heat rather than light (which also affects cooling), energy-efficient bulbs begin to look more attractive.

High-Efficiency Lighting

Efficiency-minded consumers have a large selection of recently developed, highly efficient bulbs to choose from. However, unlike conventional bulbs, where selection generally involves only a few decisions, these require more knowledge to make a proper decision. The first decision is to spend considerably more money for the more efficient and longer-lasting bulbs. This investment is especially appealing for hard-to-reach fixtures, where you want to replace bulbs as infrequently as possible. Note also that these bulbs are not yet available in local supermarkets or hardware stores; you may have to go to an electrical supply house or lighting store. Also check with your utility; some utilities have had special programs to encourage their use. Energy expert Amory Lovins says that the benefit of these bulbs are so great that they are more than "a free lunch," they are "someone taking you out to lunch."

To get the most out of your investment, you should note the following:

- These bulbs should be installed only in fixtures that are used for long periods.
- They must fit the fixture and not be too heavy for it; some of these bulbs have odd shapes and are heavier than traditional bulbs. (Or may require an adapter.) Also the bulbs must be appropriate to the type of lamp—for example, not too small for its reflectors.
- Some have their own peculiarities. Compact fluorescents, for example, won't work with dimmers. Others may not work well in certain conditions (temperature, humidity, and so on). Check the package.
- Check the quality of light; most are the same as or close to incandescent, including compact fluorescent.
- Be skeptical of manufacturer's claims. There is a fair amount of hype around energy efficiency, so read the claims carefully. *Home Energy* suggests you look for power rating, lumen (visible light) output, and lifetime. Be wary of claims for "percent energy" or dollar savings unless you know how the savings were calculated.

High-efficiency bulbs do not provide natural (full-spectrum) lighting. As elsewhere, variety may be the best solution: Use some of these bulbs and provide for natural light elsewhere.

| | COMPARING EFFICIENT BULBS | | |
| | Improved Energy | Lifetime | Extra Cost |
Type	Efficiency	(Compared with Conventional Incandescent)	
Krypton	10–15%	About the same	About the same
Krypton-long life	Small	1.5–4.5×	30%
Tungsten-halogen	10%–15%	2.5–3.5×	3–5× incandescent
Compact fluorescent	300–400%	7–13×	20–50×
Circular fluorescent	300–400%	12–15×	10–15×

Adapted from *Home Energy* (Jan.–Feb. 1989)

FULL-SPECTRUM BULBS

A number of bulbs have been specially developed to more closely mimic the sun's natural light (full spectrum). They are available in both screw-in and fluorescent style. The only brand that has had health-related claims verified for it is Vita Lite™, whose bulbs are said to provide 91 percent of the spectrum. Tests at Harvard Medical School have shown Vita Lite™ to help with calcium absorption and research at MIT and the National Institute for Mental Health to alleviate seasonal affective disorder (SAD), otherwise known as the "winter blues." Full-spectrum bulbs cost about three times as much as conventional fluorescents and must be purchased from Vita Lite™ representatives, natural food and speciality lighting stores. (See "Selected Resources.") Full spectrum bulbs it should be remembered are not a total substitute for natural sunlight; one expert equates forty hours under one as equal to half an hour of natural sunlight.

Artificial Area Lighting

INCANDESCENT

You can achieve overhead incandescent lighting with a number of different incandescent bulbs, ranging from standard to different energy-saving selections. Duro Test Watt Saver™ bulbs were used for area lighting in the Demonstration Kitchen.

FLUORESCENT

In general, fluorescent bulbs are economical. Their life expectancy is seven times greater than the incandescents'. They also radiate far less heat and triple the light for the same amount of current. Standard fluorescent lights provide approximately 55 to 65 percent of the natural light spectrum.

Many professionals in different fields have expressed concern over the possible ill health effects of conventional fluorescent lighting. Fluorescent bulbs actually dim every $\frac{1}{120}$th of a second, and although the phenomena is not visible to the naked eye, it may cause eye strain and headaches. More severe psychological and physical reactions have also been claimed. In addi-

tion, scientists at the U.S. Food and Drug Administration are concerned that excessive exposure to the fluorescent's narrow spectrum of ultraviolet light may increase the chances of getting skin cancer. A 1982 Australian study saw a doubling of skin cancer risk from long-term exposure. (Full-spectrum bulbs also emit ultraviolet light but in more natural proportions.) One solution to this later concern is to use solid plastic covers that do not transmit the ultraviolet light.

Some people are also annoyed by the buzz of the fixture itself. Newer electronic, or "high-frequency," fixtures speed up the dimming so the eye cannot perceive it; they also do not buzz.

Because of the spectrum of light they emit, traditional fluorescents do not cast things, including food, "in a good light." Full-spectrum light will make the food you prepare look more appetizing.

SELECTION GUIDELINES

Lighting demands vary with fixture type, room size, room shape, and the wall and ceiling reflectance, so the actual specific needs of your kitchen are impossible to predict here. Nevertheless, the table that follows can serve as a starting point. In using these figures, keep the following two guidelines in mind:

- Use the lower numbers if the fixture and surrounding surfaces are smooth and light-colored—that is, if they are good reflectors—and use the higher numbers if they are rough or dark-colored.
- Use lower area lighting figures if task lighting is provided for all work surfaces, use the higher figures if task lighting is not provided at all.

From this you can select the bulb size to suit your needs. By installing dimmers (rheostats) you can further adjust the light level according to the mood, task, and time of day.

KITCHEN AREA LIGHTING RECOMMENDATIONS

The following figures were prepared for *The Smart Kitchen* by solar engineer Daniel Bauch and will probably be lower than those recommended by light bulb manufacturers, who, he and others feel, have been raising their recommendations needlessly.

Area Lighting Recommendations

Incandescent

Small room, 80 square feet (8' × 10')

6'–7' ceiling	182–308 watts
10' ceiling	224–392 watts

Medium room, 140 square feet (10' × 14')

6'–7' ceiling	280–462 watts
10' ceiling	322–546 watts

Large room, 252 square feet (14' × 18')

6'–7' ceiling	420–700 watts
10' ceiling	504–840 watts

Fluorescent

Small room, 80 square feet (8' × 10')

6'–7' ceiling	130–220 watts
10' ceiling	160–280 watts

Medium room, 140 square feet (10' × 14')

6'–7' ceiling	200–330 watts
10' ceiling	230–390 watts

Large room, 252 square feet (14' × 18')

6'–7' ceiling	300–500 watts
10' ceiling	360–600 watts

Mixed Lighting

For a mixture of incandescent and fluorescent, add 1.4 times the amount of the fluorescent watts to be replaced by incandescent.

In choosing bulbs and fixtures, use *lumens* as a point of comparison. A lumen is a unit for measuring the light output. It is more useful than watts, which is a measure of electrical power consumption. The number of lumens supplied by a 100-watt bulb can vary from 6,000 to 9,000 for fluorescent and 1,000 to 2,000 for incandescent.

More is not always better. Too much light improperly placed results in glare, which will impair vision. The upper-threshold lighting level is only 50 "foot candles." This is a modest amount, similar to the illumination at floor level under an ordinary 1,500-lumen, 100-watt bulb in a frosted-glass ceiling fixture located in a 10-by-14-foot room with bright walls and ceilings. Studies have shown that increased lighting intensity will not necessarily improve performance for tasks

---

Standard Incandescent and Compact Fluorescent Bulbs Compared

Output (Lumens)	Incandescent Watts Used	Compact Fluorescent Watts Used
210–250	25	5
400–480	40	7
890–900	60	13
1210–1250	75	18
1710–1800	100	26
2610–2700	150	36

Adapted from *Home Energy* (Jan.–Feb. 1989)

---

that require clear vision. Use as many fixtures as practical in order to spread lighting throughout the room. Take a look in friends' and neighbors' homes to get a feeling for the type of effect you will get from different arrangements.

Artificial Task Lighting

Incandescent

Incandescent bulbs give off heat and should not be overused in a kitchen.

In the cooler months you may want to experiment with spot "grow lights" over work areas. These, like their fluorescent counterparts, provide more natural light. They may put out too much heat for the warmer months, however.

When summer comes, use reflector bulbs marked "R" or "PAR." They have built-in reflectors that aim the light, concentrating the beam downward; energy-saving PAR bulbs use 13 to 20 percent less power than conventional ones.

A bulb called an *ellipsoidal reflector lamp* (marked "ER") can also give you a focused beam and save you 40 percent or more on electricity, as compared with conventional bulbs. These bulbs, according to specifications, are feasible only according to the manufacturer "within cylindrical downlights that do not require a specific bulb of another type." ER lights are ideal where recessed lighting is part of the design.

Fluorescent

Small fluorescent fixtures are usually used for countertop task lighting under each run of overhead cabinets. They can be hidden behind the cabinet lip to prevent glare. Twenty watts is standard. Full-spectrum bulbs can provide many benefits as undercabinet task lights. They will make your food look better, but you can also create an area for growing herbs, starting seeds, and so on. I have been experimenting with this in the Demonstration Kitchen. Make sure the fixtures do not have covers which will block the ultraviolet rays. (See the following paragraph.)

Fluorescent Light Covers

Much of the energy-saving capability, as well as some of the spectrum, of fluorescent bulbs is lost when they are covered with conventional plastic covers (diffusors). This is because virtually all plastic is made with ultraviolet light absorbers. Therefore, if you use full-spectrum lighting, make sure the fixtures are appropriate. This means ultraviolet transmitting diffusors (cover or lens) or perhaps an open grid cover if the fixture is away from water. If you need a retrofit cover, check plastic supply houses for plastic without ultraviolet absorbers. One company that does not use ultraviolet light diffusors is Power Plastics. (Their fluorescent fixtures are also available with a switch, a feature I love because it eliminates the annoyance of having to hold a button in until the bulb is lit.)

Remember that it is not safe to leave bulbs uncovered in areas where they can be accidentally hit or splashed with water.

SELECTION GUIDELINES

Choose fixtures that will allow lighting flexibility, such as track lighting, several small fluorescent units in place of one large one, incandescent fixtures that can accept a range of bulb sizes, swivel and gooseneck fixtures, and even fixtures on retractable arms. Take care to avoid costly and uncomfortable overlighting.

KITCHEN TASK LIGHTING RECOMMENDATIONS

Activity	Recommended Wattage
Fluorescent	
Over sink, over eating area (separate from workspace), etc.	2–20 watts
Other task lighting	20 watts (32″ part)
Incandescent	
Fixture over sink	150 watts
Task lighting (no overhead cabinets)	70 watts per area floodlight, 100 watts regular

Switching

Switches for area lighting should be located at doorways, whereas controls for task lighting are convenient to the task area. All the artificial lighting in the Demonstration Kitchen is controlled by rheostats. They permit the level of illumination to be adjusted as need and mood dictate. Rheostats at half level reduce energy usage by about 25 percent. Moreover, bulbs last much, much longer when turned on and off by dimming action, as opposed to switching action. Linear-type (sliding) dimmers are recommended because they dim all the way down before switching off, as opposed to rotary dimmers, which can be switched off at any intensity. Lutron[R] linear dimmers were chosen for the Demonstration Kitchen because of their high quality and the fact that they make a three-way dimmer. This means the light can be controlled by two different switches—very useful in a kitchen that has several entrances. Lutron is also the only manufacturer I have encountered making fluorescent dimmers.

ROOM COLOR

Light room colors, because of reflection, spread lighting around. Other colors can reduce monotony and change the atmosphere of the room. Colors with shorter wave lengths (green, blue, and violet) create an impression of cold, whereas colors with longer wave lengths (yellow, orange, and red) appear warm. Use warm colors on the north side or in areas where there is minimal sunlight. On the south side the emphasis should be on cool colors. Semigloss paint will reflect more light than will flat paint. Gloss paint should be avoided because it will create glare. Use semigloss sparingly for the same reason.

REFLECTABILITY OF COLORS

Color	Light Reflected
White	80–90%
Pale yellow, yellow, rose	80%
Pale pastel (beige, lilac)	70%
Cool colors (blue, green pastels)	70–85%
Full yellow hue (mustard)	35%
Medium brown	35%
Blue, green	20–30%
Black	10%

Source: *Other Homes and Garbage.*

MIRRORS

Mirrors are not often used in kitchens, perhaps because they tend to steam up. Despite this, they are a wonderful way to brighten a kitchen and make the room appear larger. In the Chinese system of design, *Feng Shui*, mirrors or other reflective surfaces are recommended in the kitchen to provide for a more peaceful atmosphere and flowing cooking movements.

THERMAL COMFORT

Ever notice that your kitchen is only comfortable in winter, when the oven is on? Ever wonder why you feel chilly at home even though the thermometer reads in the 70s?

The answer to the mystery of thermal comfort is pretty simple: It has to do with how heat enters and leaves your body. There are two good reasons to consider thermal comfort as a factor in kitchen design: (1) We spend a lot of our waking time there (on average close to 50 percent), and (2) most kitchens incorporate such hard materials as enameled steel, plastic laminate, finished wood, tile, and glass, which can make a room colder. When such material is in direct or indirect contact with cooler temperatures (such as the outside air at night), its surface temperature becomes lower than the inside air temperature (which may be in the 70s). Window glass is very cold to the touch, a tile floor is almost as cold, and a bare tile wall is cooler to the touch than cork, drapes, cloth wall coverings or wall hangings, or even wood.

Surfaces that are cool to the touch, if they make up a large percentage of the surfaces in a room, make your body *feel* cool even when you are *not* touching them. Here's how that works:

Normal body temperature is about 98°F. Your body is constantly burning up food (calories) and losing heat to the air around you in order to maintain this temperature. You feel comfortable if the rate at which your body loses heat is within correct limits.

1. If the rate is too slow, you feel hot and start to sweat to speed it up, because the evaporating water will take heat with it.

2. If the rate is too fast, you feel cold and start to burn up more food or even shiver.

The rate at which your body loses heat—and thus, your comfort—depends largely on the surface temperature of the objects around you.

Why surface temperature rather than air temperature, since that is what thermostats measure and weather forecasters talk about? Well, your body doesn't know about thermostats and weather reports; it loses heat in three ways: *conduction, convection,* and *radiation.* Conduction is heat moving between things in contact; convection is heat being carried by a moving thing, such as air or water; and radiation is heat being carried by invisible rays, like the way heat is given off by a wood stove.

Although the body conducts some heat to the air around it and some of that heat moves away by the convection of moving air, most of its heat is lost through radiation. (You might say your body is one big radiator!) Since radiation happens through space from one solid thing to another, the rate of radiation has to do mainly with the temperature of solid things around you. The bigger the difference in temperature (and the nearer objects are), the faster the heat will move. Put your hand an inch away from a cup of hot tea, then do it with ice water, and you will feel how this works.

So, where does that leave us in the kitchen?

- By adding surfaces covered with poor conductors, such as wood, fabric, cork, and so on, you will have a more comfortable kitchen. Add cushions to chairs (with removable, washable fabric covers), add throw rugs with nonskid pads, and add washable drapes and wall hangings where appropriate (away from cooking areas, and the like).
- Cover windows at night with heavy drapes or window insulation. These are the coldest surfaces, and

some attention here will pay back in comfort and fuel savings. Window insulation has been available commercially only since about 1980, but a variety of tight-fitting, insulated curtains, shades, shutters, and lightweight removable panels are now available in window covering and energy stores.

- For summer the best strategy is to block the sun's heat with shading, window insulation, or heat-reflecting films. Awnings and rollup shutters or the European type that are hinged to swing out at the bottom are good. Foliage is better. There is nothing like a well-placed grape arbor, shade tree, or tall hedge. These take planning and patience, but using foresight, fast-growing varieties, and inexpensive awnings to "tide you over" will pay off in natural beauty and comfort. Split bamboo shades are an inexpensive temporary (three to eight years) measure. They are most effective if they can be hung outside your windows.

THREE TREES FOR THE FUTURE

Trees are particularly important in keeping energy costs down in air-conditioned spaces. Research has shown that just three trees planted on the sunny side of buildings can cut cooling costs by as much as one third. But the trees not only save on the expense of conditioning but have beneficial affects on air pollution. Even residences without air conditioning should have the trees planted for their shade, beauty and ability to keep the atmosphere healthy.

ENVIRONMENTAL CHOICES

There is little doubt that a relationship exists between light and health, although exact needs are debatable. There is also considerable disagreement concerning the effects of regular fluorescent lights on both the body and the mind. Because of the possible ill effects of standard fluorescent lighting, minimizing its use, especially by those who think they may be sensitive, should be considered.

Maximize the natural light in the kitchen through natural-light-transmitting window and skylights or genuine full-spectrum bulbs.

If fluorescents are to be used, consider (a) mixing them with full-spectrum bulbs (make sure they are not shielded by nonultraviolet covers) or even incandescents, and (b) using high-frequency or other better ballasts.

Chapter 5:

ACOUSTICS AND NOISE REDUCTION

One of the most bothersome elements that cooks must contend with is noise in the kitchen. According to the U.S. Environmental Protection Agency (EPA), the kitchen, with rare exception, is "the noisiest room in the house."

This situation is somewhat unavoidable, considering the amount of noise-generating equipment and activities going on there. The sounds of the refrigerator, freezer, dishwasher, blender, food processor, mixer, exhaust fan, and pots and pans can make even a well-designed workspace inhospitable. Even though appliances are used only for short periods, according to the EPA, "it is the intensity, random intermittency and periodic or cyclical characteristics of the noise that are especially annoying." (Much of the source material for this chapter, including all quoted material, is from the EPA's publication *Quieting: A Practical Guide to Noise Control*.)

The use of such sound-reflecting elements as plastic laminates, metal, and finished wood further aggravates the problem, and using such sound-absorbing materials as cloth and unfinished wood in the kitchen is impractical. Although sometimes better acoustical floorings such as rugs, cork, and rubber are employed, their use must be carefully considered. See Chapter 6. Curtains are only of minimal value, although large, safely placed drapes that are easily removable and washable are a good option in some settings.

The most effective strategy is preventing or reducing noise output from appliances is at the source: selecting quieter equipment and installing it properly. Next is to employ techniques that reduce the overall sound level within the room, such as creating an acoustical ceiling. Also locating the kitchen as far as possible from noise-sensitive areas and soundproofing it from the rest of the house reduce the overall effect of the kitchen's noise output.

ACOUSTICAL MEASUREMENTS

Most of us are familiar with measurements for electricity, sound, weight, height, and so on. But few of us have ever even heard of acoustical ratings. Here is an introduction to acoustics.

The main objective in quieting down a room is to choose sound-absorbing surfaces as finishes, rather than sound-reflecting or sound-transmitting ones. The sound absorbers are generally soft and/or porous materials, and their ability to absorb sound can be compared by looking at ratings that might be expressed in two different ways.

One way to rate sound absorption is the *noise reduction coefficient (NRC)*. A perfect absorber would have an NRC of 1.0. Any material with an NRC of .6 or higher is worth using. Try for .7 or .8. Any building material or component that is sold for its acoustical value will have an NRC rating.

Another measurement is the *absorption coefficient*, which is just the NRC expressed differently. By translating the NRC's decimal into a percentage, you get the absorption coefficient. For example, an NRC of .1 means a 10-percent absorption.

NRC (AT NORMAL NOISE LEVEL)	
Heavy carpet (on heavy foam)	.570
Glass (ordinary)	.180
Plywood	.170
Heavy carpet (on concrete)	.140
Wood	.100
Parquet flooring (on concrete or asphalt)	.070
Gypsum board (½")	.050
Plaster (rough)	.040
Linoleum (on concrete)	.030
Plaster (smooth)	.020
Concrete	.015

Source: Northern Sound

KITCHEN ISOLATION

The ability to close off the kitchen minimizes the intrusion of its noise on the rest of the house. (The kitchen should be capable of being shut off not only to confine noise but to limit odor, fumes, and even fires from spreading. There are times, too, when one wants to be able to restrict children's, pet's, or guests' entry.)

The process of soundproofing a kitchen from other living areas includes (1) building or modifying walls for a low sound transmission capacity, (2) fixing the doors to seal tightly, and (3) replacing lightweight, hollow doors with solid-core doors. According to the EPA, "solid core [doors] . . . should be equipped with soft rubber or plastic gaskets at the top, sides, and at the bottom. Hinged or sliding doors may be used providing good edge seals are maintained. Such an installation will confine the noise to the kitchen area.''

The construction of noise-reducing walls is not difficult but is too lengthy a topic for inclusion here. A number of good pamphlets on the subject are listed in "Selected Resources."

Noise Prevention at the Source: Quieting the Appliance Itself

You can substantially reduce the kitchen noise level by choosing appliances with their noise factor in mind. See for yourself, some appliance models are considerably more tolerable than others. If you are sensitive to sound, make sure you don't buy any mechanical device without first hearing it in operation.

The noise of such countertop appliances as the food processor, blender, or beater can be quieted by rubber or cloth pads; experienced cooks routinely place a folded dishcloth beneath the bowl when using an electric beater in it to reduce the amount of noise generated.

You can minimize noise from large appliances by installing them with some foresight—for example, by "wrapping" the appliance in acoustical material or insulation. The dishwasher in the Demonstration Kitchen has fiberglass board on three sides. Provided you don't interfere with air flow, you could do the same with the refrigerator. Noise-sensitive people can obtain special sound-absorbing materials from acoustical specialists. (Such insulation can also save you some energy dollars; see ''Improving and Maintaining Refrigerator Performance'' in Chapter 9.)

Large, heavy appliances—washing machines, dryers, and refrigerators—tend to transfer their vibrations to the supporting floor. You can isolate these vibrations from the floor with pads of such resilient materials as sponge rubber, ribbed neoprene, or solid rubber under the appliance's legs or corners. Pads measuring ¼ to ½ inch (6mm to 13mm) in thickness with an area of about 2 square inches (13cm²) should provide adequate vibration isolation for most large appliances. A hard plate on top of the pad will distribute the appliance load uniformly, which will prevent screw-type legs from sinking too deeply in the pad. You may need to adjust the legs somewhat to prevent them from rattling against the hard plates.

The appliance should never make rigid contact with a wall. There should be a space of at least 2 inches (5cm). Appliances built into or enclosed by counters, dishwashers, disposers, compactors, and so on,

Proper Installation of Appliances for Quiet Operation

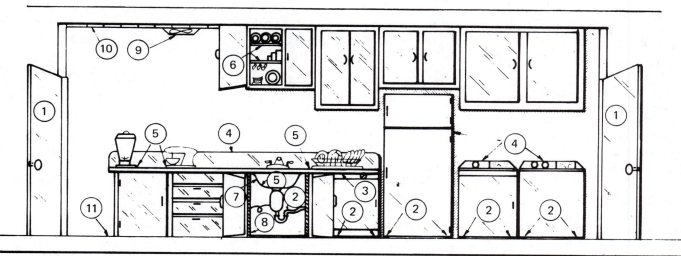

(1) Install solid door with gaskets
(2) Use vibration isolators & mounts
(3) Isolate appliance from cabinet with rubber gasket
(4) Insert rubber gaskets behind cabinets and appliances to avoid wall contact
(5) Place rubber pads under small units, dish racks and in sink basins
(6) Install rubber or cork tile on backs and shelves of cabinets
(7) Apply vibration damping material
(8) Install acoustic tile
(9) Install exhaust fan on rubber mounts
(10) Install acoustic ceiling
(11) Install carpet or foam backed tile

Recommendations for Reducing Kitchen Noise.
Source: Quieting: A Practical Guide to Noise Control (1978).

should be installed with a perimeter strip-type gasket or spacers made of soft rubber to isolate the cabinets vibrationally from the machine. "A strip gasket ¼ inch (6mm) thick and ½ inch (13mm) wide attached to the top and side edges of the cabinet opening into which the appliance is to be installed would provide adequate isolation" of the vibration.

Use flexible plastic or rubber hoses when installing a waste disposer, dishwasher, or washing machine to minimize transfer of vibrations to the walls. Otherwise, the walls will act like sounding boards, amplifying the machine noise.

In installing waste disposers (not recommended for ecological reasons—see Chapter 14), you can keep the sink from vibrating (making disposer noise worse) by inserting a soft rubber sleeve-type gasket between its mounting flange and the sink basin.

According to the EPA, with large appliances you should:

1. Install ribbed neoprene or soft rubber pads under the legs of the units.
2. Adjust screw-leveling legs to prevent units from wobbling.
3. Tighten all loose parts and panels to prevent them from rattling.
4. Install soft rubber gaskets around pipe openings and along the perimeter of washing machine, dryer, and dishwasher doors to prevent noise leakage from inside the machine.
5. Run your fingers lightly over the surfaces of appliances in operation to find areas of greatest vibration. At these points install vibration damping materials on the inside surfaces. This will tend to suppress the vibration and reduce the noise output.
6. Apply glass fiberboard on the interior surfaces of the cabinets to reduce the noise buildup in these reverberant enclosures.

Additionally, "the more technically competent person might try mounting motors and pumps on resilient isolators and inserting rubber sleeves around pipes and conduits at points of support or contact with large cabinet surfaces."

Quieting the Attached Cabinet

Appliances built into wall cabinets tend to vibrate excessively. Strip gaskets placed behind the cabinet, creating a space between it and the wall, prevent the wall from acting like a sounding board. "Such gaskets will also reduce impact noise radiation caused by the stocking of cabinet shelves and the closing of drawers and cabinet doors."

Soft rubber or cork tile on the shelves and back surfaces of the kitchen cabinets will "minimize the impact noise caused by placing dishware or food supplies in the cabinets." And you can make the closing of the cabinet doors quieter by "placing soft rubber bumpers or small strips of foam rubber on the inside edges of the . . . doors."

The Exhaust Fan—A Special Case

Exhaust fans that are noisy will be used less. Before purchase, find out the *sone*, or noise rating, of exhaust equipment. A helpful resource is available from the Heating and Ventilation Institute (publication #11). Always try to mount the exhaust fan outside the house and secure the ductwork—for example, by boxing it in tightly with plywood. If the noise level is still too high, replacing a section of the duct with a material that might reduce the transmission of noise caused by vibration (as opposed to the noise of the moving air itself) is a possibility, but it is debatable how much this will accomplish. Moreover, this can cause problems of fire safety if you use such combustable materials as canvas (actually recommended in one kitchen design book). If you can find a synthetic product that could serve as a sound break and is fireproof—for example, something used by stove manufacturers—you might give it a try in really bad situations.

You should also install exhaust fans using rubber mounts. "Most ceiling exhaust systems use high speed, noisy propeller fans that are mounted rigidly to the ducts, which in turn are connected to the ceiling by means of the fan grilles. These structural paths carry the fan vibration to the ceiling, which acts like a large sounding board and amplifies the noise." To cut down this noise, the EPA suggests that you

1. Isolate the fan from the duct with rubber grommets or resilient spacers.
2. Isolate the duct's grille from the ceiling with a soft sponge rubber gasket or spacers.
3. Operate the fan at its lowest speed.

It is much more difficult to quiet a hood-type fan installed directly above the stove because the space is so limited. At the least you can operate the fan at its slowest speed. You can also keep the oil and grease from accumulating on the fan blades and thereby clogging up the pores of the filter pack. If possible, install the fan on rubber mounts. When replacement of a ceiling or hood exhaust fan is due, remember that squirrel-cage-type fans are less noisy than propeller blade units.

Proper Installation of An Exhaust Fan

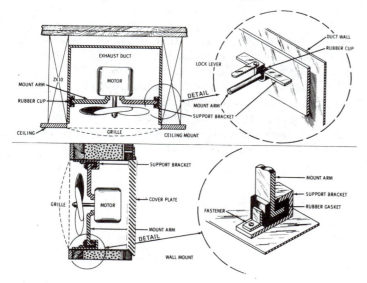

Source: Quieting: A Practical Guide to Noise Control (1978).

Floors

If you want a really quiet kitchen, choose flooring with some acoustic value, but there definitely are trade-offs to be made (see Chapter 6). Thick foam padding under the flooring material makes a remarkable difference. Carpet laid over concrete will absorb 14 percent of the sound; if the carpet is put over heavy foam backing, the absorption jumps to 57 percent. Foam-backed vinyl is probably the best bet for a floor with some acoustical value and compatibility with kitchen needs.

Walls

The walls are usually taken up with appliances and cabinets, which are hard-surfaced, sound-reflecting, and sound-transmitting. Thus, any remaining wall area, however small, should be carefully considered as an important candidate for sound-absorbing components, since a mix of wall, ceiling, and floor treatments is most effective in stopping sound reflections.

An effective, although expensive acoustical (and insulating) wall-covering material often employed by solar builders is called Sempatap.™ Similar in looks to wallpaper, it can be used on walls, on ceilings, and under carpets. Apparently, it also smoothes out rough walls. It is available in both a finished version and a version for use under paint or ordinary wallpaper. Also available are Vicracoustic™ panels, which are sound-absorbent sheets covered with vinyl.

Helpful, too, is covering one or two wall surfaces with a soft finish, such as cork tile, heavy drapes, or padded vinyl wall covering. Drapes and unfinished cork should not be close to cooking and washing areas, and they can be effective even in an adjacent dining area. The padded vinyl will tolerate water but not the heat of cookers. Commercially available wall panels with a high NRC can also be used, as well as such professional acoustic materials as Sonex™.

Ceilings

The easiest kitchen surface to turn into a sound absorber is the ceiling. In the Demonstration Kitchen I decided to emulate an acoustical ceiling used in industrial settings: an outer perforated surface through which sound travels and is then absorbed by an underlayer of sound-absorbent material—in this case, fiberglass. This design is used in various ways around us—telephone booths being one familiar application. With this design you have the added advantage of access into the ceiling—something you might be very thankful for if you need to reach plumbing, wiring, and so on.

The materials used for the Demonstration Kitchen's acoustical ceiling are high-quality, tempered pegboard, fireproof vinyl cloth, and fiberglass insulation (with no vapor barrier).

To install, first fill the spaces between the floor joists with bats of fiberglass insulation. Next, tack the vinyl to the joists to prevent minute pieces of fiberglass from descending through the pegboard. Then screw the sheets of pegboard to the floor joists. Planning is important so that the pegboard panel edges end up on the joists and so that you can attach the trim easily. The pegboard should also be painted with a high-gloss, washable paint before it is mounted.

Trim, selected to complement the room design, can be screwed to the joists where the edges of the pegboard butt.

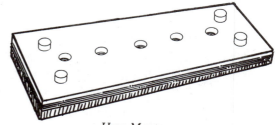

Hole Matrix.
Use to increase the number of holes in pegboard used for an acoustical ceiling.

According to acoustical expert F. Alton Everest, to get better sound absorption, the percent of holes in the pegboard should be increased from the manufactured level, which is about 5 percent, to 12–15 percent. For better sound absorption, as Alton advises, you can make a jig that sits in four peg holes with a line of additional holes in the middle. This form will make it easy to drill an extra series of holes perfectly.

Selecting Ceiling Panels

There are several good commercial ceiling panel systems available that are hung from the ceiling. The most commonly known is Celotex.™ These require suspending a metal framework from the existing ceiling (6 inches or more below it) and clipping acoustical panels into this grid. Ventilation and lighting fixtures can also be inserted into the grid, and it can conceal plumbing, electrical, and ventilation equipment. Panels that are soft, contain fiberglass or mineral wool, and are covered with washable plastic film have the best qualities. The Vicracoustic™ and Sempatap™ panels mentioned earlier are also worth investigating.

Choose panels according to NRC (the higher the NRC, the better), price, and decorative value. For sources, check the yellow pages under Acoustical Contractors or Acoustical Materials.

Chapter 6:

FLOORING

Many people are surprised to learn that one of the first decisions I made when designing the Demonstration Kitchen was to remove the expensive ceramic tile floor that had been put down by a previous owner. To many people, tile floors are the ultimate in kitchen glamour. There is no question that they impart a beautiful look, and if you equate luxury with cost, they certainly are luxurious. However, after examining the qualities of all stone and ceramic floors and the alternatives for kitchens, I would put them at the bottom of the list.

To my way of thinking, their indisputable aesthetic value is outweighed by the fact that tile floors—as well as marble, flagstone, terrazzo, stone, and the like—are cold and hard to stand on. It is no accident that a large percentage of tile floors are laid in consistently warm climates. The physical qualities of these materials are such that they hold absorbed temperatures for long periods of time. This may have advantages in warm locales, but in other climates this can be an uncomfortable drawback.

An even more important consideration is the fact that these floors are hard. This means they are hard on the feet, legs, and back, an aspect that may subtly be conditioning people away from cooking. If your back or feet ache after spending time in the kitchen, why would you want to return? Though builders and interior decorators may encourage the use of these materials—particularly tiles, for from their point of view they are commendable—the cook may find out otherwise, the hard way.

Any stonelike floor is also unforgiving. There is no glass or china that will survive falling onto this type of floor; and when they break, the shards scatter widely. And although these floors are certainly washable, their grout lines may not present the most easily cleanable surface. Finally, these floors are heavy, possibly creating structural expenses, as well as noisy, reflecting every sound.

Ceramic tiles are very popular in commercial kitchens, where their durability is prized. These working kitchens are subject to continuous abuse and require daily "swabbing" (often into a built-in drain); thus, it is easy to see where designers and builders got their inspiration. However, if you visit a commercial kitchen, you are not likely to see the workers standing directly on the tiles. They will be standing on platforms—or skids, as they are known in the trade. Skids are a kind of overfloor or boardwalk traditionally made of wood slats nailed to crosspieces. (Today they are also being made of plastic.) The skids allow spills and other slippery material to fall through to the floor, making for a safer environment as well as providing a softer surface for the kitchen staff.

MATERIAL SELECTION

After eliminating tiles, stone, and other similar hard flooring materials, I proceeded to examine the other options available for the Demonstration Kitchen. The most important considerations were

- Was it easy to clean?
- Was it durable?
- Was it relatively soft?
- Was it beautiful?
- Was it suitable for the chemically sensitive?

VINYL OR LINOLEUM

Sheet vinyl and linoleum both provide suitable kitchen flooring. Among these materials are many variations in cost and quality. Sheet vinyl is more expensive and durable than linoleum, and it is available foam-backed and with no-wax finishes. Foam-backed vinyl has excellent acoustical qualities.

Solid vinyl tiles have characteristics similar to sheet vinyl. They can be considerably more expensive, but if one tile gets damaged, it can be replaced. Asphalt tile is the least expensive, but is also the least durable. It has poor resistance to grease and stains.

All of these materials can scratch and dent. In the least expensive lines, color or design is only superficial, so the finish and decorative effect can easily be marred. It costs quite a bit more to get the color or design integral and thus resistant to damage.

For those who want the look of stone and the practicality of vinyl, vinyl tiles that mimic all these materials are available.

CARPETING

Kitchen carpet is soft, sound-absorbent, and resilient under foot. However, in an area prone to grease, spills, and heavy traffic, maintenance may become too demanding. Homeowners must commit themselves to frequent cleaning as well as replacement. On the other hand, it is an inexpensive way to cover a floor and can be quite satisfactory with regular vacuuming and the use of soil-retardant sprays.

Kitchen carpeting should be made from entirely synthetic materials (nylon, acrylic, Olefin™), the pile should be short and dense, and it should have a thick backing. Indoor/outdoor carpet, which is a more practical material due to the likelihood of water and other liquid contact, has a rough look and unpleasant feel that may be aesthetically unappealing. Remember, carpets can outgas harmful fumes that would not be tolerated by the chemically sensitive or those looking for a "low-tox" environment. One strategy is to let the carpet and backing outgas somewhere else for three months or so before installation.

Small throw rugs set at well-used work stations have become popular in kitchen spaces. Though these reduce fatigue and can be removed for easy cleaning, they can be a cause of accidents. To minimize slippage and serious injuries, use only a well-secured or properly backed mat.

RUBBER

Rubber flooring is being more widely employed in industrial settings and spreading to home use, too. It apparently has many advantages. It has excellent acoustical qualities; it is certainly soft. But it also has several limitations. These floors apparently continue to have a rubber smell for quite some time, and they may be particularly problematic for those with sensitivities to petrochemicals. Smooth rubber, although water-resistant, tends to get slippery when wet, and oil and grease may stain. Although new designs with a continuous raised pattern reduce this hazard, they create a new problem: a floor with hundreds of small grooves for dirt to sit in.

CORK

I considered cork tiling for the Demonstration Kitchen for quite some time, since it absorbs sound, is forgiving to dropped dishes, and is kind on the feet and back. It can also be sealed against water. But finally its reputation for low durability kept me away. Since cork tile is made by compressing cork with petrochemical binders, it is a poor choice for those with sensitivities to these substances.

WOOD

Wood flooring was the choice for the Demonstration Kitchen. Its aesthetics are classic. Its fibrous nature makes it a warm material that is easy on the body and less damaging to breakable objects. I used oak flooring inlaid with walnut that I had specially milled locally. This allowed me to create a simple pattern in the floor that easily competes with the most expensive floors for beauty. Other suitable woods include pecan, maple, birch, and cherry; the darker woods may be somewhat less revealing of dirt.

You must resign yourself to the fact that a wood floor will not remain unmarred. There will be some dents, scratches, and spots where something worked its way through the finish, but if you look at any wood floor, you'll find this to be true. After all, it's only a floor. Moreover, unlike other floors whose beauty can be destroyed by wear, those defects are less disturbing in wood.

Laying a wood floor in the kitchen takes extra attention. High-quality wood should be used to minimize natural imperfections and should be air-dried on the building site or other heated space for at least a month to minimize shrinkage. The wood should be stacked so that air can circulate, in a spot with an even temperature. When installing the floor, be very careful to make end cuts and joints snug and the nailing tight. Of course, you will want to make sure there is a solid underlayment. This attention has paid off on the Demonstration Kitchen floor, which after almost five years of use shows no shrinking, warping, or splitting.

FLOORING COSTS PER SQUARE YARD (INSTALLED)	
Vinyl sheet	$13–42
Linoleum	$20–30
Vinyl tile	$ 4–14
Indoor/outdoor carpet	$10–12
Rubber tile	$ 8–20
Rubber sheet	$15–47
Cork	$ 6–14
Hardwood	$ 6–13

Source: *The New York Times*, January 1987

Selecting Wood Floor Finish

POLYURETHANE

There are two types of urethane oil-modified urethane and moisture-cure urethane. Oil-modified urethane, is what you are most likely to find in the hardware store. It is easy to use and durable. It will off-gas for about 3 weeks, but the worst will be over in the first 24 hours. I have found the fast-drying type to be less durable. Moisture-cure urethane, despite it's innocent-sounding name is not considered suitable for the homeowner. It is highly durable but will off-gas for long periods of time.

VARNISH

Most varnishes today are made from synthetic materials but should not off-gas for long periods. The alkyd varnishes are easily applied and durable.

ACRYLICS

These are not as durable as other finishes, but they are nonvolatile.

SWEDISH FINISH

A "Swedish finish" was chosen for the Demonstration Kitchen, since it has a good reputation for long life acid and alcohol resistance. Although we are very happy with the finish, I am not happy with what I eventually learned about the finish's contribution to indoor air quality. Subsequent to its application, Dr. Thad Godish of Ball State University, an expert on formaldehyde, expressed concern about the level of this controversial substance, and John Girman, of California's Indoor Air Quality Program, although less concerned about formaldehyde, had reservations because of its emission of butanols. Dr. Godish thought the formaldehyde might dissipate in six months; Girman thought the butanols could last a lot longer. The question is, do you want to live with the finish as it off-gases since both chemicals are known to have negative health effects? The company states that the product's constituents are within regulations and are not harmful.

NONTOXIC FINISHES

See "Selected Resources" for the address of Woodpecker's Tools, which makes such nontoxic finishes as natural resin floor lacquer.

ENVIRONMENTAL CHOICES

Tile or concrete are the best choices for the chemically sensitive but not for the cook. Wood and hard vinyl are next best choices and should not prevent problems except for the most sensitive. Those with chemical sensitivities also have the option of a nontoxic wood finish. Otherwise, urethane or a prefinished flooring are best for the kitchen. Those applying floor finishes that have any problematic "volatile" ingredients (check label) should wear an organic-vapor respirator and rubber gloves. Some volatiles include mineral spirits, methyl alcohol, and formaldehyde. Also, the floor should be allowed to dry with its door(s) and windows closed until dry (to keep dust out) and then opened for as much time as possible. The windows in adjacent rooms should be open through the entire process.

If you choose vinyl, avoid soft vinyl, which may contain volatile plasticizers; a vinyl that will break when bent is a better choice.

Concrete and tile (laid without adhesives) are excellent for those with serious sensitivities, but, as already discussed, they have many ergonomic disadvantages in the kitchen environment.

Be sure that the glue used to lay any flooring and carpet backing does not contain formaldehyde.

Chapter 7:
SMALL WONDERS IN THE KITCHEN

Today some small appliances are as important in the kitchen as the stove. The following is a discussion of some important electronic assistants.

THE FOOD PROCESSOR

A food processor is like having a second chef in the kitchen. Its ability to do tasks rapidly makes it a real asset when working with fresh food. The processor is a pleasure for quantity food preparation—jobs such as shredding, chopping, and slicing vegetables; whipping egg whites; and puréeing various foods. Homemade bread can be featured regularly with its assistance, and fresh pasta can be made on demand with an attachment to the processor. I've always felt that a processor would pay for itself from the less expensive meals you can prepare from fresh ingredients.

Even in small households a mini-unit can speed up routine jobs such as chopping herbs and onions, grating cheese and bread crumbs, and puréeing salad dressings.

THE BLENDER

The blender has become such an integral part of the American life-style that cookbooks today regard it as casually as they do the stove. There are certainly many jobs that would be extremely tedious, bordering on impractical, without this tool. Though less versatile than the processor and to some extent a duplication of it, the blender does do some jobs better—for example, making smoothies, puréeing soups, grinding nuts, and transforming crackers into meal.

Glass blender containers are best. Although glass is vulnerable to breakage, plastic blender containers scratch and discolor unattractively. You should also get a model with removable blades; it is easier to remove food after processing, and there is less waste at the bottom. Moreover, these blenders are much more convenient to clean and safer: You are less likely to stick your hand in the container to remove something, thereby cutting your fingers, if you can simply remove the blades by opening up the bottom.

THE TOASTER OVEN

In Chapter 11 the toaster/broiler/oven is presented as an energy-saving alternative to full-size ovens. Because their capacity is less than conventional ovens, they are more energy efficient for small jobs. I find these multifunction appliances to be one of the most useful tools in the kitchen and consider them essential for both families and individuals. The toaster oven is ideal for defrosting frozen baked goods as well as other foods. It is suitable for cooking as well as reheating single and two-person servings of foods that would normally be placed in the oven at a considerable waste of space and energy. Instead of using a skillet to pan-fry meat, fish, grilled sandwiches, and such, you can use the toaster oven. Since you need no added fat, the nutritional quality of these foods is improved.

THE MINI-VACUUM

That small vacuum cleaner commonly known as a Dustbuster℗ makes a valuable addition to your collection of kitchen cleanup tools. It pays for its modest cost by easing some of the annoying and repetitive kitchen cleanup tasks—for example, removing crumbs from drawers and under the cooktop. Miraculously, these mini-vacs get in there and do the job. Likewise, they are wonderful for small dry spills that are common in the kitchen—particularly such powdered substances as flour, sugar, and dishwasher soap.

For about twice the price there is a similar-size vacuum designed for use in wet areas as well. Given the abundance of liquids in the kitchen, this dual purpose mini-vac may be worth purchasing.

THE COMPUTER

Personal computers may someday become a standard kitchen appliance. The machine that has revolutionized our lives in so many ways may also hold the key to organizing many of the everyday cooking tasks, including shopping, meal planning, and monitoring of special diets.

I was eager to experiment with a computer in the Demonstration Kitchen and received support in doing so from the Kaypro Company. Although the technology of the Kaypro 4 I use has since been surpassed, its exterior design is considered to be seminal by industrial design experts.

One feature of this computer that makes it especially suited to the kitchen is its size—something that should be looked for in any PC to be used in the kitchen. Measuring just 18 inches wide by 8 inches high by 22 inches deep, it fits comfortably in a Hoosier cabinet, where it is protected against fumes, grease, and moisture during cooking. Designed to be portable, it closes up easily, providing additional protection. These are attributes worth considering in choosing a computer that will be used in the kitchen environment.

Unfortunately, at this point the computer has not found the acceptability in the kitchen we had hoped for. It may take another generation and more facility with PCs, but one day they will be very helpful in solving dietary problems—more so than any fabricated food has been. The following sections explore areas where the PC can help. See "Selected Resources" for a list of food related computer programs.

Meal Planning

The realization that diet is closely related to health has put a new responsibility on those who prepare foods to keep meals in line with both general and specific dietary needs. This is where a PC in the kitchen can really prove itself.

By using a nutritional analysis program, it is possible to break down any recipe, meal, or diet into its nutritional constituents. With this information the layperson can easily plan meals in accordance with current dietary guidelines. For example, the "dietary goals" established by the U.S. government in the 1970s suggest that Americans reduce consumption of total fat, saturated fat, refined sugars, salt, calories, and alcohol, and increase consumption of complex carbohydrates. Some authorities cite such specific recommendations as 30 to 35 percent of total calories from fat (with 10-percent saturated and the remainder coming from polyunsaturated and monosaturated sources), at least 45 percent of total calories from complex carbohydrates, and a limit of approximately 300 milligrams of cholesterol and 5 grams of sodium in the daily menu.

Diet monitoring by computer can be of special benefit to those with specific health problems. An article in the *National Dairy Council Newsletter* (1981) tells the story of a computer executive who had just had a heart attack. He explained how his wife was using a computer program to modify her recipes according to the doctor's instructions. The article goes on to say: "In the future when home computers are more widespread, home cooks may call in a recipe to find out at once the nutritional analysis of the day's menu, supplement missing nutrients for the family and check the presence of the ingredients—either forbidden or required in a special diet—for medical reasons."

Diabetics will also be able to plan and analyze their diets and exchange foods with simplicity. The same goes for people with high blood pressure, food allergies, weight problems, and other defined food-related health concerns.

Programs can even coordinate exercise in relation to weight loss and actually tell you how many calories you will theoretically burn at different activity levels. With details like this you can chart the expected outcome of changing your food habits and exercise patterns.

Recipe Indexing

Though you may not want to transcribe all your cookbooks onto diskettes, a data base can help you to index your favorite recipes to take advantage of foods on hand, on sale, and in season. By setting up a file containing fields of predominant ingredients, a selection of appropriate recipes for any single food or even a combination of foods can be called up with ease. A computer program can also help to scale recipes proportionately to fit different needs. In the future, when cookbooks become "cookdisks", you will be able to retrieve cooking assistance rapidly with far broader scope than ever.

Shopping and Pantry Storage

The computer can store information about your food inventory on a file program. Although in small households this may be of little value, it could be quite helpful in large families and where substantial amounts of food are preserved. Additionally, price information and sources could also be included. A similar file can be developed for gardeners to keep track of yearly crops, varieties, yield, and use so that home food production can be intelligently planned. For anyone interested in monitoring the yearly food budget, the computer and spreadsheet software are the tools.

Entertaining with Ease

If you want to preserve menus for future use, including where the recipes are located, any adjustments necessary (was there enough of each dish to go around?), who was present (so you don't serve guests the same meal next time), and any particular food likes or dislikes of those you entertain, you can do this with a basic data base program. Each time you invite someone to dinner, you can pull up their file for a complete "history."

Computer Bulletin Boards—A Nutritionist in Every Kitchen

Computers can communicate with other computers via the telephone by utilizing a modem. The modem makes it possible to "talk" to other people and experts about food, recipes, diet, and so on. This is the closest one can come to having one's own nutritionist or cooking expert literally "on hand."

The Ergonomic Chair

Computers demand a comfortable work station. Proper positioning at the keyboard can make the difference between an enjoyable and a back-breaking experience. Especially in the kitchen, where you may find yourself working at desk height (24 inches), counter height (36 inches), or possibly somewhere in between (and here the rising counter is handy), a chair that can be adjusted to suit the place as well as the user is a bonus. We have been using an ergonomic "secretarial chair" that has a pneumatic height control. The fact that this particular chair is also on wheels means it can be easily maneuvered to other kitchen locations when the cook would prefer to be seated.

The Stereo

Many people enjoy cooking to music. It is also nice if the kitchen can provide some way to utilize educational tapes. One option is small speakers connected to the house stereo system. A radio, preferably with a cassette player, can provide more choices and give those in the kitchen the opportunity to personalize their entertainment.

The Television and VCR

The television has become a common feature in many kitchens today and can be a convenience there (but not if it diverts the cook's attention or interferes with personal communication). A video cassette recorder is a wonderful vehicle for learning cooking techniques, but there are problems operating the machine in the kitchen. For example, to cook from a video you should be able to stop or review the tape while you're cooking. But this is difficult and possibly dangerous with wet or messy hands. A foot pedal similar to those used with dictaphones would make the VCR a much more versatile tool under these circumstances. But, alas, none exists.

Chapter 8:

SAFETY

It should not be surprising that the kitchen is the most dangerous room in the house. The confluence of fire, electric, gas, hot water, sharp implements, motorized gadgets, heavy pots, and so on, creates myriad opportunities for mishaps. As a result 40 percent of all household accidents happen in the kitchen.

· Unfortunately, safety is not a topic given enough attention by those involved with designing and building kitchens. The indexes of design books written by professionals for the layperson illustrate this point. Among all the popular kitchen books I reviewed, only one explores the subject in any depth; two others mention safety only in connection with construction, and one merely alerts you to such appliance safety identifications as "UL (Underwriter's Laboratory) approved."

Overall kitchen design should seek to minimize the movement of heavy, hot, or otherwise troublesome items. This means that the ideal design in terms of safety is one with a counter that contains, *without interruption*, sink, workspace, stove, workspace. Where this is not possible, you should think about the details of kitchen activity—for example, an adjacent workspace is important at the stove top and ovens, particularly if it can tolerate hot pots. Also, insufficient counter space can create dangerous clutter.

FIRE

Some remarkable statistics: Sixteen percent of fatal fires in the U.S. begin in the kitchen. There are more than 130,000 known kitchen fires reported each year, but one expert, Dennis Smith, suggests in his *Fire Safety Book* that there are probably five to ten times that amount that go unreported.

Cooking oils and greases, clothing, towels, waxes (heating paraffin on the stove), spilled combustable liquids (alcohol and cleaning fluids), and flour and other combustable powders are the principal kitchen materials that can be ignited. Contact between the cooking elements, or flame, and these materials is most frequently accidental and comes with such a surprise that reactions are often hasty and misguided. Moreover, grease accumulation on stove or exhaust system very often serves as a medium for a small fire to spread rapidly.

Obviously, kitchen fire safety is of utmost importance. But how many kitchens have even rudimentary firefighting equipment? And how many people have any idea what to do if a fire does break out?

Smoke Detectors

Unfortunately, because of emissions generated by the cooking of food, commonly available smoke detectors, as presently constructed, cannot be used in the kitchen. Both the photoelectric and ion chamber detectors will go off inappropriately, and they can become desensitized by grease, fumes, and so on. Thus, no responsible maker of popular smoke and fire detectors recommends installing them in kitchens. Since most kitchen fires start while people are present, fire precautions and firefighting equipment are more important considerations.

Fire Extinguishers

Every kitchen should have at least one fire extinguisher for oven and small fires. Fire extinguishers have ratings, based upon their ability to extinguish different kinds of fires. The most versatile for the kitchen and home in general are those rated ABC. They can extinguish (A) paper, wood, cloth, and some plastics; (B) grease or inflammable liquids; and (C) electric fires. At the least, it must be rated BC. Be sure to get one that is not too heavy for any prospective user, and make sure it has a gauge to check its pressure. Hang

---

KITCHEN FIRE STRATEGY

Never try to carry a burning pan from the house, or you risk spreading the fire. However, you should try smothering it with the lid, some baking soda, a cookie sheet, or a fire blanket. For oven fires keep the door shut and turn the oven off. You may also try opening the door a crack and using an appropriate extinguisher.

Do no more than try to cope with a small fire. If you can't control it, get everyone out of the house, closing the kitchen door behind you. Call the fire department.

it in an obvious place, away from young children and not right near the range. An exit is an excellent location.

Halon extinguishers, which depend on a nontoxic gas, may be better for kitchen use than the more commonly available dry extinguishers, which leave a residue difficult to clean up. Although only rated BC—that is, not suitable for paper or wood fires—they are all right for "limited use" on paper fires. (Unfortunately, halon gas is associated with the destruction of the ozone layer and I am reluctant to recommend it for this reason. In fact, it is possible that the use of the gas will eventually be banned. Hopefully a suitable replacement will be found.)

Fire Blanket

One of the most practical discoveries I made in researching kitchen safety is an interesting piece of fire-fighting equipment that is hardly known in this country: the fire blanket. Hundreds of thousands of these fiberglass blankets are sold each year in England, and though they are used here in industrial settings, they are generally not marketed to the American homeowner. Since a fire extinguisher can actually spread some fires, a blanket is especially appropriate in the kitchen.

Blankets work on a basic principle known to all: If you deprive a fire of oxygen—that is, if you smother it—it will be extinguished quickly. As a representative of one fire blanket manufacturer said to me, "If it doesn't work, you missed!" I think this is a piece of equipment that should be standard in all kitchens and homes. (See "Selected Resources.")

Baking Soda

Once again, this remarkable substance is useful in the kitchen. Baking soda has excellent fire-fighting capabilities, particularly when grease is the culprit. A labeled container permanently placed near the stove is a simple inexpensive precaution.

Water Hose

The kitchen is a good place to locate a fire hose. Coiled under a sink and permanently hooked up to a water source at one end and a ball valve that is easy to turn on at the other end, a hose can provide another level of defense.

Note: Water should not be used on a grease fire, since it can spread it.

Sprinkler Systems

Built-in sprinkler systems are now available for the home. Though they are not a small investment, they are not as expensive as people might think (about 1 percent of the total building cost). They are very reliable and do not go off unnecessarily. Builders of new homes would be wise to look into their cost, as well as insurance discounts.

ELECTRIC

One of the most surprising things I learned while working on this project was how many people suffer electrical shocks in the kitchen because they wrongly assume that appliances that are turned off have no electricity in them. But this is not so: Even though a toaster, blender, broiler, waffle iron, electric frying pan, radio, TV, coffee maker, or whatever is not switched "on," as long as it is plugged in, parts of it are still "live." A plugged-in appliance, even when "off," can shock or kill you if, for example, it falls into water, is cleaned with a damp rag, or you touch a live part and a ground, such as a faucet, at the same time.

Water and electricity can be a deadly combination. Making contact with an electrical current while standing in water or even on a damp floor can transform what might otherwise be a light shock into instant death. Consumer products that have been related to this kind of electrocution hazard include hair dryers, electrical power tools, TV sets, radios, small kitchen appliances, and sump pumps.

HOW TO USE A FIRE EXTINGUISHER

Know how the extinguisher's safety and switch work and how far to hold the extinguisher from the fire.

Because extinguishers have different spray patterns and power, the National Fire Protection Association recommends that people familiarize themselves with their equipment. For example, trying it out on a small fire outside on a windless day; then you won't be surprised if you have to use it. The cost of recharging is a small price to pay for the experience gained.

Here's how to work extinguishers (*PASS* is the instructional reminder):

1. *P*—Pull the pin.
2. *A*—Aim.
3. *S*—Squeeze the handle.
4. *S*—Sweep from side to side at base of fire.

Be careful: Do not hold the extinguisher too close to the fire. The propellant might blow the burning grease onto walls, or other inflammable surfaces. Use on small fires only.

Unplug It!

Because of these accidents, Underwriter's Laboratory (UL) and the Association of Home Appliance Manufacturers launched a public relations campaign called "Unplug It!" The campaign's purpose is to get us into the habit of unplugging kitchen appliances (and for that matter, bathroom appliances) when not in use. So, unplug it!

WARNING: IF YOU THINK THE POWER IS OFF WHEN THE SWITCH IS OFF, YOU'RE WRONG.

KEEP AWAY FROM WATER.

Everyone knows that electricity and water are a dangerous combination. But did you know that an electric appliance is still electrically alive even if the switch is off? If the plug is in, the power is on. So when you keep appliances near water, keep them unplugged.

ALWAYS UNPLUG SMALL APPLIANCES.

Public Service ad from Association of Home Appliance Manufacturers and Underwriters Laboratories Inc.

Ground Fault Circuit Interruptors (GFCIs)

There is another, very effective way of providing electrical safety, without having to unplug appliances: *ground fault circuit interruptors,* or *GFCIs.* The layperson can think of GFCIs as "super circuit breakers," but they are more accurately described as "electric adding machines." They continually watch the current going into appliances (hot load) versus the current leaving appliances (neutral load). Whenever a hazardous amount of current seeks ground via anything other than the circuit—*such as your body*—the GFCI trips *very quickly*: quicker than a circuit breaker and, more important, quicker than a heartbeat, which prevents most electrocution or severe electric shock injuries.

The GFCI is extremely sensitive to even small electrical changes. These "ground faults" can be caused by worn or defective equipment as well as by accidents. GFCIs may not entirely prevent a shock, but at least you will not get a fatal one. As a matter of fact, two times during the construction of the Demonstration Kitchen serious shocks were prevented by GFCIs.

GFCIs must be installed in an accessible location, so they can be tested once a month by the residents. This is to ensure that the contacts are clean and in good working order. The test can be performed by anyone, and a record card is provided to help assure regular testing. GFCIs are available in three types: (1) installed in circuit breaker box, (2) installed in outlet, or (3) portable.

Enough Outlets

It is a popular practice to use three-way plugs, extension cords, and other devices that overload, or "bottleneck," electrical outlets. This is especially common in older kitchens, where the plethora of electric kitchen appliances people use nowadays was not anticipated.

In light of this I was very happy to come upon strips, or "raceways," of electrical outlets, one of which is called Plugmold.™ The strips are often seen in shops and industrial settings. They consist of 1 ¼- by ⅞-inch metal strips that contain multiple prewired electrical receptacles. All receptacles are spaced at 6, 9, 12, or 18 inches. They usually come in stainless steel and a buff color (which can be repainted to any color with an oil-based paint, although the company suggests testing the paint first).

The Demonstration Kitchen has Plugmold™ mounted underneath all the overhead kitchen cabinets, far away from curious little fingers. I can think of no better kitchen electrical system than raceways of outlets backed up with GFCIs.

Three-Prong and Polarized Plugs

Many appliances are affixed with three-wire cords and plugs. The third wire serves as a ground; in the event of an electrical fault in the product, the current will be drained away and not expose the user to a shock. With them, first, it is necessary to make sure that the ground circuit is completed at the outlet for this safeguard to be effective. In other words, you must have properly installed grounded wiring. Second, *never* cut the ground pin off of the plug. Some older homes are wired with a two-wire system that does not provide the ground circuit; manufacturers usually provide instructions for coping with this situation. If in doubt, consult an electrician. There are usually simple ways to provide access to a ground.

Take a close look at a new electrical appliance plug. Chances are that one prong will be about ⅛ inch wider than the other. This is a *polarized plug;* it will fit

SAFE EXTENSION CORDS

Motor Size	120 Volt Appliance Load		Extension Cord Size and Lengths			
	Watts	Amps	#18	#16	#14	#12
¼	600	5	74'	118'	188'	300'
⅓	720	7	60'	95'	152'	241'
½	1200	10		70'	111'	177'
¾	1680	14			79'	126'
	1800	15			65'	112'
	1920	16				108'
1½	2400	20				87'

only one way into a polarized socket. This innovation was made to increase appliance safety, since the hot (or live) wire can be identified at the outlet, and then this wire can, in turn, be the one that is switched by the appliance switch. Extension cords are also made with polarized plugs. Do nothing to defeat this feature.

Extension Cords

Use the appropriate-size extension cord for the appliance. This is especially important for air conditioners and freezers. Grounded appliances must have three-wire, grounded extension cords, and polarized plugs need polarized cords. If you have a problem putting a new plug into an old or substandard extension cord socket, I suggest you discard the extension cord. The size of extension cord wire is marked on the cord in fine print and is also printed on the cardboard sales label. The common sizes are 12, 14, 16, and 18; the lower numbers are the heavier wire. The marking will also show the number of wires; thus, 12/3 means three wires size 12, and 14/2 means two wires size 14. Use the table above to determine which size wire is required for the job. The measurements in feet given in the table are the maximum extension cord lengths for the particular size wire carrying the amount of current shown. Equivalent watts and motor horsepower ratings are also given with the current. Appliances with motors will last longer if you use one half the lengths shown, especially if they will have long-term use on the extension cord.

Electric Safety Checklist

According to the Consumer Product Safety Commission, 35 percent of electrically caused fires are related to cooking equipment. Please observe the following rules:

1. Read and follow manufacturer's instructions concerning their products.
2. Check appliances for loose plugs, frayed wires, and so on. They can spark.
3. Add more outlets if necessary. Overloading of outlets, or "bottlenecking," can cause overheating and fires. Also, make sure that the circuit and fuses (or circuit breakers) are adequate for the appliances on that line.
4. Make sure fuses or circuit breakers are well identified on the box so that they can be switched off quickly by anyone.
5. Be aware of these signs of poor wiring: frequent flickering; regular blowing of fuses or tripping of circuit breakers; and outlets, plugs, and wires that are warm to the touch.
6. Overwattage in lamps causes overheating and fire. Do not exceed recommended lamp wattage. A "roasting" smell is an indication that you are using a bulb with too-high wattage.
7. Tape appliance cords and extension cords together when the connection is permanent.
8. Do not run extension cords near toasters, ovens, ranges, radiators, or any other high heat source.
9. Prevent fraying of long cords and extension cords by not running them under carpets or mats or through doorways.
10. Don't shorten cords by wrapping them up tightly, for they can heat, dry, crack, and consequently cause a fire. Shorten the wire instead.
11. Keep electric cords away from any water source. Any appliance near water must have waterproof wire (not cloth covered, as was used in the past or sometimes today for a decorative look).
12. Don't interchange cords from different electrical appliances.
13. Children are the most frequent victims of accidents involving electric cords. Both children and electric cords tend to be at floor level—a bad combination. Children have been known to chew, suck, and, of course, pull on electric cords. Minimize these problems through inspection and repair and by situating outlets above children's level. (There are no exposed outlets in the Demonstration Kitchen.) Cap unused outlets or install rotating outlets, which must be turned 90 degrees to be used. Special plugs are available at hardware stores.
14. Discard or repair any appliance that causes the slightest shock, or even a "tickle" or funny feeling, when you touch it.

GAS

There is no question of the need to be warned of gas leaks, but at this writing there is no commonly available gas detector or alarm system to recommend. The danger of large leaks is evident: Explosion, fire, and loss of life can result. But small leaks can sicken you, and this is no mere trifle. Unfortunately, the technology that is used today for gas detectors is sensitive not only to gas but to many cooking emissions, making them unsuited to kitchens. I hope in the future an effort will be made to develop an alarm that would be gas-sensitive alone. This would be a great boon in terms of both safety and health.

GAS LEAK STRATEGY

When you smell gas:

1. Immediately extinguish matches, cigarettes, candles, and so on.
2. Check that pilot lights have not blown out.
3. Most building codes require an in-line shutoff valve, called a gas cock, for each gas appliance. Shut it off and call the gas company.
4. Open windows and leave the area if possible.
5. After the problem is located, remember to reignite all pilot lights.

MISCELLANEOUS CHILD SAFETY CONCERNS

The foregoing sections include many pointers about child safety. This section discusses additional concerns.

One thing to keep in mind In general: Sharp corners anywhere are a hazard to kids.

Electric

Outlets should be installed out of reach whenever possible. Swivel outlets are available that protect children, as do outlet covers. GFCIs will protect children as well as adults. Shorten appliance cords and/or tack them down so they can't be tripped over. To tack down wires, use insulated staples, duct-type tape, or special wire covers. (Also see number 13 in the foregoing "Electric Safety Checklist.")

Poisons

- Keep all poisonous household products in original containers. If you must transfer them, do so to childproof containers. Never use a food container.
- Empty all containers before discarding.
- Keep food and household products well separated.
- See "Cabinets" later in this section.

Garbage

Garbage, including the plastic garbage bags, should be out of the reach of young children. In the Demonstration Kitchen the can is hidden behind bifold doors that can be latched. (Bifold doors have two or more sections that fold away to one side without projecting very far into the room, enabling them to comfortably span wide areas.) By hanging the doors a few inches from the floor, you can create an enclosed area to feed animals that children cannot get at.

The cabinet under the sink is a usual garbage (and storage) site and an area that can easily be made childproof with a latch.

Refrigerator

The refrigerator should be made childproof if possible with a safety latch, since medicines and heavy items are potential sources of trouble. Deep freezers must have a latch. Special hardware is available in hardware stores.

Cooktop/Oven and Microwave

Buy these appliances with knobs that must be pushed in and turned. Dials located on top of cooking surfaces rather than on the front surface are less tempting. The oven door should probably have a childproof latch; wall ovens are less accessible than under-the-range models. Microwave ovens should be totally inaccessible to youngsters. (See Chapter 11.)

Small Appliances

Small appliances are best out of sight in childproof cabinets when not in use. They are very attractive to youngsters and dangerous if used improperly.

Small Utensils

Sharp-edged utensils must be stored in childproof spaces.

Cabinets

According to a major study by the American Association of Poison Control Centers in 1983, 90 percent of poisonings occurred in the home and 64 percent of the victims were under age six. Nondrug substances accounted for two thirds of the poisonings; the greatest number were caused by such cleaning substances as bleaches, disinfectants, and detergents.

Cabinets that use "press-touch" latches rather than knobs are less appealing to children. All below-the-counter cabinets should have child safety catches.

Where there are no resident children but frequent young guests, childproofing hazardous locations is a courtesy that will be appreciated. A number of different devices are commonly available in hardware stores.

A nice idea from Arlene Stewart's little book *Childproofing Your Home* is to create a special kids' cabinet. Fill it with convenient breakfast and snack items, plastic utensils, unbreakable dishes, and the like, so a child can serve him or herself without climbing all over the kitchen.

Swinging Doors

These are not recommended where small children are present. Also, if used often, they should have a window.

Flooring

Avoid throw rugs without nonskid backing and on very smooth flooring.

Kitchen Stool

Stepladders, step stools, and even highchairs are a child's stairway to trouble. Attaching them to a wall or inside a closet with a spring-loaded hook and eye or other device can help limit the danger.

The Clock

Hang your clock so children can see it without having to climb. We used a Bulova battery-powered wall clock that was rated water-resistant, a feature that should help protect against kitchen moisture. It's nice, too, to have at least one battery-powered clock for when the power goes out.

First Aid Kit Inventory

The kitchen is a prime site for housing a first aid kit. Not only do many accidents happen there, but people tend to go to the kitchen as well as the bathroom to tend wounds.

A well-stocked first aid kit includes:

Assorted Band-Aids®, including butterflies	Syrup of ipecac
	Sterile gauze
Waterproof adhesive tape	Sterile pads
Surgipad® dressing	Small mirror
First aid cream	Needle
Alcohol swabs	Matches
Hydrogen peroxide	Finger cots

Part II:

APPLIANCES AND ENERGY EFFICIENCY

Some 20 to 40 percent of household energy is consumed in the kitchen. This is obviously a formidable amount, and part of my concept for the Demonstration Kitchen was to see if this could be reduced. Indeed I did find that energy savings can be obtained from knowledgeable selection and maintenance of lights, dishwashers, stoves, and—most significantly— refrigerators. Not surprisingly, the expense of inefficient appliances falls hardest on the lowest income groups, who spent 25 percent of their income on energy in 1980 as compared with 4 percent for the average household.

Before the fuel crisis of 1973, kitchen design barely considered energy; remarkably, things haven't changed much since then. Most kitchen guides and studies do not broach the subject. Furthermore, when I received the results of a free energy audit from my local utility, I was amazed to find that among all the worthwhile suggestions listed in the computer analysis of our home's energy status, there was no mention of appliance efficiency. It certainly is a lot simpler to replace a refrigerator and save 40 to 50 percent on its operating cost than it is to insulate the floor, which is one of the suggestions I did receive.

What really shocked me was what I learned about the relationship between refrigerator efficiency and the need for new power plants, including nuclear. A calculation from the prestigious Lawrence Berkeley Laboratory in California is quite an eye opener. As reported in John Rothchild's *Stop Burning Your Money* (1981), scientists there estimated (in the 1970s) that if everyone in California had an energy-efficient refrigerator, the state could save 5 percent of its energy, or the energy generated by two nuclear power plants. The two power plants (at that time) cost $3 billion to build; 16 million refrigerators cost $750 million. It would actually be cheaper to give the refrigerators away than to build the nuclear plants—and safer too!

Thus unexpectedly, choosing efficient kitchen appliances can have far-reaching effects. The nice part is that there are appliances that can satisfy both consumer and environmental needs. Conservation is an energy alternative with many positive attributes: It is a simple strategy, it is about five times cheaper than providing "new" energy, and it is a good deal safer. It can create new jobs through innovative technology, it frees scarce resources, and it can ultimately result in more effective design and better health. "Consumers want the services that energy provides, not energy itself," says Dr. Arthur H. Rosenfeld, director of the Center for Building Science at Lawrence Berkeley Laboratory. (The center is responsible for much of the basic research on appliance efficiency and air quality in this book.)

What also cannot be ignored is that the fuel burned by power plants adds to the pollution that destroys the Earth's ozone layer, contributes to the greenhouse effect, and generally affects air quality. Anything we can do to reduce the use of of fuel helps.

This part of *The Smart Kitchen* focuses on refrigeration and cold storage needs, as well as selecting dishwashers and cooking units.

LEGISLATED EFFICIENCIES

U.S. government regulations help to make major appliances more efficient. After years of resistance by manufacturers and a veto by President Reagan, Congress passed the National Energy Conservation Act in 1987. This law establishes minimum efficiency standards for home appliances and heating and cooling equipment. The standards for dishwashers took effect on January 1, 1988, and requires an air-dry option. The standards for most other appliances take effect in 1990.

These standards will mandate appliances to be 10 to 30 percent more efficient than the average model before the legislation. The American Council for an Energy Efficient Economy (ACE[3]), a Washington-based public interest organization, estimates that this will save the average household about $30 a year. But even more important, it will reduce the need for many new power plants.

THE ENERGYGUIDE LABEL

Have you ever noticed black and yellow labels glued to the front of major appliances? These government-mandated Energyguide labels are a very valuable consumer aid, enabling "comparison (energy) shopping." The energy efficiency ratings (EERs) that appears on the labels provide an *estimated annual operating cost* for that particular appliance. Presently, refrigerators, refrigerator/freezers, freezers, dishwashers, water heaters, clothes washers, room air conditioners, and furnaces must all bear the Energyguide label.

The labels will continue to be important even with the higher appliance standards. This is because the standards eliminate only the least efficient models. Appliances will still be made with a broad range of efficiencies, and since some, like the refrigerator, have a lifespan of fifteen to twenty years, your choices can have a long-term effect. In 1986, if you used the Energyguide label and purchased the most efficient refrigerator available (Whirlpool ET17HK1M), it would have cost you $60 more, according to ACE[3]. But the extra expense would have been paid back in thirty months from reduced energy consumption—a 45-percent rate of return. After this period, the unit would continue to save about $24 dollars a year for the life of the refrigerator. (By 1993, when the standards are fully in effect, payback periods may only be one year!)

Using the Energyguide Label

Following is a detailed diagram of the Energyguide label. You should be aware that the "estimated annual operating costs" that appears on it do not necessarily

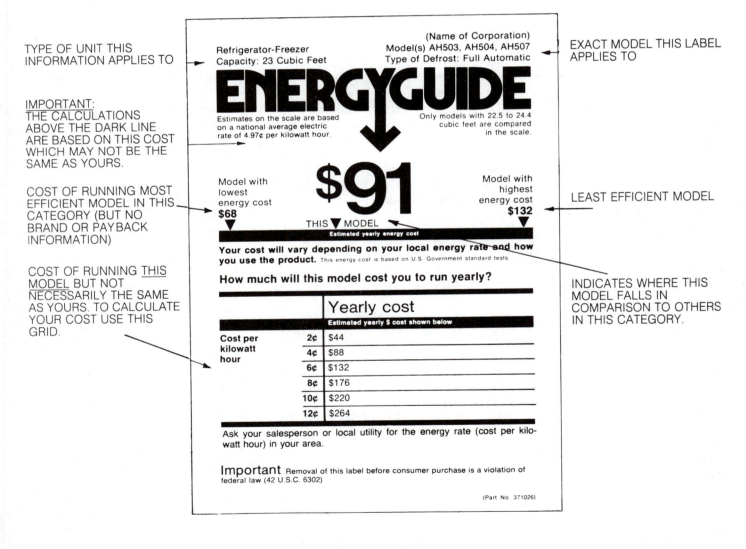

ENERGYGUIDE LABEL

predict your *actual* operating cost; that depends on personal use and your local utility rates. (The utility rate used for the Energyguide label calculations is found in very small type on the upper-left side of the label. However, a grid of rates is included on the label, and all you need do to estimate your actual cost is find out your local electric rate, easily obtained from your bill or utility company.)

One big limitation of the Energyguide label is that although energy consumption for the most and least efficient of this type of appliance is also given for reference, brand and model numbers are not provided. The government leaves it up to the consumer to find more efficient models on their own. But do not despair—help follows.

By the way, even if you don't know your electric rate (expressed as cents/kwh) the Energyguide label will still help you judge how efficient an appliance is, relative to others like it.

AMERICA'S' MOST ENERGY-EFFICIENT APPLIANCES

There is a way to find the key information missing from the Energyguide label. It is contained in an inexpensive publication by Howard Geller called *The Most Energy Efficient Appliances*, published by ACE[3]. The pamphlet lists—by brand name, serial number, and cost—the most efficient refrigerator/freezers, freezers, dishwashers, clothes washers, air conditioners, heat pumps, water heaters, gas furnaces, oil furnaces, and oil burners. Also included is the council's formula for determining the actual energy expense of different products. The booklet is updated every year and at this writing costs $2. Another publication that will help you compare other features of refrigerators and freezers is available for a small charge from the Association of Home Appliance Manufacturers. (See "Selected Resources.")

If you read no further in *The Smart Kitchen* or do not want to learn the details of refrigerator purchase in the next chapter, and if you are buying or helping someone else buy a new refrigerator, get a current copy of *The Most Energy Efficient Appliances*. Using the information in that booklet alone will recoup the price of *this* book in less than two months.

AVERAGE ANNUAL ENERGY REQUIREMENTS OF ELECTRIC HOUSEHOLD APPLIANCES

	Est. Kwh Consumed Annually	Est. Monthly Cost*	Est. Annual Cost*
	Food Preparation		
Blender	1	$ .01	$ .08
Broiler	85	.57	6.80
Carving knife	8	.05	.64
Coffee maker	140	1.10	11.20
Deep fryer	83	.55	6.64
Dishwasher	165	1.10	13.20
Egg cooker	14	.09	1.12
Frying pan	100	.67	8.00
Hot plate	90	.60	7.20
Mixer	2	.01	.16
Oven, microwave (only)	100	.67	8.00
Range			
with oven	596	3.97	47.67
with self-cleaning oven	626	4.17	50.08
Roaster	60	.40	4.80
Sandwich grill	33	.22	2.64
Toaster	39	.26	3.12
Trash compactor	50	.33	4.00
Waffle iron	20	.13	1.60
Waste disposal	7	.05	.56
	Food Preservation		
Freezer			
Automatic defrost 16.5 cu.ft.	1,820	12.13	145.60
Manual defrost 16 cu.ft.	950	6.33	76.00
Refrigerators/freezers			
Automatic defrost, 17.5 cu.ft.	1,500	10.00	120.00
Manual defrost, 12.5 cu.ft.	600	4.00	48.00

*Based on 1987 national average cost of 8 cents per kwh.
Source: Edison Electric Institute (1985) and American Council for an Energy Efficient Economy (1989)

Chapter 9:

REFRIGERATION

Virtually every American household has a refrigerator; many households have more than one (in the basement, garage, den) and often a free-standing freezer as well. But most people are amazed when they find out how much they spend to run these appliances each year. According to all the experts, refrigerators can account for as much as one third of household energy expenditure. They also account for about 7 percent of the United States' total electric usage.

THE COLD FACTS

Just in case you haven't bought a refrigerator lately, an 18-cubic-foot, frost-free model used anywhere from $120 to more than $250 worth of electricity yearly, depending on the unit and where you live. These figures actually represent a decline in refrigerator energy consumption over earlier models; older units were much less efficient.

Consumers who have recently purchased a refrigerator may have made a wise investment. I am tentative about this because there is a serious concern that (1) refrigerators are still not being made energy-efficient enough, and (2) even with Energyguide labels available, households are not necessarily ending up with the most efficient models.

Why? One reason is that about 65 percent of all refrigerators are not bought by the user; they are purchased by contractors and other disinterested parties. Another reason is that many consumers don't seem concerned with long-term savings, although that may be changing. According to one study done by Pacific Gas and Electric in the early 1980s, consumer concerns, in order of importance, were (1) price, (2) features, (3) brand, (4) suitability, and (5) energy efficiency. (More recent studies show that energy efficiency may be moving up in importance.)

Another reason efficient refrigerators aren't being selected is that only 27 percent of consumers believe there are differences among refrigerators, according to Dr. David B. Goldstein, who conducted a study of residential energy use for the Lawrence Berkeley Laboratory in Berkeley, California. But there are actually models that differ from each other as much as 100 percent (50 percent for units made after 1990). Dr. Goldstein also contends that we will spend $50 billion in the next twenty years to build power plants for the energy that will be "wasted" by inefficient refrigerators.

FUTURE COOLERS

The experts believe that refrigerators could use as little as 200 kilowatt-hours a year. This translates into an astonishing $16 *a year* (at the 1989 average electric cost of 8 cents per kilowatt-hour). The average unit now in use consumes about 1,300 kilowatt-hours per year, the average new model just under 1,000. This projected energy savings could be obtained through a better self-defrosting system, elimination of door heaters (or adding switches for them), and by a more effective separation of the refrigerator section from the freezer section. Adding a more efficient compressor motor and additional, more, and better insulation could further reduce energy usage. And decreasing the number of defrost cycles not only saves energy, it lessens food dehydration. The Japanese, Germans and Danes are already mass-producing such units.

In the U.S., Larry Schlussler, a Ph.D. formerly with the University of California's Quantum Institute, has

---

THE ENERGY TELLER™

An instructive way to find out how much an appliance costs to run is to use a device called an Energy Teller™, a little computer designed for this single purpose. You simply plug your appliance into it, plug the Energy Teller™ into a receptacle, enter your local kilowatt rate, and watch your electric bill grow, penny by penny. The Energy Teller™ sells for about $50, but it's conceivable that it could save you a lot more than its cost if the knowledge you gain causes you to act. It certainly taught me a big lesson about refrigerator efficiency, for even though I had read a lot about how inefficient older units were, I never imagined that our twelve-year-old unit could be an offender. Well, after only one day I began to think it was my patriotic duty to replace it! At 9.8 cents per kilowatt-hour, it was costing us more than $260 a year to run. The Energy Teller™ is available from the Brookstone Company. Share one with friends, family, or community groups.

founded the Sunfrost Company to manufacture super-efficient refrigerators. His 16-cubic-foot model, for example, uses 180 kilowatt-hours per year compared with the present day range of 960 to 2,400 kilowatt-hours per year. A 70-to-80-percent savings!

Other advantages to Dr. Schlussler's design include a higher humidity level, offering better-quality food storage, quieter operation, and greater ease of cleaning (the inside contains no drains, vents, and the like). Sunfrost refrigerators are available in both DC and AC, with any exterior desired. They are comparatively expensive and are really only cost-effective for solar electric homes (where substantial money is saved by not having to install electric service), but they certainly demonstrate that the technology is available. If you can live with a long-term return on your investment, look into getting one; you'll definitely be the first on the block, and you'll show your concern for energy conservation.

STATE AND UTILITY AID

The weight of concern over power wasted by older, inefficient appliances is reflected by the fact that many utilities presently offer rebates or other benefits to encourage consumers to purchase energy-efficient refrigerators. These companies' actions acknowledge the reality that it is cheaper to conserve energy than to build new power plants. If your utility doesn't have a rebate program, find out why not. Also a warning from Amory Lovins, energy expert and co-director of the Rocky Mountain Institute, who says that areas without refrigerator rebate programs are "probably dumping grounds for inefficient models that don't sell well in other parts of the country."

BUYING A REFRIGERATOR/FREEZER

The following information pertains to refrigerators, combination refrigerator/freezer units, and freestanding freezers. For simplicity, however, I will refer to them all as "refrigerators." As far as separate freezers are concerned, chest-type units are generally considered to be a more efficient design than upright models, since cold air does not tumble out when the door is opened. However, some people do not like the inconvenience of digging for food in the chest.

Appliance Payback

Energy-efficient appliances cost somewhat more to buy than their less efficient counterparts, but not always by a great amount. Moreover, this is an investment in the future. The initial energy savings will help balance the purchase price, and after that period you continue to reap the benefits for the life of the unit (as

in the earlier example). Consider the money saved from lower fuel bills as tax-free income.

The time it takes to recoup your investment is called the *payback*.

Factors Affecting Efficiency

The energy efficiency of a refrigerator is determined by many factors, such as size, insulation, method of defrosting, number of defrost cycles, temperature of freezer space, condensation controls, type of motor, design, and luxury features. Choices encompass refrigerator alone, freezer alone, or the more common combination units. Combination units are available with a top freezer, bottom freezer, or the freezer and refrigerator side by side. Before going into the specifics of making a good choice, keep these strategies in mind to reduce your operating costs:

- Large refrigerators can be more efficient per cubic foot than small ones. Use the information available in the publications mentioned earlier and EER ratings to determine how this factor applies to your needs—for example, if your family may expand.
- Consider some of the energy-free cold storage ideas ("Out-of-Refrigerator Food Storage") that appear at

---

HOW TO FIGURE APPLIANCE PAYBACK

To calculate how long the payback will be when you buy a more expensive, but more efficient appliance, use this formula:

$$\frac{A}{B} = \text{years until payback is realized}$$

A = the additional cost of the more expensive refrigerator

B = the difference in estimated operating cost of two models per year, calculated from their Energyguide labels

Example: I priced two large side-by-side refrigerator/freezers. One was priced at $1,489 and cost an average of $83 a year to run (according to the Energyguide label). The other was priced at $1,329 and cost an average of $121 a year to run.

$$A = \$1,489 - 1,329 = \$160$$
$$B = \$121 - 83 = \$38$$
$$\frac{A = 160}{B = 38} \quad 4.2 \text{ years}$$

Thus the payback is a little over four years. The average unit is expected to last twenty years. After the four-year payback period, the nontaxable energy savings of the more efficient unit over the sixteen years would be more than $650 (16 years x $38).

the end of this chapter. If you utilize any of them, you may be able to reduce your refrigerator needs substantially.

- Consider a manual-defrost refrigerator. They are always the most efficient to operate but will require extra labor on your part. (See "Effortless Defrosting," later in this chapter.)

SIZE

Next to paying for it, the hardest part of buying a refrigerator is sizing it properly. In general, energy cost is affected by the size of the refrigerator. The bigger it is, the more *total* energy it uses. However, as mentioned, for technical reasons large units can be more efficient per cubic foot than similar units, so check ratings and divide by cubic feet.

A unit that is too large will result in wasted energy, whereas one that is too small may mean more frequent trips to the store. Also, if you pack food too tightly inside, the lack of adequate air circulation may increase operating costs and not keep foods satisfactorily cooled. (If the refrigerator is too large for your present needs, fill unused areas so it does not have to constantly cool the empty spaces. Bottles of water and the like will do the job.)

The following are the usual "standards" for sizing a refrigerator. In the fresh food section, 8–10 cubic feet is judged adequate for a family of two, plus 1 cubic foot for each additional person, plus 2 more cubic feet if you do a lot of entertaining; the freezer space should provide approximately 2 cubic feet per person. Note that these figures are on the high side and should be adjusted based on your life-style, other storage options, and such.

INSULATION

The more the better—polyurethane foam is preferred, since it has the best insulating qualities. If you think insulation doesn't matter, touch the outside of an older refrigerator. I bet it's cold.

Unfortunately, chlorofluorocarbons (CFCs) used in making refrigerator insulation are associated with the destruction of the ozone layer. If and when a safe replacement comes on the market, you should give it preference. One promising technique utilizing "evacuated panels" with a vacuum similar to thermopane windows may appear in the future.

(See also "Adding Extra Insulation to the Refrigerator," later in this chapter.)

METHOD OF DEFROSTING

The defrost capabilities significantly affect the amount of energy the refrigerator/freezer uses. Auto-

matic defrost units utilize 20 to 40 percent more electricity than those with manual defrost. Units are available with the following defrost options: manual, partially automatic, and automatic.

Manual-defrost units are the most economical, if you know how to use and defrost them. (For example, making sure foods, particularly liquids, are always covered will reduce frost build-up.) Frost should not be allowed to get thicker than ¼ inch.

Partially automatic defrost or *cycle defrost* is a hybrid. The freezer must be manually defrosted several times a year, whereas the refrigerator does not require defrosting. In general, the best partial-automatic is more economical than the best fully automatic unit. (To calculate the cost of differing features, contrast the EER labels of comparable models.)

Automatic defrost requires no effort, but you pay for this convenience.

EFFORTLESS DEFROSTING

1. Plan to defrost when food supplies are low (for example, before a big shopping day). A cool day is best.
2. Put up a few pots of water to boil.
3. Put any perishable food in a picnic cooler. (Inexpensive styrofoam™ ones work very well.)
4. Unplug the refrigerator, unscrew the fuse, or throw the circuit breaker rather than turning it off. This is much safer, and you don't have to remember what temperature it was set at before.
5. Put pots of hot water in the freezer. Close the door.
6. Leave the unit for a few hours and then clean up loosened ice.
7. Wash out the inside with baking soda or other mild sanitizing solution. Dry all inside surfaces with a towel.

NUMBER OF AUTOMATIC DEFROSTING CYCLES

In most automatic refrigerator/freezers defrost cycles occur every sixteen to twenty hours. Units with reduced frequency also have reduced energy needs.

TEMPERATURE OF FREEZER SPACE

A zero-degree freezer is a must if you store a lot of food, particularly for long periods. Some new freezers have a special "super-freeze" area that should lengthen the storage life of food. Freezers located in single-door refrigerators may only give you 15°F, which is not cold enough for long-term storage. If it is called a "frozen food storage compartment" or "food freezer" you can expect it only to store *already frozen foods* several months. Those described as "freezer compartments" or "sections" are suitable only for storing ice cubes.

CONDENSATION CONTROLS

Contradictory as it sounds, heaters are installed to prevent condensation on the outside of refrigerators. To reduce energy use, most good-quality units have switches to turn these heaters off during dry weather. (For how to add a condensation control, see "Adding Your Own Energy-Saving Switch" in this chapter.)

TYPE OF MOTOR

The lower the wattage (shown on the ID plate), the better. More efficient motors, however, may be somewhat noisier.

DESIGN

Overall configuration is very important. The most common units come with top freezers, followed by side-by-side models and the much less common bottom-freezer models. Side-by-side units are the most expensive to buy and run and, while exceedingly popular these days, I do not find this a well-conceived design. Although small items may be easier to find in the door, many people say they find the two compartments too narrow, and foods seem to get buried at the back of the shelves. Surprisingly, my preference—the bottom freezer format—is the least popular, although it seems the most user-friendly. The eye-level refrigeration is a definite asset, since you use this section most: *No bending to retrieve items on bottom shelves.* The freezer also tends to be larger, with convenient sliding trays or baskets. Unfortunately, these modes are often less efficient than top-mounted units, although according to *Consumer Reports,* "there is no technical reason why that should be so." (At this writing Amana, Kitchenaid, and Whirlpool manufacture bottom-freezer units, whereas in 1980 ten companies made them.)

Internal layout should also play a substantial part in your choice. Check the number of shelves and their configuration. Some units have continuous shelves and some half shelves. Some are glass, others wire. The glass will limit spills but inhibits air movement and is breakable. Check the height of the shelves and the options for adjusting them. One unit I looked at had one in-door shelf that would not take anything larger than 3¾-inch items. Great for nail polish but impractically small. Test the shelves for strength and support.

See-through bins are an important convenience and can be energy savers: You spend less time looking for things. Check that sliding baskets move easily and have effective stops so that the basket cannot slip out.

Controls should be conveniently located, especially the condensation control, since you will want to use it. If the unit is to be located up against a wall or cabinet, make sure the door doesn't need extra "side clearance" to allow for removal of shelves and baskets. Most don't need any, but some units need as much as 17 inches. It is very important that the unit opens in the right direction (toward counter space) or that the door is reversible.

LUXURY FEATURES

Extra options, such as automatic ice makers and beverage dispensers, use additional energy (and of course also elevate the price.) Newer electronic monitoring panels, which give information about servicing problems or inform you when the door has been left open, considerably reduce the effective payback period. Glass exterior doors, available on some very expensive models, do not insulate as well as solid doors.

Don't be dazzled by gimmicks; look for worthwhile design features and energy efficiency.

COLD HOUSES

If you heat with wood or your house temperature is consistently less than 70° for any reason, check with the manufacturer before you buy a refrigerator. Some refrigerators will not run well under these circumstances.

USING AN OLD REFRIGERATOR

If you plan to buy a new refrigerator and keep the old one as an auxiliary, plug in the old unit only when it's needed. If you think you'll need the old unit on a regular basis, it is much more economical to purchase a new, more efficient, adequate-size model in the first place. If you do not replace the old refrigerator, take steps to make it as energy-efficient as possible. (See "Adding Extra Insulation to the Refrigerator" and "Adding Your Own Energy-Saving Switch," later on in this chapter.)

REFRIGERATOR DISPOSAL

Resist the temptation to sell the old refrigerator for a few dollars. You're not doing anyone a favor by passing it on, since it will cost a lot to run and waste valuable fuel.

As previously mentioned, refrigerators rely on CFCs in the coolant and insulation. This poses a dilemma for disposing of an old unit in an environmentally sound manner. Although refrigerator CFCs account for only 4 percent of CFC usage in the U.S., their effect on the atmosphere should not be ignored. Unfortunately no guidelines have yet been issued. My only advice is that, if possible, store the unit in an out of-the-way location until you hear of an approved disposal program. (Be sure to remove the door or detach the latch for safety.)

IMPROVING AND MAINTAINING REFRIGERATOR PERFORMANCE

Not everyone can afford to replace their refrigerator with a more up-to-date model. Therefore, it is important to increase the efficiency of the millions of units already in homes. Maintaining new as well as old units is also essential.

Placement

One morning, while having breakfast at a local eatery frequented by contractors, I happened to notice a builder friend at work on a projected kitchen layout. When I pointed out that he was putting the refrigerator next to the stove, he replied that it was the only way he could fit everything in!

Don't make the same mistake. Refrigerators should be in a cool spot away from the stove, radiators, and direct sunlight. If there is absolutely no choice and it must be near a heat-generating element, separate with a partition filled with 3 inches of fiberglass or 1 inch of foil-faced foam insulation board and shade from direct sunlight. For maximum refrigerator performance the kitchen should also be dry and well ventilated.

If there are coils in the back of the refrigerator, leave at least 4 inches behind it so that the heat ejected from them can dissipate; otherwise, the unit will not run properly, efficiently, or for very long. Leave 1 to 2 inches of air space on the sides. There should be 10 to 14 inches minimum clearance above the refrigerator for the heat to exit. Be sure not to block the flow of air from behind the unit if you are placing a cabinet above it. New refrigerators with no coils showing on the back have fans that blow the heat out front through the bottom grill. These generally can be built in without the clearances just mentioned, but you should always check the manual.

Operation

- Let hot foods cool somewhat before placing them in the refrigerator.
- Make sure all foods are covered. This is especially important in manual-defrost models.
- Don't set controls colder than necessary.
- Thaw foods in the refrigerator. This helps the unit and saves energy for cooking.
- Keep the refrigerator well stocked but allow air to circulate. If you have a lot of empty space, fill it with dummy packages, such as bottles of water.

- Keep the freezer well packed. Again, you can use dummy packages.

Care

Proper care will keep a refrigerator running efficiently and extend its life.

1. The weatherstripping around the door is crucial to your refrigerator's operation. The most common test of this seal is with a dollar bill: Close the door on the dollar and see how easily it pulls out. If it slips out easily, the gasket is too loose. This test is valid, however, only on older refrigerators with rubber gaskets rather than magnetic seals. For refrigerators with magnetic seals, put a strong flashlight inside aimed at the section of the seal you are testing and close the door. If you do this at night, you will see the leaks when you turn off the room lights.

   Check the seal closely to see that it is not broken or that it has not become loose anywhere or fouled with debris. Sometimes hinges and latches must be tightened and adjusted and the seals changed. Original replacement gaskets are often unnecessarily expensive, so look for other products that substitute. Other clues that weatherstripping is bad are:

   - The unit has been running longer than normal. (An increase in your electric bill would suggest this.)
   - Frost builds up quickly.
   - The walls of the unit sweat.

2. Clean the coils in back and under the refrigerator twice a year with a vacuum and brush. (Check the manual for specifics.)
3. Keep the inside of the unit clean using a baking soda solution and nonabrasive scrub sponge.
4. Get two reliable thermometers—one for the refrigerator and one for the freezer. An easily read thermometer that can be affixed to the inside of the walls is the preferred design. Check them occasionally. For food to last three to four days, refrigerators should be 45°F; for longer-term storage, 40°F is suggested. The freezer should be between 15°F and 0°F, depending on the model and setting.
5. Empty the water tray under self-defrosting refrigerators and clean it with a sanitizing solution (a little chlorine and water). Otherwise, it can become a source of mold.
6. Defrost manual units two to four times a year, depending on need. Never let the frost build up to more than ¼ inch. If you don't defrost, the unit will have to work harder to cool through the ice buildup, which acts as insulation. (See "Effortless Defrosting," above.)

7. Keep food, particularly liquids, covered in order to minimize frost.

THE REFRIGERATOR BLACKBOARD

According to experts, 2 to 4 percent of refrigerator energy is lost every day by hungry people staring into its open door for inspiration. While you are standing there trying to tantalize yourself or remember what is in the various containers of leftovers, cold air is tumbling out. A practical and amusing way to minimize this "open door syndrome" is to place a blackboard nearby to inform hungry diners of the available choices within. Also, by publicizing the next planned meal here, you can ensure that nobody eats the fixings prematurely. In the Demonstration Kitchen, I inserted a blackboard onto the over-refrigerator cabinet door. (The refrigerator door or wall are equally suitable locales.) The blackboard can, of course, also provide a good medium for other household communications.

REFRIGERATOR BLACKBOARD

Adding Extra Insulation

While working on the Demonstration Kitchen, I read about a number of do-it-yourself techniques for increasing the efficiency of refrigerators. One of these ideas, adding extra insulation to the unit, is so obvious it is almost comical. I was curious, however, to see how easily this could be done and what extra insulation would really mean in terms of electricity usage. So I decided to run some tests to find out what homeowners would gain by boxing their refrigerator in with urethane panels.

In 1984, I conducted three different tests in both the summer and winter, running the refrigerator each time with and without added insulation. To measure savings I used a meter to determine how long the compressor was on, as well as the Energy Teller™ to calculate energy consumption. I discovered that I could average a 10-percent savings (in my northeastern climate). If you live in a hot climate, you can probably save more: The summertime savings I calculated were

16.5 percent, whereas the winter savings were only 7 percent. Therefore, just adding $20 to $25 worth of insulation could save me at least $26 a year—a one-year payback. (These savings are similar to what you can expect from hot water heater "insulation wrap," which returns about a 10-percent savings.)

If you think your refrigerator will not benefit from this procedure, touch the outside of it. Is it cold? If so, this is an indication that added insulation would help.

Manufacturers are, of course, aware of the benefits of extra insulation but are afraid to oversize their units, making them harder to move through doors and fit into kitchens. The answer— it would seem, then—is add-on panels kits.

Here is what you need: Foil-faced rigid insulation (1-inch or ½-inch, depending on available space), strip magnets (adhesive on one side) or double-sided tape sufficient for all edges of the insulation, and duct tape.

1. Measure the surfaces of the unit. You can insulate the door, but you should cover it afterward with contact paper, vinyl wallpaper, plastic laminate, ⅛-inch wood paneling, or another finish of your choice for appearance. (Some coverings can easily be applied with spray contact adhesive. You can cut around the handle or change it if you like.) If your refrigerator has coils on the back, do not insulate the back! When insulating the unit, do not interfere with the free flow of air that is necessary under and sometimes behind the unit. (Check the manual.) Do not insulate under the bottom or over the back opening that gives access to the machinery.
2. Cut the insulation to size for each surface—the top, sides, back, and door (if desired). Don't forget to add on the extra thickness of the insulation itself when measuring, or the pieces will be too small. If possible, each panel should be a single piece; however, you can splice insulation boards together using panel adhesive and duct tape. (Cut the pieces and tape together on *one side* of joint only. Then, open the joined pieces as if tape were a hinge and apply panel adhesive or other appropriate glue to the exposed edges, following the instructions on the package. Close the "hinge," wipe off any excess glue, and then tape the other side.)
3. Wipe the refrigerator down with a sanitizing solution, such as Borax or Clorox. If the refrigerator is scratched or nicked, do your best to clean and seal these spots before insulating. Use steel wool, fine sandpaper, or other rust-removing treatment and then a touchup paint.
4. Make sure that the refrigerator is dry on the outside at the time you place the insulation in order to minimize sealing moisture under it. A dry, cool day is best for this job.
5. The best technique for attaching the insulation to the refrigerator is to use double-sided tape or flexible

magnetic strips with adhesive on one side. The magnetic strips are recommended, since they allow easy removal of the panels if needed. Attach the tape or strips to the insulation, running it around every edge for maximum seal.

6. Start by insulating the sides, then the back, and finally the top.

7. Once the insulation is in place, tape all seams (in other words, where the top and sides meet and where the back and sides meet) to provide an air seal that will block any conduction (which would defeat your efforts).

Note: If you live in a humid area, you might want to check under the insulation periodically for rust, mold, and such.

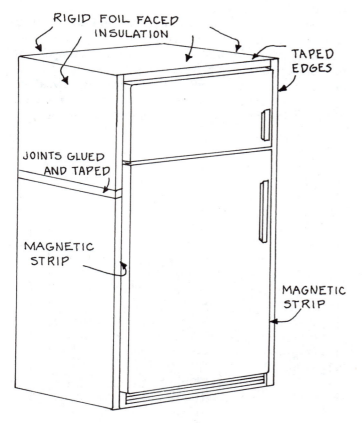

REFRIGERATOR WITH ADDED INSULATION
Adding insulation to a refrigerator saves about 10 percent on operating costs.

Adding Your Own Energy-Saving Switch

One of the most important energy-saving features many new refrigerators come with today can be added to existing units: the switch that controls the refrigerator's door heater. It sounds curious that refrigerators have heaters built into them, but they are there to prevent condensation on the outside and near the door frames in humid weather. Not only are you paying to run the heaters, but your refrigerator works harder to counteract the heat, which may also shorten the unit's life.

Refrigerators, as they are presently designed, may warrant such heaters in humid weather, but when it is dry, they are unnecessary. So energy-conscious manufacturers have installed switches in new models, enabling homeowners to regulate this feature. Installing the switch in a unit that does not have one can save you $4 a month (at 8 cents per kilowatt-hour), according to the designer of this system. Bill Keough, in an article in Rodale's *New Shelter* Magazine, explains how it is done using an ordinary 600-watt 120-volt lamp dimmer, a standard 2-by-3-by-2-inch electrical outlet box (usually called a gem box), some wire nuts, and 18-gauge (or lower) wire:

1. Check to see if your unit has this type of heater. The manual may call it a "mullion," "shell," "stile," or "anticondensation" heater, or dryer.
2. Empty and unplug the refrigerator.
3. Using the manual, locate the wires going to the heater. If you are not sure you have found the right wire, you can double-check with a VOM (volt-ohmmeter). The wire's resistance should equal the added resistances as shown in the manual's schematic.
4. If you live in an extremely dry climate, the heater is unnecessary and you can simply eliminate it by cutting the wires. Make sure you put wire nuts on the exposed wires and label them for the benefit of future owners.
5. Cut the wires at a convenient place; near a terminal is best.
6. Mount the electrical box in a convenient place. Connect the dimmer to the heater wires and install in the box. Make sure that wires are not touching the compressor or any hot spots in the mechanical area.
7. Turn off the dimmer and plug in the refrigerator. Let it run for a few hours.
8. Check the unit. If there is condensation, wipe it off and turn up the dimmer slightly. Repeat until there is no condensation. After practice you will learn where to set the switch each season and how to label the dimmer appropriately.

THE NATURAL REFRIGERATOR

The really innovative might take inspiration from Richard Villelli, who built a refrigerator that uses the seasonally cold air outside his home in Bonners Ferry, Idaho. Conceptually, it is a refrigerator with small closable vents in the rear that allow air from the outside to circulate within the box. You might be able to modify a conventional refrigerator in this manner if you know where to cut, but you will probably want to have a commercial refrigerator fabricator build the entire unit, as Villelli did. To temper the air in the natural refrigerator (and keep nosy animals away), the side with the vents faces an unheated room rather than being exposed directly to the outdoors.

Although such custom refrigerators are more expensive than standard ones, the accumulated months of free refrigeration may eventually balance this. What's more, you have the opportunity to construct it to any size and put any facade on it to fit your interior design.

OUT-OF-REFRIGERATOR FOOD STORAGE: COOL-SPOT PANTRIES

The most sensible kitchen cabinets for food storage are attached to cool outside walls and near shaded or west- and north-facing windows. Cabinets near heat sources—including cooking appliances, hot water heaters, southern walls, and even refrigerators-are not suitable for food.

For generations before refrigerators, people took advantage of the natural cooling provided by the earth itself. (Earth temperature remains a constant 40° to 50° below a 3-to-4-inch depth.) Consequently pit storage, root cellars, and even caves were employed to hold food. Most homes have a corner, cellar, or cabinet that, because of its location, stays cooler than the rest of the building. Modern home dwellers can capitalize on these ancient discoveries and possibly utilize a smaller refrigerator, thus obtaining long-term energy savings. Can you take advantage of this in your home?

Nikki has relatives who live on the outskirts of Paris in an old estate house. Their dining area contains a cupboard that holds not only everyday dishes but also butter and cheese. The butter is always spreadable and the cheese can continue to ripen. Many European homes have similar setups.

Perhaps I was thinking of this during the construction of a dining room addition where we were up against an existing stone wall and floor. Rather than remove or bury the wall, we built a long storage unit around it. Now the cool stone maintains the temperature anywhere from 40°F to 60°F, depending on the season. We have used it for five years to store grains, beans, oil, root vegetables, beverages, canned goods, and such.

I encourage you to look for space within or in close proximity to the kitchen that could house a natural pantry. This free cooling space may even allow you to buy a smaller refrigerator. It must be cool and not exceedingly dry if you wish to use if for fresh foods. The best spot is on the northeast or west side of the house. A kitchen cabinet can be used, or a closet, or, as you will see, even the crawl space under your house. You

should test the area with a thermometer and hygrometer, commonly found in hardware stores, for proper temperature and humidity readings.

The table on the next page will help you to determine what you can store effectively in your cool-spot pantry.

The Crawlspace Pantry

To demonstrate how this technique might be used in limited spaces, I experimented with a cooling closet located in the crawlspace of the Demonstration Kitchen. I cut a hole in the floor in an accessible but out-of-the way location. There I suspended a tin box fabricated in a metal shop and provided access through a tightly fitting trap door that matches the floor. The storage area can be as large as you like, just as long as you maintain the floor's integrity.

I use recessed (nautical) hardware on the door to eliminate protrusions and accidents. To prevent condensation from forming on the inside, I sprayed the outside of the box with Sweat Stop™, a spray-on product manufactured specifically to eliminate sweat on pipes. Housed in the crawlspace pantry are containers of oil, grains, beans, and such, as well as suitable produce.

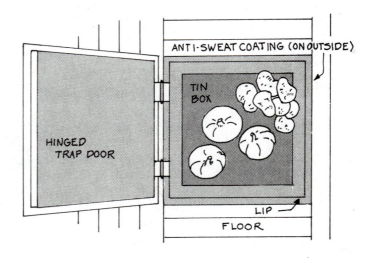

DEMONSTRATION KITCHEN CRAWLSPACE PANTRY

If your planned location is excessively cold, you will have to place insulation in strategic locations around it, insulate the exterior of the box, or line it with heavy paper. If it is too warm, you may have to vent it to the outside to bring in the cool air. Store food appropriate to the atmosphere and temperature (see the following table, "Storage Requirements"). If ventilation is pro-

STORAGE REQUIREMENTS

Fruit

32°F–40°F, 80%–90% humidity:	Apples, grapes, oranges, pears
40°F–50°F, 85%–90% humidity:	Cantaloupe

Vegetables

32°F–40°F, 90%–95% humidity:	Beets, brussel sprouts, cabbage, carrots, celery, parsnips, rutabagas, turnips
32°F–40°F, 80%–90% humidity:	White potato, endive, cabbage
35°F–40°F, 60%–70% humidity:	Onions
60°F–70°F, 60%–70% humidity:	Sweet potatoes, pumpkins
50°F–60°F, 60%–70% humidity:	Winter squash, tomatoes

Other Foods

Below 68°F, in closed containers:	Grains, nuts, seeds, beans, oils

Adapted from *Encyclopedia of Chemical Technology*, Vol. 2

vided, fruit and root vegetables, which require air to circulate around them, can be stored there on perforated trays mounted within the box.

After I built our crawlspace pantry, I was interested to see a similar design for a wine cellar in Thomas Cowan's *Beyond the Kitchen*.

The Cabinet Pantry

To build a cool-spot pantry into a cabinet or closet you essentially need to isolate it from the rest of the room, as well as possibly venting it.

1. Determine whether the space is cool and humid enough by monitoring it with a thermometer and hygrometer. Adjust the exterior insulation if necessary so that the pantry stays in the acceptable range (see the previous table, "Storage Requirements"). In new-construction situations consider building the cabinet with a removable back panel so you can adjust insulation as needed. If an existing space is too cold, rigid insulation panels can be inserted. If more humidity is needed, keep a bottle of water in the area.
2. Insulate the door and walls that interface with the house to R-12.
3. The best design includes a top and bottom screened exterior vent, particularly if it is to be used for ripening fruit. These should be adjustable and closable but need not be air-tight. (Keep vents open except in the coldest weather and adjust as needed.) If only such foods as bread, oil, cheese, butter, grains, beans,

and such in closed containers are to be stored, vents are not necessary, but they are nonetheless helpful for temperature control.
4. Install shelves. Provide racks or baskets for circulating air around fruit and root vegetables.
5. To keep track of the interior temperature easily and accurately, you may want to obtain a remote reading thermometer. Hardware stores sell remote-reading indoor/outdoor thermometers (range about 25°F to 150°F). They are also available from scientific supply houses (see "Selected Resources"). These devices let you read the temperature without opening the cabinet door.

The California Cooling Cabinet

According to *Home Food Systems*, an excellent book by Roger Yepsen, Jr., many homes in California were once built with "cooling cabinets." In this unique design, the cool air from the crawlspace or basement is drawn through the cabinet and out a top chimney-type vent. The floor of the cabinet is a strong wire mesh to supply air, the shelves are wood slats, and the vent is usually a 6-inch duct. The cool air circulates from under the house to the warmer roof vent. The door is tight to prevent drafts. The chimney vent is screened to keep animals out.

Foodstuffs cannot be packed tightly in the cabinet, or air flow will be restricted. For an illustration of this system, see the adaptation to compost systems in Chapter 14.

Chapter 10:

DISHWASHING

There is no question that the presence of the kitchen robot known as the dishwasher can be extremely influential in determining whether or not people cook. Without the inhibition caused by the thought of a stack of dirty dishes, people are inclined to cook more. Although not a necessity, and not inexpensive, the short-term expense of a dishwasher is easily balanced by the payout in less expensive, more nutritious meals. Nikki and I have observed that we would never entertain as much as we do if it weren't for the presence of this appliance.

Additional monetary savings are garnered because dishwashers can save substantially on the amount of hot water used as compared with washing dishes by hand. According to a study done at Ohio State University (1988), the average dishwasher uses 9.9 gallons of water as compared with 15.7 gallons on average for an equal amount of dishes hand washed.

Handwashing Dishes Efficiently and Comfortably

Handwashing dishes properly can reduce the amount of water used to only 5 gallons of water if the water is "ponded." Ponding water means filling the sink or a pan with water and washing and rinsing with this water. In a two-basin sink one basin has soapy water and one rinse water; the water is replaced as needed. The best system is a three-basin sink, which gives you an extra rinse. Always air-dry dishes, since towel drying is *very* unhygienic. And make sure you have an aerator or other water-saving device on the faucet. Aerators reduce the flow by 40 to 60 percent and yet have good intensity without much splashing.

Note also that being able to sit while washing dishes may add some joy to this thankless task. For more on this, see "Kitchen Sink Seating," in Chapter 3.

SELECTING A NEW DISHWASHER

Dishwasher design has benefited from the increased concern for energy efficiency. This is due to the introduction of low-energy, or short, wash cycles; cold water rinses; internal hot water heaters; and air-dry cycles.

The selection of dishwashers has become much easier as the result of the Energyguide labels. (See the introduction to Part II for a complete discussion of Energyguide labels.) This guide is invaluable, but you should also look for some features listed below that are not reflected in the Energyguide figures. Also check a copy of *The Most Energy Efficient Appliances*, mentioned in the beginning of this part, which lists the most efficient dishwashers available.

According to the Association of Home Appliance Manufacturers, 80 percent of the cost of running a dishwasher is heating the water. The following are the important features to consider in selecting a dishwasher because they affect the amount of hot water you use:

- **Built-in hot water heater.** For dishwashers to work properly, they require water heated to 140°F. One way for you to get this hot water, of course, is to keep your household hot water heater set this high—quite a waste of energy, since no other domestic household needs require water this hot. However, now many dishwasher manufacturers have installed internal hot water heaters so that domestic hot water (usually 120°F) is boosted by a heater within the unit itself. This feature is highly recommended, since it can save up to 10 percent of your home's total hot water bill. Some units may even be able to heat cold water, especially useful when the dishwasher is located some distance from the hot water heater.
- **Less hot water usage.** Dishwashers vary in the amount of hot water they use. By selecting a model that uses less, you conserve energy and another dwindling resource, water. Check manufacturer's literature for comparisons.
- **Variable cycle selections.** Formerly, dishwashers had very few choices of cycles; you used the same amount of water no matter how dirty the dishes or how full the unit. Shorter cycles can save up to one third in electricity. Machines now come with a range from "light wash" to "pot wash."

All dishwashers made after January 1, 1988, must have an option to dry without heat. This saves an estimated 15 percent on the unit's electricity.

Most units will air-dry with a fan; some machines use other mechanisms to dry, such as the heat absorbed by the dishes during the hot wash.

Some new models of dishwashers are being made with internal diagnostic systems to warn you of operating difficulty. At least one company makes a model that lets you program it to go on at another time in order to take advantage of lower electric rates. But since the average dishwasher uses only about $32 of electricity per year (at 8 cents per kilowatt-hour), the advantages from this feature alone are probably small. Also, manufacturers recommend that you be present when running a dishwasher, in case there is a malfunction. (To compute possible savings, compare the cost of comparable models, using the payback formula provided in Chapter 9.)

LOCATING THE DISHWASHER

Dishwashers should be located next to a sink. This facilitates both plumbing and loading. Whether it is to the right or left of the sink should be determined by proximity to dish storage. Try not to install it next to the refrigerator, since the dishwasher emits heat; if this is unavoidable, insulate to R-12 between the units. If you live in a cold or seasonally cold climate, make sure the water line is far from outside walls or insulated or both. (See "Note" in the section "Using the Dishwasher," which follows.)

Also make certain that when the unit's door is open, it does not inhibit any other activity or interfere with other open doors, such as the oven, refrigerator, or lower cabinets.

Although dishwashers are installed almost universally below the counter, this is not necessarily the best spot. At this height loading and unloading is difficult for many people, as well as exposing it to curious children. Dishwashers should be capable of being installed 1½ to 2½ feet above floor level; this may give much better access, visibility, and safety. I have not seen this done, but there should be no reason it can't be (but I suggest you check with the manufacturer before attempting it). Moreover, you should not do this if you will lose significant counter space or if you can't reach the controls.

THE FINNISH DRYING CABINET

The Finnish drying cabinet has been in use in Finland for more than sixty years but is virtually unknown in North America (although similar open wall racks were used in colonial America and are seen in English kitchens today). The cabinet's purpose is to allow dishes to air-dry in a dust-free and out-of-sight locale.

This device is basically a kitchen cabinet which has had its bottom removed and its shelves replaced by dish racks. The cabinet is generally mounted over the sink, but I mounted a metal drip pan underneath so that it can be hung next to the sink. I also added a wine glassrack. Dishes, glasses and utensils can then be washed, placed directly in the cabinet, and left to dry off the counter. Close the doors and the dishes disappear from view as well. (Note that though the cabinet frees up counter space that is normally used for a dish rack, water will drip on the counter as washed dishes are placed in it. I generally place a dish towel on the counter to absorb the drips.)

I used pocket door hinges on the cabinet so the doors could slide into either side of it, providing maximum access when loading wet dishes. This door format is not necessary to the design, but produces a cabinet that is not only easier to use, but safer—no bumped heads on open doors. As an alternative, the doors could be eliminated entirely.

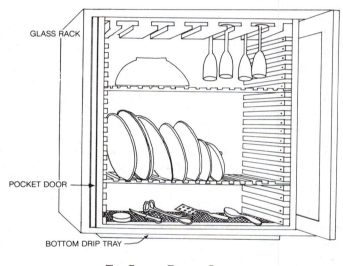

GLASS RACK

POCKET DOOR

BOTTOM DRIP TRAY

THE FINNISH DRYING CABINET

INSULATING THE DISHWASHER

You can install rigid fiberglass insulation around any dishwasher, as I did in the Demonstration Kitchen. The small cost of boxing in the unit will be repaid in better efficiency plus reduced sound level (for more information on sound insulation, see Chapter 5). Insulation may be especially productive in cold climates, when a dishwasher is installed along an exterior wall and outside temperatures may influence water temperature and efficiency of the machine.

USING THE DISHWASHER

1. Use only when full. If you feel your dish use is such that you will not fill the machine within a rea-

sonable amount of time, use the "rinse and hold" cycle. This cycle will clean away food debris so there is no odor or dried-on food, but it will not give a thorough cleaning. (Don't overuse this cycle, since it uses 3 to 7 gallons of hot water.)

2. Don't prerinse dishes in the sink if you do dishes once a day. If you must prerinse, use cold water. Normally, just scraping off food debris is enough for new dishwashers.

3. Use "air-dry" to dry, or shut off the unit before the drying cycle and open the door. One good way of doing this is to learn how long the wash cycle takes (by timing it) and then set your kitchen timer to remind you when to open the door.

4. Always use the shortest cycle for the load.

5. Run at off-peak hours if this electric option is available.

Note: If your dishwasher does not seem to work as well in the winter as it does in the summer, the hot water line may be getting chilled. Test the nearby faucet with a candy or meat thermometer. Let the water run until the temperature stops rising. It should be about the same as the temperature set on the water heater. If it isn't:

- Move the pipe and insulate it. Actually, all hot water pipes should be insulated. The insulation pays for itself in three to four months, is easy to install, and will mean much less waiting for hot water.
- Try running the machine during the warmest part of the day.
- Get an add-on hot water booster.
- Let the water run at the faucet until hot and then turn on the dishwasher.

Chapter 11:
COOKING

The stove, or as the Europeans call it, "the cooker," is the heart of the kitchen. Almost everything else in the kitchen is there to facilitate what will eventually happen on the stove top or in the oven. And since you may have to live with your decision for quite a while—stoves and ovens have an average lifespan of more than fifteen years—it pays to spend some time making a choice. In the past one had to decide only between a gas or electric stove, but today, with separate wall ovens and cooktops, you can have either fuel or both. But that is only the beginning of the choices; there are now convection, microwave, self-cleaning, and continuous-cleaning ovens, (and combinations) plus different kinds of gas, electric, and smooth cooktops.

Cooking experts know that there can be substantial variation in the quality of foods prepared in different appliances. Food cooked in a coal- or wood-fired oven has a robust taste and crusty exterior. When you compare the end product, electric and gas ovens are almost always vastly superior to microwave ovens. And, knowledgeable cooks almost universally choose the gas flame over the electric coil.

Because of my love of good food my preference for equipment is influenced here, more than in any other area, by performance. However, there are other important factors, such as the appliance's impact on health, safety, ventilation needs, and the like, and they, too, will be covered in this chapter.

To begin with, I believe the area of stove design needs some innovative thinking. Although there are more choices than ever before, most of the new options do not offer any great improvement over their predecessors. For example, though most professional cooks agree that a gas cooktop and an electric oven are the preferred appliances, you cannot buy a single unit that contains both features. Rather, the focus is on such equipment as microwave ovens which present new marketing opportunities but do little for the *art* of cooking. It is my opinion that unless the kitchen industry begins to put more emphasis on better conceived innovations, we will microwave away thousands of years of glorious culinary history.

Moreover, practicality is often sacrificed for aesthetics; professional ranges are purchased for appearance, with no consideration given to the appropriateness of the tool to the household, or its energy consumption, or the airborne pollution it produces.

GAS VERSUS ELECTRICITY

In my estimation there are advantages and disadvantages to both gas and electricity in terms of cooking performance. These are enumerated a bit later in this chapter. But first, here is a discussion of these two most common cooking modes from other angles. You must balance these considerations for yourself.

Safety

Anything that produces high heat can obviously present safety problems. The open gas flame is a potential cause of fire; gas leaks are not only inflammable but can sicken and even kill. Electric stoves can start fires from both the coils and electrical malfunctions. Furthermore, you can burn yourself on a gas flame or hot grate or on an electric coil. In fact, electric coils practically invite trouble if the unit does not warn that a heating element may still be hot, though switched off. (The most dangerous models do not give warning even when an element is on.)

Since fire and personal safety are a concern with all units, proper installation, maintenance, and operation are essential.

AVOIDING INDOOR AIR POLLUTION

The cooking of food itself, by any method, creates unwanted vapors and other airborne substances such as grease. Both gas and electric burners also cause indoor pollution through the incineration of airborne particles such as dust. In addition, cooking with gas creates a unique problem that should not be ignored. Burning gas generates significant indoor air pollution. This includes most particularly, nitrogen dioxide (NO_2), carbon monoxide (CO), and to a lesser extent nitrous oxide (NO), aldehydes (including formaldehyde), and particulates—all of which can cause or aggravate a variety of ailments. Emissions are the greatest from poorly adjusted burners.

Animal and human epidemiologic studies have linked nitrogen dioxide (NO_2) to greater risk of infectious respiratory disorders. According to Brobeck and Averyt's *Product Safety Book*, published under the auspices of the Consumer Federation of America, (and other authorities) concentration of exposure is more dangerous than length of time of exposure. Even a very short exposure to a large amount of nitrogen dioxide may "significantly increase susceptibility to nose and throat, as well as breathing irritation and disease . . . Higher levels of exposure [to NO_2] also increase airway resistance, and over time produce emphysematous lesions in the lungs." People already suffering from such respiratory disease as asthma are more seriously affected. Nitrogen oxides are also extremely irritating to the eyes and lining of the upper respiratory tract.

Carbon monoxide (CO) has no color, odor, or taste but is very dangerous. Even small amounts in the air diminish the level of oxygen in the blood. As the amount of carbon monoxide increases, those inhaling it can experience "shortness of breath, a slight increase in pulse, tightness across the forehead, headaches, and flushed skin." If the levels of the gas further increase, "breathing difficulty, coma, convulsions, and death can occur." Even low levels of carbon monoxide make the heart pump harder, so heart patients, anemics, and infants are extremely vulnerable to this pollutant.

Exposure to formaldehyde (the most common aldehyde) irritates the eyes, nose, and throat and causes "nausea, headache, dizziness, memory loss, and many asthmalike symptoms." Asthma or emphysema sufferers and those with allergies can have more serious reactions. Some people become sensitized to formaldehyde, and thereafter contact with products containing even a miniscule amount of the chemical become a problem. Formaldehyde emissions are not a problem unless the appliance is not properly tuned. Laboratory studies have also linked formaldehyde to cancer, although the effect of long-term exposure to low levels of the chemical is unknown.

Because of these combustion by-products, it is important to address air quality, particularly if you use gas, live in an energy-efficient home or poorly vented space such as an apartment, or are susceptible to environmental pollutants. Some segments of the gas industry are unwilling to admit there is reason to be concerned. The Gas Research Institute and some appliance manufacturers, however, are searching for ways to reduce emissions, even though they don't feel they are "threatening." This research is reportedly aimed at burner inserts and new-type burners that would reduce combustion by-products; their introduction to the market will be welcome. One European company may introduce a ceramic-topped gas cooktop; if vented, it could mean the best of both worlds. Another innovation is the "infrared jet-impingement" burner which are about 50 percent more efficient than conventional ones and emit much less nitrogen dioxide. In the meantime, as you will see in Chapter 12, there are ways to vent air even from energy-efficient homes, as well as cleaning the air of those toxins associated with gas combustion.

Even electricity has its health effects, since there are a small number of people who complain that they are "electrosensitive," experiencing headaches and other physical discomforts from the small amount of electromagnetic radiation emitted by electrical appliances (such as electric stoves). This is not as far-fetched as it may sound. Dr. Robert Becker, co-author of *The Body Electric*, and other researchers are warning that "electropollution"—the excessive electromagnetic background that surrounds all of us from appliances, TV, radio, microwave signals, major power lines, and the like—is as much of a concern as air and water pollution.

Fuel Efficiency

The question of fuel efficiency is less crucial than one might imagine because cooking appliances don't consume or waste immense amounts of energy. This does not mean that efficiency should be ignored, but that other factors—cooking capability, emissions, and safety—have more weight in this decision. In terms of "end use efficiency," even the American Gas Association admits that electricity is more efficient (45 percent versus 79 percent). This means that you get 34 percent more heat for your dollar out of electricity at the burner. (However, when hidden costs such as the power needed to generate electricity and power lost through transmission are figured in, electricity does not do so well.)

More important is the introduction of electronic ignitions to gas appliances. Not only do these automatic starters bring a 25-to-50-percent energy savings for just a small increase in purchase price, they eliminate the pollutants generated by the continuous gas flame. An electronic ignition is required in the U.S. in all gas stoves manufactured after January 1, 1990.* It should be be mandatory in your kitchen, too.

Some people have the pilot lights in conventional stoves turned off. This should be done only by a qualified person; some utility companies will do this for free or at a nominal charge.

Note: When lighting a burner or oven by hand, ignite the match or lighter *before* turning on the gas.

*At this writing they are mandatory in Arizona, California, Hawaii, Michigan, Minnesota, Oregon, New York, and Wisconsin.

THE COOKTOP

Since the cooktop is used more than any other appliance, this selection can have an enormous effect on the user's feelings about cooking. Choosing a separate cooktop and oven is generally more expensive than buying a traditional range, but it does provide more options. The discussion here will help you make comparisons no matter which mode is selected.

Cooking Performance

As mentioned earlier, most experienced cooks prefer gas stove tops. Although electric stove tops have been improved dramatically in the last few years, it is doubtful that they will ever equal the flame when it comes to cooking control. The appeal of gas is in the ability to manipulate the heat by small degrees, and to change the intensity of the heat dramatically and instantly. With gas, you can adjust the flame precisely because it is highly responsive and visible.

With electric burners you must trust the dial rather than your eye. Although after a while you do develop a feel for its heat and can try to compensate for heat retention or lag time, conventional electric burners, by their nature, cannot be as responsive as their gas counterparts. It should be noted that many new electric ranges are being made with improved elements that do respond more rapidly, as well as controls for adjusting the number of heating coils to correspond to the size of the pot (for energy efficiency and safety).

Another consideration is that electric cooktops are much more efficient when flat-bottomed pots and pans are used, whereas with gas cooktops you can use any vessel you like.

Cooking with electricity is much more popular in Europe than it is in North America and some of the better European-style electric cooktops with smooth, easy-to-clean burners are becoming more available in North America. These European "solid disk hobs" (disks of cast metal set in heat-resistant material) are not all identical, as the heating element may take one of three forms: (1) *protected element*, where a built-in limiter reduces power when heat is not being conducted, for example, if the pot boils dry; (2) *automatic element*, where the thermostat maintains a preselected temperature and is self-adjusting to correspond to the heat generated by the pot and its contents; and (3) *unprotected element*, which merely responds to the thermostatic setting on the dial and reaches a higher temperature than others.

Some users report that the hobs take longer to heat than is desired and may not produce enough heat for sautéing. The hobs themselves may also stain or need to be "seasoned" (heated and oiled) to prevent rusting. On the other hand, spills are much easier to clean than on other burners, and the chances of a fat flareup are virtually eliminated. Further, there is virtually no indoor air pollution produced with hobs. For more information, see "The Smooth Cooktop," later in this chapter.

Superburners

Many people are attracted to "superburners" in both electric and gas cooktops. Usually just one burner has this extra BTU output, which gives quick, intense heat when needed. Superburners are handy for heating up a large pot of water for corn or canning, but they are not at all necessary.

Note that superburners on some electric stoves require that a different coil be inserted. This extra effort may inhibit their use.

Griddle/Grills

I am very enthusiastic about the use of griddle/grills, which allow the grilling of foods indoors or alternately have a large griddle surface. These devices are available as separate appliances, integrated into the cooktop or as a drop-in option (least likely to be used).

The function of the griddle can be duplicated by placing any flat pan over the burners, but the real advantage of the built-in griddle is its size. The widespread, even heat lets you cook about twice as many eggs, home fries, pancakes, or grilled sandwiches as could be accommodated using a single burner.

The grill opens up an entirely new dimension in dining. Grilling can enhance the flavor of foods and help broaden the variety on your table. Today people need new ways of making appealing low-calorie, low-fat, and high-fiber meals. Bean- and vegetable-based burgers, for example, which are gaining popularity, can be made more gustatory on the grill. Grilling such vegetables as corn, asparagus, tomatoes, or eggplant, or stewing a pot of mixed fresh vegetables or beans over the "coals," imparts an essence of the outdoors. (Studies of the harmful effects of barbecuing are only associated with high-fat foods, particularly meat.) This is a superb example of a cooking innovation that can really add to the dining experience.

Griddle/grills are fueled with either gas or electricity. Note that some gas stove tops have built-in electric griddle/grills, so do not assume that just because the other burners have a flame that the grill will too.

In some units, a large gas burner heats volcanic stones, which then radiate their heat to the food placed on the rack above them. Other models have just an electric coil, and the flavor is more akin to conventional oven broiling.

As far as the griddle operation goes, the source of heat is not relevant to taste. Electric is probably easier to maintain at a fixed, even temperature, which is desirable in certain cooking situations. Significantly, electric griddle/grills create much less air pollution than do gas units.

Other features to consider are ease of cleaning and a fat-collection device. Ask for a demonstration of how the stovetop and griddle/grill opens for cleaning. Look at the quality, sturdiness of grates and griddle, hinges, heavy metal versus nonstick coating (the latter does not brown foods well). The ability to close the griddle/grill unit, especially if it is not used regularly, will help keep it clean and adds an extra heat-resistant counter surface.

It is imperative that you have good ventilation when you use the grill. Therefore, you must plan on installing an efficient exhaust system. See Chapter 12—particularly the section "The Task Exhaust System."

Interchangeable Stove-Top Inserts

Some stove tops are available with interchangeable inserts of grills, griddles, smooth cooktops, and the like. These seem like a nice way to expand versatility, but this is not always so. Human nature being what it is (particularly in this era of "convenience cookery"), you should seriously look at whether you are the type of person who will go to the trouble of removing and replacing the inserts. If you think you are, make sure to provide accessible storage space for the parts when not in use.

The Grate

Each individual burner in a gas cooktop should have its own grate. Some models have two grates affixed together, supposedly for better pot stability. However, these double grates are significantly heavier, and may be unwieldy and difficult to wash. Double grates also make stove spills more difficult to clean up; you may have to move a pot of spaghetti on the other half of the grate to take care of the tomato sauce spillover.

Controls

Controls may be situated on the front face of the unit, or on the top at the front, side, or rear. Those at the front of the top are best. Reaching for a control behind or even to the side of the burners puts hands, arms, and sleeves dangerously close to hot burners and pots. Controls located on the front face of the unit are in too easy reach of curious children and hard to see.

Downdraft Exhaust Systems

Built-in downdraft exhaust systems are a new addition to the stove world. They work by creating a low-pressure stream over the cooking surface. Despite the fact that their placement is in direct opposition to the natural principle that heat and gases rise, they are quite popular. Do not expect the downdraft exhaust to be as functional as other systems, especially when cooking with tall pots or woks, or at high heat. In addition, they can be disturbingly noisy. I would not purchase one unless it was available with an exterior mounted fan (which makes it quieter), and only after a demonstration. In all the time I spent looking at kitchen equipment, I never found one of these units hooked up in a showroom. When I did finally see one in operation, I was not impressed with its ability to remove cooking odors and smoke. Not surprisingly, I observed a significant amount of fumes rising and escaping the system entirely. Also, ventilation experts have warned me about the large fans used in them. Apparently they are powerful enough to create negative pressure in your house (akin to a vacuum), which could cause non-vented furnaces, chimneys, and the like to reverse direction—potentially a very dangerous situation. (See Chapter 12.)

The Smooth Cooktop

The idea of a smooth cooking surface is an appealing notion—cooking utensils can be moved around easily, no spills splashing over and under burners, and so on. But the North American "white ceramic" design has been a failure. For one thing, these ceramic cooktops, which have electric burners beneath the smooth surface, use 15 percent more electricity than conventional electric cooktops because some of the heat is conducted to the surface between the cooking areas. In addition, it is easy to forget that the surface is dangerously hot - even though there may be an indicator light. (Do not consider a ceramic cooktop unless it has a warning light for *both* on/off *and* residual heat.) Finally, food spilled on a smooth cooktop will burn, causing unsightly stains that are difficult to remove.

The smooth cooktops popular in Europe, made of a special glass-ceramic material, are now being marketed more heavily in North America. Their design is superior to the American version, since they usually include a temperature limitation control (to prevent burns and burnt-on food) and a residual heat warning (which prevents burns by indicating you when the surface is safe to touch). The glass-ceramic material is said to conduct heat well, which combined with the increased surface contact with the utensil should mean better energy efficiency. They can also accommodate more than the usual four utensils and maintain desired temperatures even at low levels. Often, too, you can see through the surface, which helps with controllability.

Like electric burners, smooth cooktops work best with undamaged flat-bottomed utensils.

The Magnetic Induction Cooktop

The magnetic induction cooktop is about as "space age" as you can get in the kitchen today. This appliance resembles the smooth ceramic cooktops visually, but it uses a totally different technology to create heat: magnetic fields. Since iron must be present in the cooking vessel in order for the interaction to occur, the unit may come with a small magnet to test the suitability of particular utensils.

This cooktop is exceptionally safe in terms of burns because, remarkably, the surface gets hot only where the heated cooking vessel has reflected heat back. It is astonishing to be able to put your hand down comfortably right next to a pot of boiling water! (Accidents are prevented by a built-in safety device that protects such items as jewelry, cutlery, and other small iron-containing utensils from being heated on the surface.)

The induction cooktop is very responsive to the thermostatically regulated controls. This makes it ideal for such procedures as frying and candy making, which require specific temperatures, for simmering without fear of the pot boiling over, and for long, slow cooking of beans, grains, sauces, soups, and stews. I agree with kitchen expert Donald Silvers that they are excellent for tasks suited for a double boiler, but they are not much good for fast heavy cooking. He believes, as I do, that they make a great extra burner.

Sanyo, the manufacturer of the portable unit in the Demonstration Kitchen, claims that their induction cooker is very energy efficient—an 80-percent return as compared with 40-percent for gas and 52-percent for electric stoves. Add this to the fact that there are no emissions of any kind, and you can see why this appliance may have great potential in the future, particularly for those with air quality sensitivities.

Induction cooktops are available as both small portable units and entire cooking surfaces. Due in part to their high price, they are not yet very popular, but a portable unit may be a worthwhile adjunct to the stove top, acting as an extra burner and also offering the possibility of tabletop cookery. In the Demonstration Kitchen an undercounter "garage" was built near the cooktop to hold the portable induction cooktop when not in use.

The Halogen Cooktop

If cooking with magnetism seems strange, are you ready to cook with light? European technology employs tungsten halogen lamps (or infrared lamps) for the heating element in another smooth cooking surface. According to one English kitchen publication, they "offer the controllability of gas with the sleek, clean design of electric ceramic hobs." The publication credits them with being able to provide "instantaneous" heat.

ENERGY EFFICIENT COOKTOP USE

1. Use the appropriate-size burner for the cooking vessel. If the stove has an oversize burner in the front, don't use it for a small utensil, even though it is more convenient. This is a common habit.
2. Use the right-size pan for the job. Flat bottoms are best, particularly for electric and smooth cooktops.
3. Utensils should have tight-fitting lids. Cover them whenever possible, particularly when liquids are set to boil.
4. Unnecessarily fast boiling wastes fuel; keep heat just high enough to maintain a gentle roll. The flame should not emerge above the bottom of the pot.
5. Make sure electric coils are working properly. A worn-out element is a real power drain.
6. Try to take advantage of the residual heat in electric stove tops by turning off the power early.
7. Long-term cooking is more economical in the oven than on the cooktop but only when the oven's capacity is being utilized.
8. Keep reflectors under the range clean. Inexpensive replacements are available for both gas and electric stoves.

The reflectivity of the underlying surface affects the stove top's efficiency. According to one replacement reflector manufacturer, with good reflectors you can expect a 3- to 38-percent savings on cooking fuel, depending on such variables as room temperature, water temperature, mineral content of water, and overall range efficiency. Even a 3-percent savings nationally would be impressive, so replace any discolored reflector pans.

9. Make sure the burners are properly tuned. This will not only save fuel, but reduce gas emissions.

THE OVEN

If you are installing a separate oven, there is no reason I know of to choose a gas oven over an electric model. Experts tout electric ovens because they tend to hold the temperature more uniformly and are less drying to food. Both of these features are a function of the fact that the electric element does not burn oxygen to make heat. In contrast, when gas is burned in the oven, air must constantly be introduced to fuel the flame; this air flow dries the surface of food and often creates uneven results. Moreover, to control a gas oven thermostatically, the stove must continuously raise and lower the flame. This can create short time lags of underheating or overheating. With an electric oven the temperature is regulated in a more constant fashion.

Additionally, unless there is an electronic ignition with a gas oven, the pilot light can account for 40 percent of the oven's gas usage.

Another factor in the electric oven's favor is that the broiler is inside the oven rather than in a bottom drawer. This location usually means a larger surface area and more convenient usage. The usual position of the broiler at the bottom of gas ovens makes its use very uncomfortable.

Because of gas combustion emissions, I strongly believe that the only suitable gas ovens are those with their own venting systems. If you already own one that is not self-venting, be sure to provide adequate ventilation. Also do not forget that well maintained and adjusted burners have less gas emissions.

Our investigation of ovens for the Demonstration Kitchen revealed how important it is to compare all aspects of an appliance to make the best purchase. In looking for a single wall oven for the "Ideal Cooker" (described later in this chapter), I was surprised to discover that small differences in internal width can dramatically alter capacity. In an oven wider than the typical 19 to 20 inches by only 1½ to 2 inches, the extra space can mean room for four pies or two 9-by-13-inch casseroles on a single shelf, an impossibility in any lesser space. Also notable are broiler coils with three, rather than the more common two, loops—a small feature that provides more even cooking. A "preheat" setting, which heats the oven rapidly, saves some time and probably a little energy, too. And extra insulation also saves you a little money and keeps the kitchen cooler. (See "The Ideal Cooker" for how to add your own insulation.)

Another feature to look for is a door window. A window and light are a food and energy-saving combination: Visibility eliminates the need to open the door frequently to check on the food's progress. Each time the oven door is opened during cooking, a loss of 25° to 50°F or more occurs. The window will also mean less disturbance to such delicate foods as soufflés.

In development is the biradiant oven which is said to save about one-third of the energy ovens normally use.

Continuous- and Self-Cleaning Ovens

Despite their obvious attraction, continuous-cleaning ovens should be avoided, since the wall coating may dissipate into the air. Also, according to to Cook's magazine, the specially coated walls are "generally ineffective" and then can't be cleaned with abrasive cleaners. Others say the feature doesn't really clean but merely "degreases." Future models may have glass-ceramic walls that clean better and do not dissipate into the air.

I would not spend my money on a self-cleaning oven either, one reason being the extra expense involved provides a very dubious return. (The self-cleaning feature can add up to 21 percent to your operating costs, and ovens are not used that often for the savings from extra insulation to amount to anything.) Although they may eliminate the need for strong oven-cleaning chemicals, the self-cleaning process can produce airborne pollutants while in operation.

The heavier insulation of self-cleaning ovens may reduce fuel consumption, but you can gain the benefits of the extra insulation by adding it yourself when installing a wall (or drop-in) oven. (See "The Ideal Cooker.") Extra insulation can save 2 to 10 percent on energy costs in electric ovens, nominal amounts in gas ovens.

With a self-cleaning oven you are limited to triple-glass black doors. On the positive side, these doors stay cooler and may be a safety consideration to those with children.

If you go with a self-cleaning oven, choose a vented model. If you already have one that is unvented, provide *ample* ventilation, particularly when using the cleaning mode.

Choosing Ovens: When Small is Beautiful

Before you turn on the oven, remember the smaller the oven is, the more efficient. It makes little sense to heat up an entire oven just to bake one potato. Here a toaster oven or other small countertop oven would be much more sensible. According to *Good Housekeeping* magazine, it takes approximately 0.52 kilowatt-hours to bake potatoes in a toaster oven, compared with 1.67 kilowatt-hours in a conventional electric oven and 1.22 kilowatt-hours in a self-cleaning electric oven. Thus, a well-thought-out kitchen might have at least two, and possibly three, ovens of varying sizes.

The Toaster Oven

I have found the toaster broiler—or toaster oven, as it is more commonly called—to be one of the most original and useful kitchen tools to appear in quite a while. The fact that you are heating such a small space makes it very energy efficient.

This versatile appliance is especially appropriate to the contemporary cook, who may be preparing meals for one, reheating leftovers, or looking for speedy results. The oven function is perfect for defrosting—a feature I find appealing, since Nikki and I keep a large "freezer pantry." We can choose, for example, among our large supply of different whole-grain breadstuffs and then easily defrost just what is needed. Coupled with its capacity to toast and top-brown (broil) all in the same unit, the toaster oven is one of the best appliance buys around.

The Steam Oven

Steam ovens are not well known yet. These counter-top units resemble broilers or toaster ovens and do all the same jobs— broil, bake and toast—but can also cook with steam. Makers claim that the penetration of the food by steam means cooking in half the time of conventional ovens, and by combining functions you can crisp the exterior as well. Steam ovens provide a way to cook foods without fat and are an interesting alternative to the microwave oven. (Some ovens of the future may offer a "steam injector" option for baking.)

The Convection Oven

The convection oven is a simple and meaningful modification of the conventional oven. It is available in countertop models or as an alternate function in conventional and microwave ovens. These ovens, according to René Verdon and Jacqueline Mallorca, the authors of *Convection Cuisine*, cook up to 30 percent faster, and baked goods need 25°F less heat; by circulating the heat, it cooks more evenly and the foods "taste" and look better. I think this appliance is a much better choice than the microwave oven when looking for a faster cooking unit. With this appliance you can save time without sacrificing results or having to deal with controversial microwave technology.

The operating principle of the convection oven is interesting: An internal fan provides moving air, which heats much more quickly—sort of a "wind heat factor" akin to a wind chill factor. The fan also blows away "natural thermal barriers" (for example, moisture) that normally form on the surface of food while it cooks, insulating it. There is less odor and heat transfer to the room. Moreover, the internal fan makes it possible to cook different foods together without the odor of one permeating the others.

Convection ovens have been used in commercial kitchens for quite some time. They are made in small sizes, which are ideal for limited spaces, but the large ones work best. They save some energy and are available only in electric versions. Some of them can be used even as food dehydrators and slow cookers.

Now for their shortcomings: First, you have to know how to adjust your recipes to them. Second, since there is no uniformity in manufacture, results may vary from one unit to the next. Third, they are noisy due to the fan. And last, baking is said to be inconsistent—you can't make meringues and custards and some delicate baked goods may dry out (but not if a bowl of water is placed in the oven). It is nonetheless one of the best products of new technology to be introduced to the kitchen.

You can turn any electric oven into a convection oven with an ingenious device called the Zephyr. See "Selected Resources."

ENERGY-EFFICIENT OVEN USE

1. Don't cook with the oven door open—this common practice is quite wasteful.
2. Make sure the door seal is tight. A bad seal allows considerable heat loss.
3. Do not preheat longer than necessary. Ten minutes should be sufficient. Preheating is not necessary when broiling.
4. Use the oven as full as possible, but not overloaded.
5. Thaw frozen foods in the refrigerator first in order to reduce cooking time.
6. Use the right-size utensil for the quantity being cooked. Flat, shallow casseroles cook faster than deep ones. Cover when possible.
7. If you use glass or ceramic baking dishes, you can lower the baking temperature 25°, since these materials retain heat better than others.
8. Don't keep checking the progress by opening the door. An oven with a window and lit interior eliminates the need, as do reliable recipes.
9. Keep the oven clean, especially the heat-transfer surfaces.
10. Lining the oven with foil can reduce indoor air pollution by keeping the interior clean. Before doing this, however, check the manual so as not to interfere with the oven's operation.
11. Clean self-cleaning ovens right after use to take advantage of residual heat. Always scrape off what you can first, in order to hasten the process.
12. Don't use the oven to heat the house. This is not only inefficient, it can be dangerous.

The Microwave Oven

Despite the fact that the microwave oven is one of the most phenomenally successful appliances of the twentieth century, the Demonstration Kitchen does not contain one. As a matter of fact, this appliance's effect on the art of cooking was one of the strong motivating forces in the creation of the Demonstration Kitchen project. My impression of this appliance definitely runs counter to the trend, which, according to industry statistics, will see 80 percent of American homes containing microwave ovens in the 1990s.

You can call me old-fashioned, overly cautious, or a food snob, but I think there's good reason to resist the temptation of the microwave, although it does save time and cleanup in the kitchen. Somebody said, "There's no such thing as a free lunch," and here I think the metaphor is really appropriate.

You must acknowledge that the microwave oven does not replace the conventional oven unless you plan on only microwaving prepared storebought offerings or relearning cooking from scratch (and even then it has its limitations). You also must not care too much about the quality of such foods as meat and baked goods (more on this) and have no need to do quantity cooking (most are smaller than conventional ovens). Thus you can plan on purchasing both a microwave oven and a conventional oven (or an expensive combination unit).

Will microwave ovens someday serve up unpleasant surprises? This is a question we would do well to ask now in light of our experience with food processing, additives, and pesticides. Like these technologies, which were thrust upon consumers, will the far-reaching effects of microwaving food prove equally disturbing?

One thing is for sure: Microwave ovens are changing the quality of the food we eat, and not for the better. We are in the process of microwaving away 50,000 years of glorious culinary history in order to satisfy a dubious quest for convenience.

Moreover, and of great importance, there are serious concerns about the interaction between food and packaging and wrappings used in cooking, food-related injuries, microwave-related injuries, microwave emission standards, and food safety. There are also misconceptions about the oven's energy efficiency, nutrient retention, and speed.

ENERGY CONSUMPTION

Microwave ovens do not necessarily use less energy than conventional cooking does. The ovens may consume more or less energy than a conventional gas or electric appliance, depending on the quantity, type, and shape of the food being heated. Comparisons are difficult; the microwave oven is usually much more efficient than other means for cooking small amounts of food but no better than equal when cooking whole meals. Generally, microwave ovens consume as much or more energy than electric cooktops do but less than electric ovens. It should also be noted that prepared microwave foods are also energy intensive to manufacture.

NUTRIENT RETENTION

Many tout the microwave oven's ability to cook vegetables quickly and thereby conserve flavor and nutrients. Although this may be true for vegetables, it does not necessarily translate to other foods. Nutrient retention varies with cooking time, internal temperature, and product type, and with oven size, type, and power, so that in some cases nutrient retention in microwave ovens may not be that much better than in conventional ovens. Microwave ovens are also known to overcook easily, precisely because of the speed and high heat generated, which results in nutrient loss as well.

SPEED OF COOKING

Microwave ovens are designed for reheating prepared foods, and they do this very rapidly. They are also very quick at boiling water, cooking vegetables, reheating, and the like. However, some foods, such as noodles, rice, and pasta, which have to be rehydrated, require as much and sometimes more time to cook by microwaves than by conventional methods.

The microwave oven also does not do that well when compared with the pressure cooker ("the thinking cook's PC"). Once pressure is achieved (about 5 to 8 minutes):

- Asparagus spears take a mere 1 to 2 minutes under pressure; microwaving takes 8 to 10 minutes, plus 3 to 5 minutes "resting" time.
- A pound of green beans cut in 1-inch segments calls for zero to a minute of pressure cooking, whereas microwaving needs 5 to 11 minutes, plus 3 to 5 minutes resting.
- Presoaked chickpeas require only 18 minutes in the pressure cooker; the process in the microwave takes as long as an hour, and stirring every 10 minutes is suggested.
- In every comparable recipe for potted beef, veal, chicken, or pork, microwave cooking is two to four times longer and the recipe far more complicated to follow. Only fish preparation is equally fast using both systems.

Note, too, that times for microwave cooking are extremely varied from cookbook to cookbook.

When compared with conventional oven and stove-top cookery, most foods cook an estimated 70 percent faster while using 50 percent less fuel.

OVEN-RELATED INJURIES

A pamphlet issued by South Carolina Energy & Gas states, "There has never been a reported injury attributed to microwave ovens." This, unfortunately, is not true. A 1983 study by the Consumer Product Safety Commission records 213 microwave-oven-related injuries, some of which required hospitalization. There is also good reason to believe that many microwave oven accidents go unreported, or when reported, that injuries are not attributed to the appliance.

FOOD-RELATED INJURIES

Educational material from the Shriners Burns Institute, "Burns Associated With Microwave Ovens," issued in 1988, indicates that "burns associated with use or misuse of microwave ovens had increased" during the previous two and a half years. In a letter to the *The Lancet*, Matthew Maley of the Burns Institute writes:

The underlying cause of microwave oven re-lated injuries seems to be that oven users do not understand that microwaves heat in a way completely different from conventional heating appliances. This results in actions which would probably not be considered by someone using an ordinary cooker. Haste and an attitude that microwave ovens are safer likewise results in injury. The increasing popularity of microwave ovens will result in more and more burn injuries, unless preventive measures are taken.

The Shriners Burns Institute reports frequent burns and scalds from microwaved liquids—many to children under seven months from heated formula, despite bottle makers' warnings against doing this. The problem is not only that the contents can get too hot in traditional bottles but that bottle liners, particularly if not completely full, when shaken, can explode over the baby and feeder because of the pressure built up in them.

Another safety problem unique to microwave ovens concerns the so-called "eruption" phenomenon. When clear liquids are heated in glass, ceramic, or smooth plastic containers, the liquid can become extremely hot, although not boiling, and can erupt violently when moved or stirred or when something is added to it (for example, a spoon or instant coffee).

Reports of injuries are all the more alarming in light of increased use by children. According to the Campbell Microwave Institute (1988):

> Children as young as six years old use the microwave oven with their parents' supervision. In fact . . . nearly nine out of ten children ages six to seventeen use the microwave. Six- to twelve-year-olds use it most often for lunch and snacks, and teenagers use it an average of three times a day.

MICROWAVE-RELATED INJURIES

Since 1971 microwave ovens have had to be made to government standards that include door interlocks to prevent operation if the door is open and limits on the amount of microwaves that are allowed to leak from them. But additional microwaves can escape if the door seal becomes loose, is disrupted by food or other debris, or is otherwise defective. For this reason an engineer at the University of Alberta recommends strict controls on secondhand microwave ovens. At present there are none.

Can a microwave oven operate with the door open, and if so, what are the dangers? There have been several published reports of injury to the hand and arm while stirring food or removing containers from a microwave oven. Two treating physicians contend that their patients received radiation burns upon brief exposure (approximately 5 seconds) and that although the skin subsequently healed, there was persistent neurological damage to the area, which they were unable to treat successfully with currently known conventional therapies (*Bulletin of The N.Y. Academy of Medicine*, April 1983, and *Contemporary Orthopaedics*, November 1989). Also, Maley's letter (just quoted) lists nine cases of burn injuries in the U.S. and England that were caused "because [the] oven did not shut off when [the] door opened."

The microwave industry believes that the federally required safety interlocks "essentially prevent operation with an open door" and deny any possible malfunction. Manufacturers further support their safety position by stating that even if this were to happen, such short exposure to radiation would not be sufficient to cause injury.

Unfortunately, proof of such accidents is difficult to document because microwave burns do not produce skin destruction, as ordinary fire or electric currents do. The damage is to the peripheral nervous system. The industry defends itself on this "lack of proof" basis. In 1986, however, a Florida jury found proof and awarded $1.1 million for radiation injuries from a malfunctioning oven.

Despite all of this, an informational pamphlet, *The Microwave Oven*, presently distributed by the Association of Home Appliance Manufacturers, states, " 'there hasn't been a documented case of human' injury from microwaves from a microwave oven."

Safety Standards

The story of how the current microwave emission standards were set is not a comforting one. According to an article in *Science* Magazine (June 13, 1980), the standards were established in the 1950s when research on microwaves was just beginning, by those concerned with military applications (where risk is inherent), not by medical or environmental experts (who strive for zero risk). Since then, industry and the military have limited the flow of information about microwaves, which makes effective criticism or confirmation impossible. And though *Consumer Reports* tests have revealed microwave leakages to be within government standards, Dr. Robert Becker, researcher and author of *The Body Electric*, says other leakage studies contradict these reports. Microwave expert Stephen Cleary of Virginia Commonwealth University asserts that "nobody really knows what the safe levels are."

In a bulletin prepared by the Center for the Biology of Natural Systems at Washington University in July 1980, low levels of microwaves were reported to produce sterility, genetic changes, changes in the transmission of nerve impulses, and possible damage to the immune system in animals. Dr. Sidney Wolfe, executive director of Public Citizen's Health Research Group, feels there have not been enough studies on their mutagenicity or carcinogenicity.

Despite their rosy reports about the safety of microwave ovens, *Consumer Reports* suggests keeping a "reasonable distance" (about 4 feet) during operation. The University of California (Berkeley) *Wellness Newsletter* advises that users "not make a practice of standing right by the oven for long periods as it cooks, and discourage children from staring into it for long periods while it is running." (This is good advice for everyone.) These warnings are also particularly important for pregnant women: there have been pregnancy complications associated with similar radiation emanating from computers.

Most disquieting, there is no outward indication of leakage before symptoms appear.

Self-Testing

According to a U.S. Bureau of Radiological Health study, "Inexpensive Microwave Instruments: An Evaluation," microwave leakage meters sold for household use are not accurate.

FOOD SAFETY

Microwave cooking is not always effective at killing trichinosis in pork or salmonella in meat. In 1987, the U.S. Department of Agriculture issued a warning that owing to the presence of large bones and the varied distribution of internal moisture, unwanted microorganisms may survive microwaving. Unless you are sure the pork has reached an internal temperature of 160° to 170°F throughout, and poultry 180°F, you are taking a serious chance.

In June 1988 the University of Missouri-Columbia warned against using special devices made for home canning in microwave ovens, since the food does not get hot enough to kill some toxins, including the deadly botulism.

FIRE

The 1983 report by the Consumer Product Safety Commission just mentioned also found a "potential fire and thermal hazard" from 210 reports of electrical or mechanical malfunction. Fortunately, only a few serious injuries were reported. Because of the possibility of "self-starting" when no one is present, it is advisable to unplug the unit while not in use and also to have a smoke alarm.

Also, certain foods, such as baked potatoes, marshmallows, and microwave bags of popcorn, are known to more easily ignite.

PACKAGING AND WRAPS

Food-packaging materials and the plastic wraps used in microwave cooking have given rise to concerns about the leaching of their chemical components into food. The U.S. Food and Drug Administration (FDA) is looking into the migration of furans and dioxins, extremely toxic substances to food, from microwavable paper trays such as those that come with commercially prepared meat dinners.

The FDA is also investigating "heat susceptor packaging" used with crusty foods like pizza. The temperatures within these containers get very hot, in excess of 400° to 500°F—conditions not contemplated when the packaging materials were originally approved for food use. A preliminary government report describes a "breakdown" of the packaging and also states that "a considerable number of volatile components of the heat susceptor packaging become indirect food additives" from microwaving. At present it is not known if this is "unhealthy," and according to a spokesperson for the International Microwave Power Institute, "there is no decent test [at this time] to determine what is happening."

The plastic wrap that works best in microwave cooking, polyvinyl chloride (PVC), has been under suspicion for a long time. Dr. Gregory Cramer, a chemist at the FDA who works on plastics and new packaging, is quoted in *Atlantic* that "The reservoir of chemicals that could migrate into foods" is "much higher" in PVC wrap than in other kinds. In a 1988 report by the Institute of Food Technologists on the migration of plasticizers in PVC films to a variety of foods, levels were highest where there was direct contact between the film and foods with a high fat content at the surface. Plastic-wrapped microwaved meats (specifically pork and chicken) measured the most contamination. Like susceptor packaging, plastic wraps were approved for food use before microwave application, with its high temperatures, was envisioned.

SOLID WASTE

The U.S. Food Safety and Inspection Service estimates that by 1991, when microwave oven penetration is expected to reach 80 percent of American households, an estimated *4.7 billion plastic containers of food* will be sold, mostly for use in microwave ovens.

TRADING CUISINE FOR CONVENIENCE

Even if there were no safety considerations, I would reject microwave ovens on the basis of poor performance. Foods cooked by microwaves tend to be soggy and overly hot; they lack the appealing crisp, browned exterior of foods cooked in conventional ovens.

If the tasteless tomato is the symbol of technological farming, then it is the demise of the crusty baked potato that is the symbol of the microwave oven.

Although many consider the five-minute baked potato a miracle, to me it is more of a culinary tragedy. No doubt civilization will survive the soggy, overly hot dismal result, but why should we put up with the denigration of good food—one of the great joys of life?

A Safeway supermarket pamphlet on microwave cooking was honest enough to admit: "Since microwaved foods do not brown (except where fats become very hot), you may want to use a sauce, baste, or topping *to color the food and pick up its appearance*" [emphasis mine]. Microwave ovens perform particularly poorly on meat and baked goods. One cookbook says it "stews, braises, poaches and steams meat to perfection"—not exactly the most favored ways to prepare meat. And under the heading for pork: "Clearly it doesn't brown." Consequently, honest microwave cookbooks tell you, for example, to finish off ribs under the broiler or on a charcoal grill, or a roast in a conventional oven. In other microwave cookbooks, "barbecued" means applying a barbecue sauce to the microwaved meat. Listed as "disastrous" in another microwave cookbook: roasts, soufflés, and bread. "Then we have the problem of the appearance of the muffins," the author continues. "Our eyes are used to seeing golden-brown tops and of course we can't get this in the microwave. However, you can use a variety of toppings to *fool the eye into believing there is a browned muffin underneath*" [emphasis mine].

If you want to make gravy, don't count on the drippings after microwaving, since there aren't any. (One cookbook suggests having a gravy base "ready" for the juices that will appear on slicing. Do you make the gravy at the table? Go back to the kitchen? I list this under "things they didn't tell you at the appliance store.")

Also according to the Safeway pamphlet, "some conventional recipes are unsuitable for microwave ovens without major changes in ingredients and preparation." Note here, too, that the ovens are made with different wattages, but most cookbook recipes assume ovens in the 600-plus range; if you've got a lesser unit, or one without variable power, you'll have to learn to adjust cooking time. ("There is no simple way of calculating relative cooking times for ovens of different power," admits one knowledgeable cookbook author.)

Since microwave cooking requires such precise timing and procedures, sometimes more demands are actually placed on the cook. You'll also need special utensils, which can be costly if you plan on doing much real cooking.

What I find all the more remarkable is that since microwave ovens are so different from conventional appliances, you must "learn to cook all over again." I can still hear the voice of a woman I came upon in the appliance department of a major department store complaining that the microwave class she wanted to attend had been canceled. ("I've got this thing home and I

don't know what buttons to push," she moaned.) Ironically, you could probably never get this woman to attend a regular cooking class, where she could learn techniques that would enable her to cook conventionally, yet conveniently.

Although newer models include browning functions, monitoring devices, and so on, they still are not, in my estimation, the best tool for the job when measured in terms of the combined taste, texture, crust, and so on, produced in a conventional oven. (I love the catalog copy describing the purpose of a browning element, to give a "finished *look*" [emphasis mine].)

"The proof of the pudding" should be in the eating, and if you've ever burned your mouth on a soggy lump of microwaved food, you know what I mean. My fear is that microwaved food will become the standard. Microwave technology today can be likened to the introduction of nuclear technology in the 1950s. At that time, pregnant women were routinely X-rayed, as it was thought that low levels of this form of radiation (ionizing) were harmless. However, in 1956, Dr. Alice Stewart of Oxford University proved that fetal X rays were significantly affecting childbirth mortality rates. Although microwaves rely on a different kind of radiation (non-ionizing), can they be so casually dismissed in light of history?

EDUCATED MICROWAVE OPERATION

As I've indicated, there are serious safety concerns about microwave operation. After studying a number of users guides and operator manuals, I was very disappointed to see that many of them are deficient in providing safe guidelines for cooks. Therefore for the many who already use microwave ovens and who I have not been able to discourage from their purchase, here is a summary of some important rules about their use—all of which do not appear together in any single operator's manual I surveyed.

These are the warnings *required* by federal law:

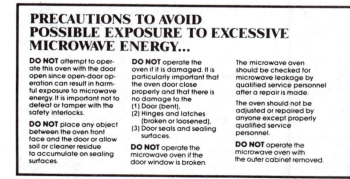

PRECAUTIONS TO AVOID POSSIBLE EXPOSURE TO EXCESSIVE MICROWAVE ENERGY...

DO NOT attempt to operate this oven with the door open since open-door operation can result in harmful exposure to microwave energy. It is important not to defeat or tamper with the safety interlocks.

DO NOT place any object between the oven front face and the door or allow soil or cleaner residue to accumulate on sealing surfaces.

DO NOT operate the oven if it is damaged. It is particularly important that the oven door close properly and that there is no damage to the
(1) Door (bent),
(2) Hinges and latches (broken or loosened),
(3) Door seals and sealing surfaces.

DO NOT operate the microwave oven if the door window is broken.

The microwave oven should be checked for microwave leakage by qualified service personnel after a repair is made.

The oven should not be adjusted or repaired by anyone except properly qualified service personnel.

DO NOT operate the microwave oven with the outer cabinet removed.

REQUIRED MICROWAVE WARNING

WARNINGS THAT SHOULD BE REQUIRED BY FEDERAL LAW

1. *Read* and *follow* the manual instructions for operation; make sure anyone else who will use the unit knows how to operate it safely, too. (When using more than one unit, for example at home and at the office, remember that they may have different power ratings and directions for use.) Keep the manual in a safe place and pass it on to any future owner.

2. If it is necessary for a child to operate a microwave oven, make sure that he or she is well trained in how to use it and knows the risks involved. Because there is no apparent flame, this does not mean the oven is not hazardous. For example, children should not peer inside while it is operating, or for that matter stand in front of it. Equally important is that they must understand how hot microwaved food can get, that they use only the proper utensils, that the oven is used only for cooking and that they put their hand in the opened oven no longer than necessary.

3. Try to stand away from the oven when it is on; four feet is the suggested distance, particularly for children and pregnant women.

4. Do not warm baby bottles in oven. Despite the fact that bottle packaging warns against this, parents, hospitals, and day-care centers continue this practice. The problem is not only that the contents can get too hot in traditional bottles but that bottle liners, particularly if not completely full, when shaken can explode over baby and feeder due to the pressure built up in them.

5. Be careful of clear liquids heated in glass, ceramic, or smooth plastic containers. The liquid can become extremely hot but without boiling and erupt violently when moved, stirred, or when an ingredient is added (for example, sugar or coffee). With new vessels, particularly smooth ones, be extra cautious and let the heated water set for a short while in the oven after you turn it off.

6. Watch out for foods unevenly heated; the jelly filling may be scalding though the pastry is only warm, and the pickle may cause a burn while the sandwich may not be hot. Frozen foods may be cold in one spot, scalded in another.

7. Sample foods for young children before allowing them to eat; watch out for "hot spots" in the food.

8. Test different foods and quantities to determine the best time and energy cycles.

9. Stir foods to distribute the heat evenly (many dishes heat from the outside in).

10. After heating moderate to large quantities of food, let the food and container remain in oven to allow vapor to decrease. Steam burns are common when items are opened too quickly.

11. Do not make hard-boiled eggs in the oven; they can explode and possibly blow the door off. Also never microwave sealed jars, an egg in its shell, or one out of its shell unless you have pierced the yolk first; pierce also baked potatoes, shad roe, sausages, tomatoes, squash, peaches, and any other food with an unbroken exterior.

12. Do not use the swing-down door as a shelf or allow children to hang on it.

13. Never turn the oven on when empty. Leave a glass of water or box of baking soda inside as a safety precaution.

14. Do not make popcorn, except in microwave bag or container. Check the power rating; popcorn packages can incinerate if subjected to too much power.

15. Do not melt paraffin in oven.

16. Do not defrost frozen beverages in a narrow-necked jar.

17. Never close a bag with a twist tie and place it in the oven. The metal in it will arc (spark), and the paper on the tie will ignite, setting fire to the bag.

18. Be careful not to overheat plastic, paper, or other inflammable materials. To reduce risk, check occasionally. If fire does occur, unplug the oven and let it burn itself out. Do not open door. If the fire spreads, follow the normal fire fighting strategy. (See Chapter 8.) Do not use the oven again without it being checked by a service professional.

19. Use aluminum foil only as directed in the manual. If you use it, check to see that it is not arcing. Aluminum foil will burn the sides of a microwave oven wherever it touches.

20. The browning element can get hot, so be cautious. Do not cover with plastic wrap, paper towel, or wax paper; they can melt and ignite.

21. Do not use any dish that gets hot in the oven (except from heated food), since it is not suitable for microwaving.

22. Do not cook in regular brown paper bags, non-microwave paper towel, or any towel or cloth with synthetic fibers. They may have metal particles or other components that can start a fire.

23. Do not dry clothing, newspaper, herbs, or food in the oven.

24. Never operate the oven when anything is touching the inside top or sides.

25. Do not deep-fry. Fat can reach "dangerously high" levels in a microwave oven.

26. Canning jars cannot be sterilized in a microwave oven.

27. Make sure nothing blocks the microwave's vents.

28. Do not use any metal utensils in the oven.

29. When directed to cover food with plastic, you must vent it. Cover the dish with the wrap and pull back a corner; do not slit the cover. Otherwise, be cautious when opening, or you can be injured by the escaping steam.

30. To minimize the possibility of chemicals migrating to the food from the plastic wrap, choose Saran™ and Glad Wrap,™ which contain fewer chemicals than PVC-containing Reynolds Wrap.™ The possibility of

migration is always greatest when fatty foods come in contact with plastic.

31. Do not cook stuffing in the cavity of a bird. Do not cook pork unless the internal temperature reaches 160° to 170°F, or chicken unless cooked to 180°F; otherwise you risk food poisoning.

32. Be cautious of baked potatoes, marshmallows and bags of pop corn which can more easily ignite from microwaving.

33. Do not microwave any prepared food not labelled "microwavable."

34. Do not use oven for any non-food purposes, such as experiments.

35. Check the door and seals periodically. If you have any questions, call the manufacturer, dealer, or local health department. Many manufacturers and health departments provide inspection services.

36. Cover the window with opaque paper to discourage children from looking into oven.

37. Do not try to repair the oven yourself. Repairs should only be done by an authorized repair service. Have it tested after repair.

38. Keep the oven's interior, door seals and vents clean.

Purchasing and Installing a Microwaving Oven

1. Purchase an oven with a service contract that includes periodic inspections. (And have the inspections done.) Buy only an Underwriters Laboratory (UL) approved unit.

2. Avoid used ovens, especially those used commercially; there are no standards required for used microwave ovens.

3. Be especially cautious of ovens made before 1971, since they had fewer emission standards. The FDA advises standing "an arm's length away" during operation.

4. Upon delivery, examine the unit for evidence of shipping damage.

5. Follow installation instructions.

6. Be cautious about mounting over a conventional oven or stove even if the manual permits this; heat and steam may damage the oven's controls.

7. Provide the oven with its own electric circuit. This is rarely done in practice but should be, as the oven can use as much as 50-percent of a circuit's amperage and overload it. This is particularly true in older homes.

8. Fill out the registration card if one is included. This will ensure that if there are any problems with the unit, the company will be able to inform you. (Registration cards are not required by law, but the dealer is required to keep your name and address on record for a number of years.)

9. Do not situate the oven where someone can sit nearby during its operation—this will avoid constant close exposure.

10. Install a smoke alarm nearby to warn of fire caused by the occasional oven "self-start." The Consumer Product Safety Commission reported more than 40 cases of self-starting, some when no one was present. Serious damage and injury was averted in a number of cases due to the presence of a smoke detector. It may also be wise to develop the habit of unplugging the oven while not in use or plug it into a switched outlet.

11. Do not take a U.S. microwave to a foreign country that uses different electric current.

Professional Equipment

Commercial cooking ranges are often chosen by those interested in the professional look or the assumed capability they provide. I must point out initially that installation of one of these units in the residential situation violates manufacturer's instructions, which usually say "designed for commercial use only." This stipulation may void the warranty on new stoves and may even affect your homeowners insurance coverage (which usually does not include commercial installations).

Almost everything about professional ranges is *large*. They may be appropriate for volume feeding, but in normal households they are apt to be a waste of energy and space. The stove top alone on a professional range may be serviced by up to three pilot lights, which keep the surface hot enough to suffice as a warming area without even igniting the burners! Also, because the burners are designed specifically to hold restaurant-size utensils, conventional pots may be unstable, readily overheated, and even damaged. There will be two to three more pilot lights for the oven.

Many single-oven models lack a broiler and also, since the professional oven and griddle are not meant to be turned on and off for short periods of time, they take a long time to heat up and cool down. The oven, too, is designed for volume; unless you use it frequently for 20-pound turkeys and half a dozen pies at a time, a lot of air is heated unnecessarily. Additionally, many professional ovens, particularly lower-cost and older models, are poorly insulated, using extra fuel and generating excessive heat in the kitchen. Normally the oven door is not insulated at all, even on new models, creating enormous burn risk, particularly in households where there are children.

Safe installation requires a 3-inch clearance and fireproofing all around (brick, sheet metal, and so on). Some manufacturers require a 6-inch clearance where the stove abuts such combustible surfaces as wood or laminate.

Kitchen expert Ellen Cheever feels people are attracted to these units as "status symbols" or "proof of the chef's culinary talents." Writing in *Kitchen & Bath Business*, she summed up her objections: First, the burners use 15,000 to 20,000 BTUs an hour, and the ovens 18,000 to 30,000 BTUs an hour. Only 9,000 to 12,000 BTUs are needed for home cooking. Because of the high gas usage you may even have to put in a larger gas line. Second, residential equipment provides safer design and easier maintenance. Industrial stoves were not built with the home cook or children in mind. Third, the high heat may create a fire hazard. Fourth, the parts are large and heavy and will not fit into a residential sink. Fifth, the 36-inch depth may not fit through doorways, and the weight, 400 to 800 pounds, may be more than your floor can support easily. Last, you will need a larger ventilation system, since homeowners' systems are not designed for the output of professional stoves. (Probably a fan rated at 1,000 CFM is needed—almost ten times larger than normally required.) These drawbacks do not seem to be counterbalanced by the benefits, especially since grills, griddles, and rotisseries have been introduced to residential equipment. Ms. Cheever recommends that cooks who do a lot of cooking may want to consider two residential ranges instead.

Those of you who have your hearts set on a commercial stove should check into new units made by commercial range makers. These "gourmet" ranges are modeled after restaurant equipment but engineered "exclusively" for the home. They can be installed flush with the wall and contain electronic ignitions. Features include six burners, large ovens, and griddles, and they meet the safety standards of the American Gas Association.

Those with existing industrial stoves should address some of the safety and insurance problems mentioned above.

Wood Stoves

Wood stoves, which have gained popularity for heating purposes, are often overlooked as an auxiliary cooking appliance. They are ideal for slow cooking of beans, stews, soups, and sauces and for "keeping a kettle on." Any stove or even fireplace insert with enough flat surface to set a pot on will do. For me the dividend is not so much energy savings but the outdoor smoked flavor that is imparted to food.

Look for energy-conserving stoves with features that include catalytic converters (to reduce smoke emissions) and an outside air inlet. Remember also that any wood stove that cannot be closed up when not in use will rob the house of heat in the winter.

The best way to learn wood stove cooking is to experiment with the amount of fuel, types of fires, and so on. Iron trivets and bricks and the like are a great aid in controlling the heat.

Check "Selected Resources" for information an annual wood stove buyer's guide that will provide a little wood stove inspiration.

The AGA

Cooking enthusiasts should be aware of the legendary AGA stove, designed by a Swedish Nobel Prize-winning physicist. These remarkable enameled-iron cookers, popular in Europe, have been finding a new following in North America despite their $6,000-plus price tag and great weight (1,000 to 1,400 pounds). The AGA to many is more than a stove; it's a way of life. The AGA bakes, broils, boils, fries, grills, toasts, stews, steams, roasts, and simmers—*all at once*. The secret is lots of design ingenuity and retained heat: The stove stays warm all the time. It is said to cook faster than conventional stoves, yet it is easy to maintain and safe to the touch. Traditionally fired with coal, it is now available in a gas version, too. They must be vented to the outside.

The Ideal Cooker

Nikki and I designed and had fabricated an "Ideal Cooker" to incorporate many of the elements we thought should be in a stove—most notably a gas cooktop and electric oven in one stainless steel (over plywood) commercial-looking unit. With this design we were able to choose an appropriate cooktop and oven in terms of size and mode, and still have the look of professional equipment to fit the interior decoration scheme. Although stainless steel is an extremely durable and attractive material, it is quite expensive and requires attention to keep it looking good. An interesting alternative is a metal-like plastic laminate.

The Ideal Cooker houses an electric oven, a four-burner gas cooktop with integral griddle/grill, lots of convenient storage spaces, and an eye-level utility shelf with a built-in exhaust. (A fifth burner, provided by a portable magnetic induction cooktop, is close by.)

The Ideal Cooker's electric oven measures 27 inches from the kitchen floor to its open door. At this height the shelves can be positioned at approximately waist level. According to Cornell University research, the oven floor should be between 1 and 7 inches below "bent-elbow" height for maximum comfort. The 1-inch distance means less bending and better visibility, whereas 7 inches makes lifting easier. Many workers prefer the compromise of 3 inches. We choose to modify this suggestion slightly, installing the oven a bit lower so that its top surface is accessible and can be used to set hot casseroles on and as a warming station, utilizing the heat given off by the oven. (Ordinarily, cabinets are built over wall ovens.) In addition, the top surface is available as a site for a future appliance, such as a convection oven. The oven's position still provides clear visibility and access, and minimizes uncomfortable bending and the problem of wrist burns from ovens situated close to the floor.

The cabinet design allows for a half-inch of rigid fiberglass insulation on the sides of the oven to increase efficiency and to keep the kitchen cooler during the warm weather. (If the oven is to have cabinets above it, the top should be insulated too.)

The cooktop was installed to the right of the oven. Seventeen inches above burner level is an 8-inch-deep stainless steel storage shelf that runs the length of the cooktop and doubles as the hood of the exhaust system. (Actually a shelf a little deeper, perhaps 10 to 12 inches, might have been better. For more on this see "The Task Exhaust System," in Chapter 12.) The design was inspired by professional kitchens, which often have a shelf and/or broiler mounted at shoulder height, enabling the cook to easily reach utensils, timer, and such and to monitor different tasks simultaneously. The toaster oven that we set here duplicates the professional chef's arrangement—especially useful for defrosting, toasting, or warming foods while other cooking is going on.

Below the oven are two deep drawers hung on heavy full-extension slides; under the cooktop are small drawers and open horizontal and vertical shelves and slots to store baking sheets, trays, racks, the wok, oversize pots, and other cooking utensils. Our specially mounted pot rack, discussed in the following section, was installed over the unit.

To the right of the cooker is a peninsula that extends perpendicular to it, creating an "L" and a complementary work area; a very handy locale to hold tools and ingredients in a "ready position" when cooking. A "garage" below the counter houses the magnetic induction cooker. (Any portable burner could be used.)

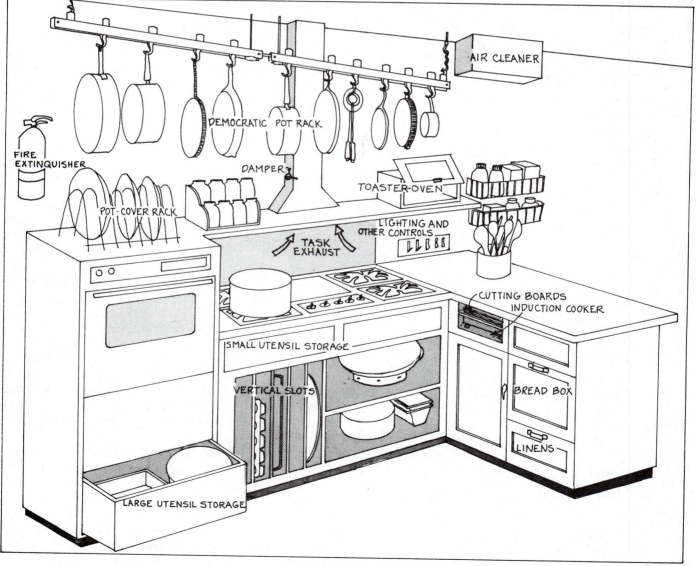

The Ideal Cooker

Stove Installation

Use of noncombustible materials around stoves is a very important part of safe kitchen design that is occasionally overlooked, sometimes with disastrous consequences.

The wall above and 2 feet to each side of the cooker should have no wood, plastic finishes, curtains, or *anything* that can burn. Tile, metal, steel, and painted drywall are your best options; brick and stone masonry are fireproof but hard to keep clean. Be cautious when placing shelves and cabinets over the cooker, unless they are metal.

A cooktop should never be placed in front of an operable window.

The cooktop should provide access only from the front, particularly in kitchens where young children are present, according to the Shriners Burns Institute. Stoves at the end of the counter negate the protection afforded by being able to cook on the back burners. The institute also recommends that you establish a "safe zone" for children while cooking is going on—you may want specify an area with tape—and that you do not use deep-fat fryers when children are at home.

The Democratic Pot Rack

Pot racks are practical as well as decorative; they free up drawer space, put pots and pans at easy reach, and provide a nice display of kitchenware.

One fault is that very often small pots and pans hung overhead are difficult to reach. I picked up a technique from professional kitchens that solves this problem, which is simply to hang the pot rack at an angle so that one end is higher than the other. I dubbed it the "democratic" way because with small pots hung from the low end and large pots from the high end, all are equally comfortable to reach.

Taylor and Ng make a nicely designed ceiling pot rack called the Track Rack System,™ which is easily hung askew. This rack consists of two metal slats within which the hooks slide. If you find the hooks slipping when the rack is at an angle (and this will vary with the severity of the incline), glue a small piece of rubber on the hooks where they rest on the slats. This adds friction so they don't travel on their own but can still be moved when needed. (Small pieces of inner tube cut into half circles work perfectly.) Hang the rack so that one end is about twice as low as the other, but adjust according to the size of your pots and workability. To keep the pot lids in easy reach, I placed an office file rack (available in any stationery store) on top of the oven. (Other racks, designed specifically for pot lids, are also available.) The "democratic" principle can, of course, be applied to other style racks as well.

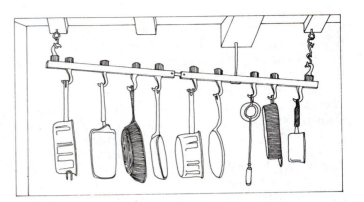

DEMOCRATIC POT RACK

I've heard it said that pot racks are grease and dust collectors, which is a valid concern. We have not found this to be the case, but that may be because of the utensils' frequent use. If this is a concern to you, large drawers with extra sturdy slides are an excellent alternative. Make sure to include some manner of organizing the lids in the drawer, or it will be hard to retrieve them. The Ideal Cooker contains such drawers under the oven, plus ample open shelves under the cooktop for extra-large utensils.

ENVIRONMENTAL CHOICES

All smooth cooktops and electric burners create the least air pollution.

To be environmentally sound, gas cooktops must have an electronic ignition and be used with adequate ventilation and /or an effective air-cleaning device. Properly adjusting gas burners is important; otherwise emissions, particularly carbon monoxide and nitrogen dioxide, will be greater. The flame must be blue, not yellow, and soot should not form on the outside of pots and pans.

Electric ovens are the least polluting. The gas oven, like the gas cooktop, will create gas combustion byproducts. Do not buy a gas oven without an electronic ignition. Gas ovens with their own venting system are best. Otherwise, plan on installing efficient ventilation and/or an air filter. Convection ovens, because they require less cooking time, can also help reduce indoor air pollution.

A strategy that Bruce Small, a Canadian environmental engineer has adopted is to isolate the stove from the rest of the kitchen in a small vented room. Although this is an unusual design, it would effectively shield the inhabitants from troublesome gas combustion products (as well as offensive cooking odors). This "cooking chamber" could be an interesting design feature with windows or even a glass wall.

Part III

AIR AND WATER QUALITY, WASTE DISPOSAL, AND FOOD PRODUCTION

Smart design today must address how the kitchen interacts with the environment. Although kitchen ventilation was always necessary, adequate ventilation is *imperative* today, since new, tighter-built homes no longer aerate cooking fumes and water vapor "naturally."

Water, virtually a universal food ingredient, is subject to a myriad of pollutants; care must be taken so it is pure once it reaches the table.

On a more positive note, increased attention can be given to making the kitchen productive in areas outside of food preparation. By incorporating a space for holding recyclable materials, this important responsibility can be facilitated. And those who garden can recycle food wastes into compost more easily if the kitchen has facilities for holding them.

The kitchen can also have its own indoor garden of herbs, sprouts, and the like if a convenient space with suitable lighting and accessible water is provided. The reward: an abundance of fresh crops year round.

Chapter 12:

VENTILATION

The average kitchen generates an astonishing 200 pounds of airborne grease a year, plus heat, odors, moisture, and other elements that effect air quality, according to the Home Ventilating Institute. Both the obvious offensive odors that linger after cooking, and perhaps the less obvious emissions generated from cooking, particularly with gas, may unconsciously be conditioning us away from the kitchen. Many building materials also emit unhealthy gases. (See Chapters 2 .) This "indoor air pollution" may also be creating serious health hazards for many people.

It is essential to have an exhaust system and possibly some other method of cleaning the air while cooking. Where electric appliances are used, this is needed to remove not only cooking vapors but also the airborne particles created by the incineration of dust, hair, and such, on the coils. When gas is the cooking fuel, air quality control is mandatory in order to deal with gas combustion products (particularly carbon monoxide and nitrogen dioxide), moisture, and particulate matter. (See Chapter 11.)

"NATURAL" AIR CLEANERS

Houseplants add beauty and color to any decor, but according to scientists at the U.S. National Aeronautics and Space Administration (NASA), there's another, healthy reason to have some in the kitchen: Certain houseplants can reduce the levels of some dangerous contaminants in indoor air. Spider plants are excellent for reducing carbon monoxide from the air, as is golden pothos; philodendron (elephant's ear and heart leaf) can absorb large quantities of formaldehyde as well as carbon monoxide; and aloe vera is effective at removing formaldehyde at low concentrations.

Scientists investigating this phenomenon point out that their experiments were done in sealed chambers and that the plants' capacity may be different in houses or apartments, where there is some ventilation. Nonetheless, houseplants are an attractive way to improve indoor air quality. Scientists at NASA firmly believe the more foliage, the healthier the environment is going to be. A wall or window full of these plants could be an aesthetic as well as functional feature especially in an apartment which may be poorly vented. One NASA scientist, Dr. B. C. Wolverton has de-

signed a special plant container to enhance this effect. (see "Selected Resources.")

MECHANICAL SYSTEMS

There are a two mechanical approaches to kitchen air quality: removing (and replacing) the offending air in some way, such as through an exhaust system, or cleaning the air, as with a filter. The removal of air is not always a simple matter due to concerns about energy consumption, comfort and backdrafting. In climates where heating or cooling of interior air is minimal, the solution is quite simple; anything that encourages polluted air to depart and fresh air to enter, such as a venting window or exhaust fan is welcome.

But up until recently, the common procedure, no matter what the climate, was to mount an overhead or wall exhaust system, ignoring the fact that these systems remove heated (or cooled) air along with the offending atmosphere. As a result, after the meal is cooked, the kitchen or living space can become uncomfortably cold or hot. According to ventilation expert Richard Karg, the heat loss from running a typical exhaust fan in the Northeast costs in the range of $40 to $80 a year (1984). (This cost does not include the additional effects from the infiltration of cold air down the exhaust and the possibility of drafts throughout the house.)

Since the noise of the fan in a filter or exhaust system can be disturbing (and may discourage use), this too should not be ignored. All equipment should be "auditioned" before purchase— if not at the dealers, perhaps at a friend's or neighbor's home. In general, exterior-mounted fans are the quietest (but there are exceptions), and squirrel-cage type fans are less noisy than propeller-driven ones. A listing of commonly available home ventilating equipment, including sound levels, is available in *Certified Home Ventilating Products Directory* (#11) and the *Home Ventilation Guide*, both published by the Home Ventilating Institute.

NONVENTED AIR FILTERS

The Recirculating Hood

Standard nonvented exhaust systems are not the solution. These popular recirculating kitchen range hoods are ineffective in removing the pollutants produced by cooking. What's more, they may actually be quite dangerous. The best models are only capable of removing grease and smoke, but not steam or gases. But most often they do not even do this very well. Dr. Thad Godish, director of indoor air quality research at Ball State University, says it is very difficult to find an adequately designed unit. One reason is the quality of the filter medium itself. To be at all effective, the carbon employed in the filter must be a solid block and thick enough so that you cannot see through it. Usually poor-quality carbon in inadequate design formats is used.

Critical too is that these systems can be fire hazards due to the grease buildup that occurs under the hood and in the filter. (When such a system is used, it *must* be cleaned often.)

An Effective Air-Filtering System

In order to remove both unwanted odors and the emissions associated with gas combustion, I investigated special filtering materials such as Purafil™ (potassium permanganate), coconut shell carbon, Formaldezorb™, and Formaldepure™. Another filter called HEPA™ is particularly efficient at removing airborne particles. (HEPA was designed by the U.S. Atomic Energy Commission to remove radioactive particles from the air.) Air filters that incorporate these materials are made for industrial use or by concerns that specialize in helping people with allergic conditions.

In the Demonstration Kitchen I asked a custom air filter maker to build one for the kitchen. This system incorporates Purafil™, activated carbon, and a HEPA filter. It is designed to remove almost all the air pollution in a 10-by-12-by-8-foot kitchen in about five minutes. There are larger units for bigger rooms.

The unit is used mostly in cold weather and often in conjunction with our "task exhaust system" (below). In addition, because the type of cooking that is done in the Demonstration Kitchen does not generate much grease, I do not know whether this particular system is right for all cooking conditions. However, as with other aspects of the kitchen project, I wanted to make a point, which is that there is available technology and it should be utilized. Also, this type of air cleansing system may not be as cost effective as a well designed exhaust system. They may however be extremely desirable in poorly vented situations such as an apartment. Manufacturers and distributors of such equipment are listed in "Selected Resources."

Cleaning Your Air Cleaner

Even the best air-cleaning device will not work if the filters are clogged up. Filters should be checked and changed periodically, depending on use. Watch for grease buildup.

THE VENTED EXHAUST SYSTEM

The vented exhaust is the most available, as well as the most practical and safest system. It can be either wall mounted or a hood type, but the latter is more effective. A well designed hood and properly operated hood can remove 60-90 percent of stove pollutants where the stove is well tuned.

Because of the potential for grease fires, hood design should be an important consideration in your purchase here. One company that claims their system is particularly safe is Vent-A-Hood.™

Sizing the Fan

To determine the size of an adequate wall or ceiling exhaust fan (assuming an 8-foot ceiling), multiply the square footage of the room by 2. (Thus a 100-square-foot kitchen would require a 200-CFM fan.)

For hood fan selection multiply the length of the cooktop by 40 if the hood is mounted against the wall and by 50 for an overhead island or peninsula hood. (Thus a 36-inch cooktop would require either a 120- or a 150-CFM fan depending on style.)

Backdraft Warning: With all vented exhaust systems, whether in a hood or the built-in downdraft type, big is not necessarily better. Too powerful an exhaust in a house that is airtight can create a partial vacuum by pulling air out but not replacing it. The resulting "negative pressure" can reverse the direction of furnaces, chimneys, hot water heaters, and the like, which are not vented to the outside. This could have serious results. Therefore, don't oversize the fan, and provide for replacement air through a window or other vent during operation.

Installation

All systems should be installed carefully for fire safety, for effectiveness, and to minimize noise pollution (see Chapter 5).

Operation

You should run the exhaust for a while after cooking to thoroughly vent the area. If the kitchen can be closed off from the dining room, the fan can stay on during the meal without creating drafts or disturbing anyone.

When not in use, wall exhaust fans that are in easy reach can be covered to prevent cold air from entering the kitchen. Inexpensive interior covers are sold in hardwares stores.

The Task Exhaust System

After discussing the situation with both ventilation and environmental engineers, I have come to the conclusion that an effective exhaust system is one that is localized, just as task lighting is aimed at a particular spot. This should result in the the removal of less heated (or cooled) air and a reduced inhalation of cooking fumes (which may be hazardous), since they do not have to pass your face to reach the hood.

Also, where formerly there was only the stove to be concerned with, today's kitchen may have a separate oven and even a broiler or rotisserie at another location. A task system can connect the exhaust to each area of need, rather than having one large, less effective, room-ventilating apparatus. This also should result in more effective service and be less of an energy drain. Unfortunately, there is no commercial task exhaust system available at this time.

In the Demonstration Kitchen all cooking is centralized at the combination four-burner gas stove/griddle/grill unit. The experimental task exhaust system I designed connected an exterior-mounted fan via a duct to the area directly over the cooktop. Rather than using a hood, the duct vents through a stainless steel shelf mounted over the cooktop. (The fan was mounted outside to minimize noise; it must be sized according to the individual installation.)

I installed an in-line damper in easy reach to eliminate air infiltration when it is cold outside. In warm weather the damper is kept open to permit natural air convection to occur when the fan is not on. (Note that the fan itself should not have an internal damper, or at least this damper should be deactivated.) The fan is controlled by a rheostat. For fire protection I included a washable grease filter. All parts were made and installed by professionals.

This plan has been very effective for exhausting from the griddle/grill, where it is needed the most, as well as from the two back burners. Since the shelf housing the vent extends out only 8 inches, the fumes from the two front burners do not seem to be captured as efficiently. (No exacting testing has been done.) Thus we make a habit of using the back burners for long-term or particularly greasy or odoriferous cooking. You can see the fumes and steam being sucked up the vent. At times the open damper alone is effective without the fan; the rheostat makes it possible to adjust the speed according to need.

Increasing the depth of the shelf to 10 to 12 inches would enable the system to encompass a greater surface area. However, the shelf must not interfere with your view of the cooktop or the ability to manipulate large pots.

Since the opening in this exhaust is below shoulder level, as opposed to the usual overhead design, vapors don't have to pass in front of your face and are thus not inhaled as they travel to reach the intake—a decided advantage. And the over-the-stove shelf itself is an extremely useful element in the kitchen, providing a place for toaster/oven, broiler, and utensils—even a warming spot for dishes.

In situations where there is more than one site in need of ventilation, additional task vents and controls can be installed there and used as needed.

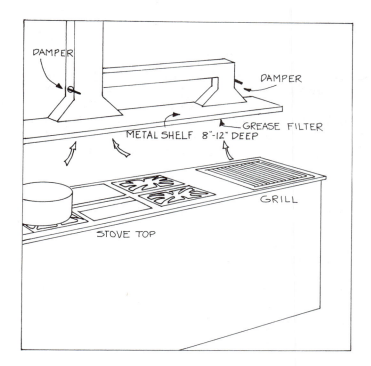

Experimental Task Exhaust System

The Heat Recovery Ventilator (HRV)

A relatively new device called a *heat recovery ventilator (HRV)* or air-to-air heat exchanger, can replace air in homes in such a way that the heat contained in the exhausted air warms the incoming air. Designed mainly for new, tight, energy-efficient homes that have little "natural" air infiltration, they may also be useful in older homes that have been weatherized to virtual solar home status. (The air in older home construction changes anywhere from once to ten times per hour; with newer building techniques from once every three hours to twice per hour.)

HRVs are available for entire homes or for individual rooms; whole-house systems will run in the thousands of dollars. In Sweden they are required in all new houses, but their use is relatively new in the United States. Therefore, you should use extra care in choosing equipment. Look for a unit that can be easily cleaned; a removable, washable heat exchange element is a must. In climates where subzero temperatures are common, a nonfrosting unit is desirable, but one that has a defrost cycle is acceptable. Installation should be done only by an experienced person. Laying out the ductwork properly is *extremely* important; see Richard Karg's *Solar Age* article, "Tips and Cautions about Air Exchangers." Also useful is the book *Air-to-Air Heat Exchangers for Houses* by William A. Shurcliff.

There are a few HRVs made just for the kitchen and they are listed in the "Selected Resources."

The Opening Skylight

One often overlooked method of venting kitchens is the opening skylight, which will vent the room through convection currents (hot air rises). The eminent architect Frank Lloyd Wright was credited with opening kitchens to the upper floor in order to take advantage of this natural air movement. I also experimented with this approach in the Demonstration Kitchen.

When used for venting, a skylight that operates by electric motor is more convenient to use than one that operates manually.

Environmental Choices

Sensitivities to gas emissions can be induced by long-term exposure. Therefore, wherever gas appliances are being used, it is mandatory that you provide adequate ventilation and/or air cleaning equipment, even if you believe you have no present reaction. The need is less stringent with electric cooking equipment, but water vapors, grease, and other airborne incinerated products should still be addressed. Moisture can cause mold growth (as well as structural damage to the house) as well as aggravate other pollution problems such as those caused by formaldehyde.

Chapter 13:

WATER PURITY, CONSERVATION, AND HEATING

The situation with America's water reminds me of the joke about the fellow who goes to a hotel for a vacation. When someone inquires as to the quality of his stay, he replies that not only was the food terrible, but it was served in such small portions! So it is with our water. Not only is it polluted, but we're running out of it: Towns and cities everywhere have had water shortages, and many localities have passed legislation to reduce water consumption.

More than seven hundred different chemicals have been found in America's drinking water, and at this writing at least thirty-four states have serious water quality problems. Contaminant levels in public water are regulated by the U.S. Environmental Protection Agency (EPA). No matter where you get your water today—whether well, spring, or public water works—it's most likely to have some sort of contamination.

Water raises other concerns as well. Fifteen percent of residential energy is used to heat hot water—both kitchen and bath—according to the American Council for an Energy Efficient Economy (ACE[3]). Since this is a significant amount, it pays to take advantage of the most efficient water heating equipment. In 1989 the average cost was $320 per year (8 cents/kwh) for electrically heated systems, half as much for gas (60 cents/therm). Here again the ACE[3] publication *The Most Energy Efficient Appliances*, listed in Resources for Chapter 9, will assist you in making the best choice. After January 1, 1990, water heaters will have to meet new U.S. efficiency standards but the ACE[3] booklet will still lead you to the best units.

WATER PURITY

Many municipal water systems will test water for free. The phone directory can help you find private and public labs for testing. For more information, contact the Water Quality Association.

Pure water can be obtained by prevention of contamination, filtration, or the purchase of water.

Prevention of Contamination

LEAD

See Chapter 3.

BACTERIA

Bacterial contamination is usually caused by septic runoff. All homes serviced by wells should have their water tested periodically. A well with bacteria can be decontaminated by disinfection fairly easily without costly professional intervention. Local labs or water plants can give instructions. If the problem persists, check the effectiveness of your septic system as well as your neighbors'. For recurring contamination, you might want to look into ultraviolet or ozone water purifiers. These systems use a powerful ultraviolet light to sanitize water and can handle up to 20,000 gallons per hour.

INDUSTRIAL POLLUTANTS

Anyone with a well should also have it tested periodically for industrial pollutants. If problems show up, look into water-filtering devices, particularly those with activated carbon.

CHLORINE

Chlorine is used in water plants as a disinfectant. It does a good job of this, but according to the EPA, in the process it can not only ruin the taste of your water, it may cause the formation of cancer-causing agents, such as chloroform. Activated carbon filters and water distillation help with this problem.

Filtration

Domestic filtering systems can range from entire household systems, individual sink systems, to small tabletop units. A filtering system that contains activated carbon can remove many contaminants, including heavy metals, chlorine, chloroform, bad taste, odor, pesticides, and industrial chemicals. They will not, however, remove fluorides, nitrates, salts, or asbestos. The best systems use a *solid block* of carbon; the block will not let any unfiltered water pass through it. The Demonstration Kitchen contains an under-the-sink unit installed at one sink.

Unfortunately, these filters may also remove some of the minerals in water that contribute to good health. The Amway filter we installed claims not to remove "beneficial minerals . . . such as calcium and magnesium." Ask about this when investigating other brands. Where minerals loss is unavoidable, find alternate sources for them. For example: iron (cook in iron pots); calcium (nuts, dairy, soy, fish with bone in, sesame seeds, dark leafy greens); magnesium (bananas, whole grains, dried beans, nuts).

Another system that reportedly works well in filtering water is called *reverse osmosis*. The best-known maker of this type of equipment is Culligan. These units remove asbestos, organic chemicals, chloride, fluoride, nitrates, silica, silicates, sodium, sulfates, copper, bacteria, viruses, pyrogens, turbidity, most detergents, pesticides, tannins, chlorinated hydrocarbons, and other chemicals; unfortunately, they also remove calcium and magnesium. Chloroform, however, will not be removed, so this type may not be suitable for use on municipal water treated with chlorine. The grids on the following page show some of the more common filters and their uses.

Water quality problems can vary virtually from home to home or tap to tap. These grids are a starting point, and offer recommendations of where you may begin to look for answers. Consult local professionals for customized solutions to your individual water quality problems.

The Purchase of Water: The Water Cooler

The office water cooler is becoming more common in household these days. This is a good alternative for people who rent an apartment or house and do not want to install a filter or lug water in from the store. Coolers are becoming increasingly popular, and some people are having them built into the kitchen.

When buying water always inquire as to its source and purity. You certainly don't want to buy someone else's contaminated water. There are very few laws covering bottled water quality.

WATER CONSERVATION

No one can afford to take water for granted anymore. Our cavalier use of this resource has caused water tables to drop, aquifers to dry up, and water to be in short supply in various parts of the country, particularly the West. Many experts feel that water scarcity will be the major limiting factor in our future.

Saving water not only reflects an active concern for the environment; it also saves you money. Less pump usage means lower electric bills, as does reduced water heating. Less water going to the septic system helps maintain its efficiency and decreases the demand for central sewer systems. It also makes it possible to install smaller septic systems and thus inhabit land that would not support a larger one.

This section explores some water-saving devices.

HOW TO SAVE WATER

1. Stop leaks. A dripping faucet at the rate of one drop per second uses 7 gallons per day, a steady drip, 20 gallons per day or 5,000 gallons a month. In 1988 the Plumbing Heating Cooling Information Bureau estimated that if the leak is on a hot water line, it could cost $40 in addition to the cost of the water itself.
2. Do not run water continuously for dishwashing and rinsing. Wash dishes in a filled sink ("ponding").
3. Use brush or cloth rather than the force of water to remove food from plates.
4. Use plastic ice trays that permit individual ice cubes to be removed.
5. Keep a bottle of water in the refrigerator for drinking rather than running tap water.
6. Vegetables should be steamed, baked, stir-fried, but never submerged in water. Use any cooking water for soups, sauces, and so on.
7. Always run the dishwasher when full, and on the correct cycle.

Aerators

Aerators do not increase or restrict the flow of water, but by adding air bubbles to the water, they make the flow seem greater than it actually is. This effectively reduces water usage by 50 to 75 percent. Most good faucets come with aerators and both faucets in the Demonstration Kitchen have them.

Faucets

Some faucets are designed better than others for reducing water use. Single-lever faucets, for example, make it easy to flip the water on and off at a predetermined mixture—very helpful when washing dishes. Some faucets are also being made with flow restrictors that can be adjusted to reduce water flow up to 50 percent. The Demonstration Kitchen contains a single-

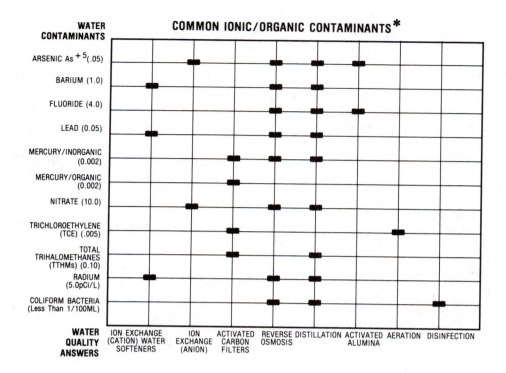

COMMON IONIC/ORGANIC CONTAMINANTS*

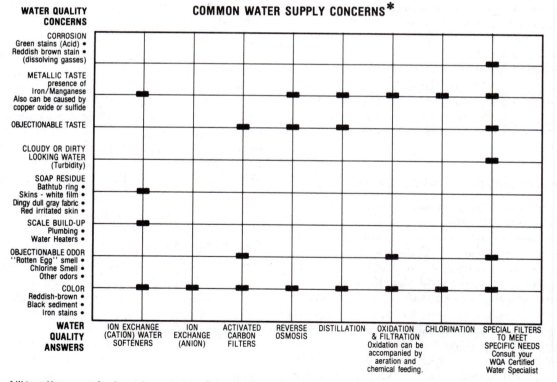

COMMON WATER SUPPLY CONCERNS*

* Water problems can vary from home to home or tap to tap. These grids offer a starting point, recommendations of where you can begin to look for answers. Consult local professionals for customized solutions to your individual water quality problems.

lever faucet with built-in aerator at the utility (dishwashing) sink.

Add-on Flow Restrictors

These inexpensive devices reduce the rate of water flow through the faucet by 50 to 75 percent. They are common in shower heads and can be added to any faucet.

Gray Water Usage

The irrigation of landscape with "gray water" (waste water) is a legal and ecological way to save this valuable resource. Generally, shower/tub, bathroom sink, and laundry (diaper free) water is best. However, in a two-sink kitchen where one sink is used exclusively for vegetable preparation, or a double sink is properly plumbed and used, gray water usage is possible from them as well. (See "Selected Resources.")

HEATING WATER

Hot water is one of the more expensive commodities in modern life, and its cost has been rising steadily. Since kitchen activities use about half of the hot water in the home, a short discussion of the many water-heating options is in order.

Thermostatically Controlled Mixing Valves

These regulate mix to automatically give you a constant temperature. They are more expensive than conventional faucets but can save 50 percent on hot water usage.

The Conventional Water Heater

Most private homes have freestanding gas or electric water heaters, consisting of a heating element or elements, an integral storage tank, and some insulation. Whether gas or electric is the cheapest option varies with location because of diverse fuel rates, but electric generally is more expensive than gas. If you are buying, compare carefully and consider both the unique health problems created by gas (see "Gas versus Electric" in Chapter 11) and the fact that in many instances heating with electricity is very costly. Gas heaters are vented, which if properly maintained should mean their are no gas emissions within living spaces, but sensitive or hypersensitive people may nonetheless not feel comfortable with them.

Here, unlike choosing stoves, there is no "performance factor"—gas and electric units both make hot water equally well. Thus, efficiency is the main consideration.

Maximum Efficiency from Your Hot Water Heater

Wrapping the water heater tank in an inexpensive insulation blanket—a ten-minute job—will save about 10 percent of your energy by reducing losses that occur while the hot water sits in the tank. (They pay for themselves in about a year or two and then continue saving an equivalent amount, year after year.) Also, all new hot water heaters should be installed with a "thermal trap," an inexpensive device that prevents loss of heat through the lines. It will save another 10 percent.

Check to see that the thermostat is not set too high. Usual settings are 110°F to 120°F, unless a non selfheating dishwasher is present, in which case you must follow the dishwasher's specifications.

Remember to drain a few gallons from the hot water heater periodically (see the owner's manual). This will remove sediment from the water that builds up at the bottom of the tank and insulates the hot water from the heating element. This is one time you don't want insulation!

Furnace Heaters

Some homes have a water heater that works in conjunction with the central heating furnace. Though this may be economical during the heating season, it may cause an enormous waste during the summer. Check your summer fuel consumption against that of neighbors who have other systems, and then consider if it pays to have a separate hot water system. In new installations, "high-efficiency condensing furnaces" (with heat exchanger) are very effective for heating water according to Howard Geller, associate director of ACE[3].

Heat Pump Water Heaters

Heat pump water heaters are a recent innovation and can save up to 66 percent over conventional electric hot water heaters. They are available as complete units or as a retrofit to an existing water heater. New technology make them even more efficient in the future.

Oil-Fired Water Heaters

These water heaters are fueled by oil and are about as efficient as gas-fired heaters.

The Spot Tankless Heater

Long a standard in thrifty European countries, so-called tankless electric and gas hot water heaters have become popular in the U.S. These small (from shoebox to backpack-size) units heat the water as it flows through; there is no tank to store hot water and no tank to lose heat. They are usually best in limited consumption applications but are also useful (1) where space is limited, (2) at the site of appliances that consume substantial amounts of hot water, (3) in places remote from the main source of hot water (to eliminate heat loss in the pipes), and (4) as a backup for some solar water heating systems. In the kitchen they are also useful for boosting the temperature of hot water to dishwashers. Be sure to get a unit with a thermostat.

Although tankless heaters make hot water only on demand, when they run, they burn a lot of gas or electricity, so they are not efficient for whole-house use.

Tankless heaters will restrict hot water flow; adding an aerator to the sink will help balance this out.

Solar Heaters

Solar heat can be an economical way to heat hot water in all but the cloudiest places (in the U.S. this means New England and the Pacific Northwest coast). A local solar dealer can show you the statistics for your area.

There are three main types to choose from—the batch heater, the thermosyphons, and the pump systems. Pay attention to price, aesthetics, suitability for house shape and site, and the reliability of the manufacturer and installer, as well as performance. Studies by *Solar Age* Magazine show that batch (or *ICS*, for "integrated collector and storage") heaters collect the most energy per square foot of collector area, with thermosyphon types second, and pump types (or *PCT* for "pump collector and tank") third. In cold climates the pump system is preferred, in order to eliminate the possibility of freezeup. Cost per amount of heat delivered is the most significant factor from a technical standpoint.

THE BATCH HEATER

The batch heater is essentially a black tank put in a well-insulated box that sits outside the house or is installed in the roof under a "window" facing south. The "window" should have two or three layers of glass or other transparent material. The black coating is generally a special "selective surface" that absorbs heat very well but does not emit much of it. Usually there are no moving parts, though some have a manually operated, insulated shutter. This unit is considered quite cost-effective. It is often used with a tankless heater as a backup.

THE THERMOSYPHON HEATER

The thermosyphon heater has an insulated tank mounted directly above an ordinary solar collector; it too is set up on the roof. Some units have added electric backup heaters in the tank and automatic drains that let warm water out of the collector bottom in freezing weather. These units perform best in warm climates and are the most popular worldwide. I would stay away from the thermosyphon systems that use freon (a chlorofluorocarbon, or CFC) instead of water in the collector. True, they work in cold climates and are efficient, but the CFC effect on the environment makes them ecologically undesirable. There are some systems that do not use CFCs.

THE PUMP SYSTEM

The pump system is still the most popular in the United States and is most appropriate in colder climates. Collectors are placed on the roof, where fluid (water or antifreeze solution) is pumped through them and then flows back to a heat exchange system. The heat is then transferred to an insulated tank that may have a backup heater. Many solar experts now prefer the drain-back variety of heat exchange module; it eliminates the need for antifreeze, requires less maintenance, and has shown itself to be highly reliable and efficient.

Chapter 14:
RECYCLING KITCHEN WASTES

It is a basic tenet of nature that new life springs from old. Ages before man began to cultivate the Earth, the soil was continuously being enriched by the rotting and decaying of once-living materials, particularly vegetation. As understanding of this process developed, farmers intentionally began to add such waste materials as straw and manure to tilled land and to develop methods for initiating and speeding up the breakdown of wastes into a more usable material that today is called *compost*. Since food waste is an important source of matter for compost, the kitchen is a natural place for the process to begin.

Moreover, both composting and recycling of newspapers, plastic, cans, bottles, and the like, save fuel, minimize solid waste accumulation, and demonstrate an *active* concern for the Earth.

THE GARBAGE AND RECYCLING CENTER

Modern eating habits have made the kitchen the center of nationwide efforts to recycle. The careful disposal of garbage and the saving of materials to be recycled is a responsibility that can be made easier with some forethought.

Garbage disposals, which grind up food and eject it through the sink line, should be avoided. These devices strain municipal sewage systems and may overload septic tanks. (Some companies claim however that their disposals grind food fine enough to be compatable with septic systems.) Trash compactors should be avoided, since they can inhibit the natural breakdown of garbage, further adding to the global solid waste problem. Further, according to Donald Silvers, writing in *Kitchen & Bath Business*, "when cans and bottles are not meticulously rinsed and the compactor is used infrequently, it quickly becomes unpleasantly odoriferous and attracts vermin even when the appliance includes a deodorizer." Silvers also notes that a 15-inch compactor will produce a weight of about 25 pounds of trash and an 18-inch compactor 40 to 50 pounds—more than many people are interested in carrying.

Since all food waste in the Demonstration Kitchen is composted (see the section "Composting," which follows), the rest of the garbage is odor free, clean, and light. Thus, it is no problem to accumulate large amounts, and a big garbage can minimizes disposal times. (Nobody likes to take out the garbage!) I recommend a 20- or 30-gallon can, but the size depends on available room. Placing it on a small dolly or adding wheels to the can makes moving it easy. Hide it behind a door, as I did. Either leave it topless, or have it cut and hinged by any metalworker for access.

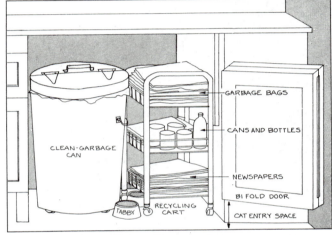

GARBAGE/RECYCLING AREA

A large garbage can (on wheels) minimizes and eases "taking out the garbage." The cart facilitates reuse and recycling. The space below the door permits pet access to food when door is closed.

Design: David Goldbeck/
Smart Kitchen Associates

In the Demonstration Kitchen the garbage can is hidden behind bifold doors hung approximately 5 inches below counter level. You can insert a hand even when the doors are closed, making small deposits convenient. When you must insert large amounts of garbage, you can easily open the doors and pull the can out. If you have a cat, you may want to use this as a protected feeding area. Leave a 3- or 4-inch gap at the bottom of the doors so that Tabby can enter. This design is especially useful if you also have a dog (or infant) that you want to keep from getting to the cat's food.

Next to the garbage can I placed a small rolling wire cart (commonly available in household supply stores) to hold extra garbage bags, newspapers, and returnable bottles. This is a small system, in a relatively small kitchen. If you have more space and many returnables, you should create a larger system, perhaps one that holds several buckets or bags, so you can presort plastics, glass, paper, and such, and take them directly to

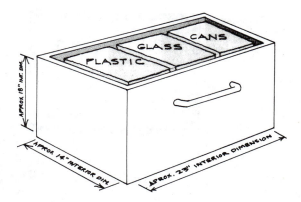

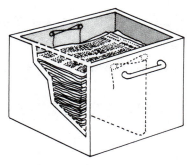

RECYCLING IN A DRAWER
Designed to hold standard paper bags.
Design: David Goldbeck/
Smart Kitchen Associates

NEWSPAPER RECYCLING IN A DRAWER
Note: Twine holder makes bundling easier.
Design: David Goldbeck/
Smart Kitchen Associates

RETRO-CYCLING
Storage space can sometimes be created in existing cabinets by combining two or more drawers. Drawers are removed and drawer fronts are attached to each other with plywood backing.

Design: David Goldbeck/
Smart Kitchen Associates

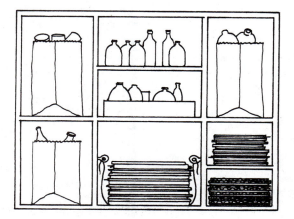

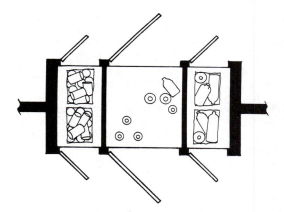

DUAL ACCESS RECYCLING CABINETS

These cabinets can be accessed from two sides. This feature simplifies both the storage of recyclables from the interior kitchen side as well as their removal from an adjacent area such as garage, mud-room, porch or foyer.

This design may be particularly appropriate for multi-unit residences (building codes and security needs having been met), providing both storage space and a way for removal by maintenance personnel.

Design: David Goldbeck/
Smart Kitchen Associates

the store or recycling center. This is going to be more and more necessary as municipalities enact mandatory garbage separation ordinances.

Kitchen designers are being called on more frequently in this regard, according to Gurney Williams III's article in *Practical Homeowner*. According to the article (which also featured the recycling features in the Demonstration Kitchen), design can be an important ally of the recycler. Kitchen drawers seem to be the most popular locale. One simple plan used a

RECYCLING SYSTEM PLANS

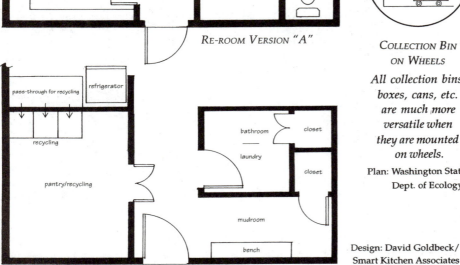

RE-ROOM VERSION "A"

RE-ROOM "B"

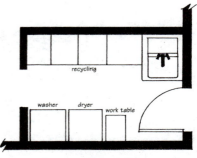

LAUNDRY/KITCHEN PLAN
Plan: Washington State Dept. of Ecology

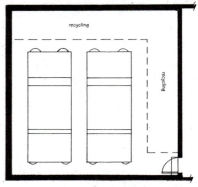

GARAGE/CARPORT PLAN
Plan: Washington State Dept. of Ecology

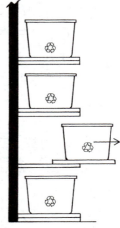

CLOSET/BLUE BOX CENTER
Design: David Goldbeck/
Smart Kitchen Associates

COLLECTION BIN
ON WHEELS

*All collection bins,
boxes, cans, etc.
are much more
versatile when
they are mounted
on wheels.*

Plan: Washington State
Dept. of Ecology

Design: David Goldbeck/
Smart Kitchen Associates

Versions "A" and "B" show a "re-room" in relation to the kitchen. In individual homes this space serves not only as a mudroom and pantry, but provides organized areas for recycling. There is no reason why multi-unit dwellings cannot include re-rooms as well, since there is probably an even greater need, given the limitations of apartment space. The re-room can serve as a location for (a) holding recyclables, (b) a waste exchange—an emerging activity which provides a mechanism for unwanted furniture, toys, clothing, and the like to be reused by another person, (c) a workshop where things can be revitalized (repaired, refinished, etc.), and (d) even a compost system for regenerating wastes. In apartment buildings, the re-room should also be used to recreate - an activity, one could easily argue, that has its own positive effect on the environment.

PRINCIPLES OF RECYCLING SYSTEM DESIGN

1. Design backwards from the local collection system. It is extremely important that the recyclable items not have to be resorted. The key to a good design is to minimize effort on the part of the recycler as this will reduce resistance to recycling. No matter whether the recyclables are to be carried to curbside or recycling center in paper bags, boxes, or cans, the design system must be based on those receptacles.

2. Location factors include site where waste is created, but more important is the distance from the exit used to carry out recyclables as they may be cumbersome and heavy. (See Collection Bins on Wheels.)

3. The recycling area should be made unsuitable to other uses. If the children start putting toys in the containers, or residents their laundry, the system will loose its ability to facilitate recycling. Likewise, avoid holding systems which may get covered up, such as those within benches (except for secondary storage), as this may inhibit their use.

4. Provide a secondary storage area, if possible. This is particularly important where recycling is voluntary and materials may accumulate before being brought to the recycling center.

5. Recycling area should be located in a an obvious location and easily used by visitors and future residents.

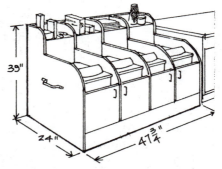

RECYCLING CENTER USING RUBBERMAID™ STACK
N'CYCLE BINS

RECYCLING AND COMPOSTING EQUIPMENT

These devices facilitate recycling and composting. Many more exist. For information about those shown here as well as others see Selected Resources, "Chapter 14, Recycling Kitchen Wastes." Note that the companies listed in the resource section may have other equipment not shown here and that the availability of equipment changes constantly.

Waste Bin AE
(Franke)

Big Box Waste Bin
(Hafale)

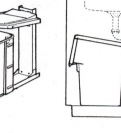
Built-in Waste Bin
(Melpa)

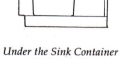
Under the Sink Container
(Rubbermaid™)

Sink with Box Set
(Blanco)

Kitch'n Composter
(Carbco)

The Green Cone
(Alsto)

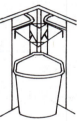
The Earth Machine
(Nova Sylva)

Double Bin
(Amerock)

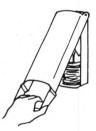
Spin-a Bin
(Feeny)

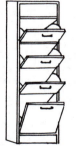
Mills Pride

Rev-a-Shelf

Dial Recycling Chute
(Minneapolis Abrasives)

Murf Recycling Center
(Nova Sylva)

Can Crusher
(Lehman)

*Stackable Recycling
Bins*
(Fidelity)

*Stackable
Containers*
(Rubbermaid™)

Newspaper Rack
(Paragon)

Newspaper Recycler
(Rubbermaid™)

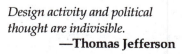

*Design activity and political
thought are indivisible.*
—**Thomas Jefferson**

single 36-inch-high drawer designed around four side-by-side plastic containers. Each container holds a standard brown paper bag for glass, paper, metal, and nonrecyclable trash. Others used more than one drawer—which, if you have the space will minimize overflow. On pickup days the bags merely have to be pulled out. Another experienced builder of recycling systems suggests that the space below the sink not be used for storage of soap, cleaning aids, and the like. This will then free it up as a convenient recycling location.

The most ambitious system I've come across used chutes that carry materials to cans in the basement. In the future such systems should be standard in new residences venting to outside containers that could be picked up regularly just as garbage is picked up.

COMPOSTING

Composting is the final stage of the Demonstration Kitchen's food cycle: The use of food waste is integrated with the growing of food, its preparation, and back again to its consumption. We have been recycling food waste for a number of years, and we can attest to the ease of the process and, more important, to the satisfaction of knowing that nothing is wasted. For those of you to whom doing *anything* with waste except throwing it out may be repugnant, consider that garbage is a "transformation that occurs entirely within the mind." What moments ago was food on your plate is now garbage in the can.

Though an agronomist might define composting as "the deliberate use and management of the biological process of decomposition to make materials available to plants as nutrients," to us it is much more. It means a respect for the processes that keep all of us alive and our "Spaceship Earth" functioning. At this writing, 16 percent of our national garbage is food, 19 percent is yard waste, and 18 percent paper—much of which could be composted and used to replace expensive fuel-based fertilizers (which poison our groundwater), as well as to replenish the topsoil currently being lost. Cynics may doubt the effectiveness of individual responses to such an enormous problem. I believe, on the other hand, that "everything counts."

RECYCLABLE MATERIALS

Materials	What Can Be Recycled	What Can't Be Recycled	Recycling Preparation
Glass	Glass containers: clear, amber, green	Milk-white glass Plate glass Light bulbs Crystal	Rinse—labels can stay on. Remove metal rings with awl, screwdriver or needle-nose pliers. Separate by color. Store—do not break.
Paper	Newsprint Corrugated boxes Egg cartons Junk mail Telephone books Computer cards and printout paper	Waxed or plastic-coated cellophane	Newspapers—keep clean and dry, stack less than 1 ft. high, tie with twine or pack in brown grocery bag or box. Cardboard—break down flat, stack and tie in small bundles. Office—stack in separate box.
Aluminum (non-ferrous metal)	All aluminum foil food wrap, TV trays, pie tins Ice cube trays Aluminum siding, storm doors, windows and gutters, lawn furniture		Trays, tins, foil— rinse, flatten and store. Other—remove foreign materials; cut into 3-ft. lengths; tie or store separately in bags or bundles.
Ferrous Metal	Most ferrous metals Separate by type: cast iron, steel sheet metal, tin	Non-ferrous and ferrous metal cannot be mixed	Tin cans—test with magnet, rinse, remove labels and ends, flatten (ends, too), store in box or bag. Bi-metal can—prepare as for tin; store separately. Other ferrous—check with local scrap dealer about preparation and selling.
Plastics	All plastic containers		Rinse, remove metal caps, flatten, store.
Organic Wastes	Non-animal food scraps, yard and lawn waste	Meat and fish scraps (breed and attract pests)	See composting instructions.

Adapted from *Householder's Recycling Guide*, NY State Department of Energy Conservation.

Composting is usually done in private homes for outdoor gardening or sometimes even in apartments on a smaller scale for houseplants and windowbox crops. The activity is simple: imitating and enhancing the natural process. The equipment is minimal: waste materials and some space.

An Out-of-Sight Compost System

I suspect that the most difficult part of the process for many people is the look and, of course, the smell of accumulated food waste in the kitchen. Attracting insects is another consideration. I was determined, therefore, to design and build a system that would minimize these problems and make the saving of this valuable resource more convenient.

What I ultimately decided upon was a design in which the material to be saved could be placed in a receptacle that was "in" the kitchen but outside of the house. I selected a place for a plastic garbage can to hold the waste under a corner of a counter that abuts an outside wall. A corner is an excellent location, since the space usually goes to waste anyway.

A can about the size of a diaper pail is perfect for this space: It fits under a counter, it is large enough to accommodate a lot of refuse before it has to be emptied, yet it is not so big as to become unmanageable when full. (The size of the container can also be varied depending on season, habits—that is, frequency of trips to the compost pile—and the like.)

I boxed in the designated compost cabinet from the rest of the cabinet and insulated it. I had an access door from the outside fabricated and installed. This door must be well made and tightly fitted—weatherstripped and secured with a sliding bolt. Do not put a vent in it or you will attract dogs, raccoons, and such. Originally I put some mothballs in with the can to discourage wandering animals, but I found there was no problem if the door is well constructed. Make sure the outside door opening is cut so the can has complete clearance. (In the Demonstration Kitchen compost area there is an unavoidable 3-inch lip at the top of the door opening, which makes removal and return of the can somewhat difficult.)

It would be best to insulate the compost cabinet's inner walls with rigid insulation as if they were outside walls or better (R-12). (You needn't insulate under the counter, but if you do, be prepared to line the edges of the wide access hole you will create with washable material such as plastic laminate.)

An entry for compostable wastes was cut into the countertop. In the Demonstration Kitchen the entry is a 6½-inch square with rounded corners. A round hole would be even better, eliminating hard to clean corners. For hygiene, the cabinet interior should be lined with plastic laminate, Kortron™, or metal. (Don't forget the underside of the counter; this is easier to do before the counter is installed.) All seams should be well sealed. If the countertop is a plastic laminate, make sure to cover the edges of the access hole with it. In the Demonstration Kitchen, the Corian™ counter provided a good natural edge. (But make sure the exposed surfaces of any underlayment are protected.) A good epoxy or urethane paint could alternately create a washable surface, but it is not preferred.

The cover for the hole was the hardest part of the design. Ideally I wanted a cover that would flip open with a foot pedal like a garbage can so that hands could be free, but I could never come up with a suitably uncomplicated approach. I finally settled on the simplest of all systems: a piece of plastic that swivels on a pivot (threaded rod or bolt) screwed into the counter. You can fasten the cover in place with a finish nut, but without one it's easier to remove for cleaning.

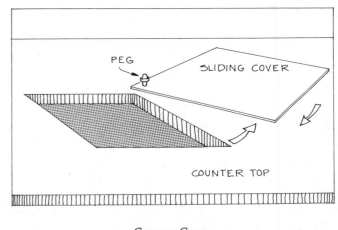

COMPOST COVER.
This simple cover swivels on a pivot for quick opening and closing and is easy to clean.

The holding can is held firmly against the underside of the counter for maximum cleanliness. I used an old piano stool mechanism which moves up and down on a threaded rod for this purpose. Since the piano stool can be adjusted by turning it, insertion and removal of the can are quite easy. The screw mechanism also makes it possible to really tighten the can up against the underside of the counter, which should keep the odor in the can, minimizing the attraction to insects and other fauna.

To prevent the inevitable fruit fly and other insects from getting into the compost container, I hang a flea collar over the edge of the can. It works very well and will not sully the quality of your compost. I also keep a small can of sawdust or wood ashes, when they are available, in a nearby kitchen cabinet. Putting in a bottom layer of one of these odor absorbers and occasionally adding some more to the accumulating compost helps neutralize the smell. A brush and bottle of sanitizing solution kept in the cabinet is handy for cleaning the can after it is dumped.

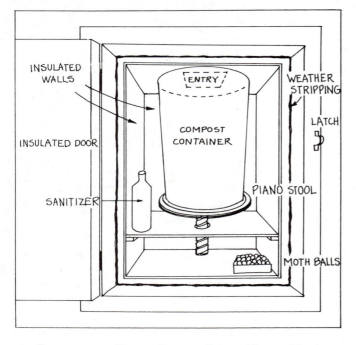

Demonstration Kitchen Compost Cabinet (Outside View)

Other Compost Cabinet Designs: Approach 1

Probably better and simpler than the piano stool method used in the Demonstration Kitchen is a system constructed by hinging the platform the can stands on at the back of the compost area. Two sliding barrel bolts mounted on the front of the platform enable it to be held in place and easily released when the can is to be removed. So that the can is held tightly, the distance from the platform to the underside of the counter should equal the height of the compost container. Placing the platform too low is better than placing it too high, though, since you can always add a piece of plywood or other shim to make up the difference.

Other Compost Cabinet Designs: Approach 2

You can add a ventilation duct to the compost holding area using the technology of the California cooling cabinet (see "The California Cooling Cabinet" in Chapter 9). The moving air provided by the cabinet should flush out bugs, moisture, and odors.

Commercial Compost Cans

Kitchen trash cans to hold food for composting are becoming more available. These covered cans are

mounted under the sink. When you open the door the can swings out and the lid opens automatically. As you close the door the opposite happens. See "Selected Resources."

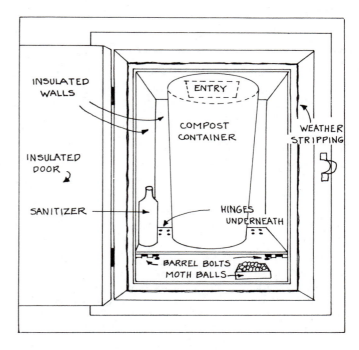

Alternate Compost Cabinet: Approach 1 (Outside View)

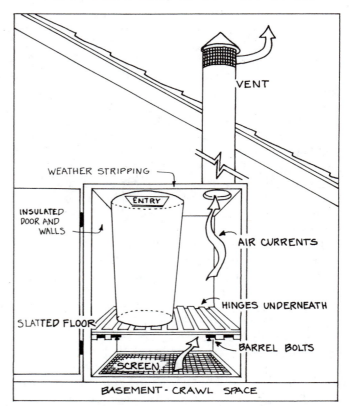

Alternate Compost Cabinet: Approach 2 (Outside View)

Outdoor and Indoor Composting

How to Compost Outdoors

The foregoing information is only the first step, or the holding phase. The technique for composting involves the accumulation and mixing of compostable materials in such a way as to promote their breakdown into usable humus, or fertilizer. Unless you are composting in an apartment, the rest of the process should take place outdoors. The materials can simply be layered in a pile, although it is better to have the heap enclosed by fencing, cinder blocks, and so on.

Begin by laying down some branches to allow air underneath. Then add food scraps from your kitchen (excluding meat and bones), to which any or all of the following materials can be added: grass clippings, leaves, pine needles, hay, straw, sawdust, ashes, and bits of noncolored paper. Manure is not necessary in composting if you use kitchen wastes. Pet or human manure should not be included in the compost pile.

Odor and Animals

If done properly, composting emits little or no odor and likewise will not attract animal infestation. There are two techniques for composting—one in which air is excluded (anaerobic) and one in which air is a vital element (aerobic). In the anaerobic system (which, by the way, is faster), the covering necessary to exclude oxygen also keeps out animals and controls odors. The outdoor waste pile is covered with a thick layer of soil or black plastic, held down around the edges, and left alone. Anaerobic composting is well suited to backyards with close neighbors.

In aerobic composting, the heat generated by the process repels insects and animals. Food wastes, as we have all experienced, give off a characteristic ammonia odor as they decompose, similar to dirty diapers. The addition of such carbon-containing materials as sawdust, paper, dry grass, and weeds, as well as the stirring in of air, neutralizes this smell. Turn the pile periodically. If the heap smells foul, it is telling you

to turn it more often. The ideal proportion is 50 percent dry matter, 35 percent food waste, and 5 percent soil or finished compost. Wood ashes, limestone, or crushed shells occasionally sprinkled on the heap will further neutralize odors. The compost should be moist but not soggy. Water the heap if it dries out, or simply add moist layers as the process continues.

Note: In freezing climates, save some dry leaves or grass clippings in cans or bags and use to cover food waste added to the compost heap in winter.

How to Compost Indoors

Making compost indoors is like making it outdoors except on a smaller scale. Carolyn Jabs, a writer with experience using this technique, suggests composting in large plastic jugs with the tops cut off, or in any short, fat, waterproof container.

Wastes should be chopped or pureed in the blender or food processor, or you can use only foods that are already quite small, such as coffee grounds, tea leaves, vegetable parings, and such. The wastes should be layered with soil (make sure it is not sterilized), and after the first few days stir it *daily*. Small amounts of grass clippings (from a suburban friend) or hay (from a stable) held in a plastic bag can also be mixed in. It is the mixing and stirring that will kill off any odor-causing bacteria. Keep moist but not soggy, and do not add garbage to a container that is already in the process of composting; start a new one.

The decomposition should take about two weeks, yielding fertilizer or humus for houseplants, window-box, greenhouse, or an unusual gift for a plant-loving friend.

See "Selected Resources" for a little-known guide to indoor composting. Bookstores and libraries will have many books on outdoor composting.

Environmental Choices

If you are mold sensitive, you should probably be cautious about storing food wastes. The best compost cabinet design in this case would probably be one based on the California cooling cabinet because of its vent.

Chapter 15:

FOOD PRODUCTION

One of the underlying themes of the Demonstration Kitchen is to develop the link between the preparation of food and its production. For this reason I set up a number of different systems within the project to demonstrate how this might occur. This is distinct from any outside gardening that one might do; thus, there are ideas for both the city and country dweller.

THE SKYLIGHT

The benefits of skylights in relation to light and heat are heralded elsewhere in this book (see "The Skylight" in Chapter 4.). Few people capitalize on this resource, however, to grow food.

The 3- by 4-foot skylight is located in the eaves of the roof and reaches the kitchen via a 4½ foot-long light shaft so that it was possible to install shelves (about 5 inches deep) along one shaft wall. To allow maximum light to pass through, and for safety, I chose plexiglass for the shelving. This has become an experimental spot to start seedlings in the spring, grow herbs year round, and dry fresh herbs, too. (Our particular situation allows access to the skylight shaft, and thus the plants, through a small door conveniently situated in the second-floor bathroom. This type of access should be considered when designing this feature.)

We further developed the skylight by hanging a wire basket on a small pulley beneath it. By loosening the pulley cord, we can easily lower a pot of frequently used herbs. (This pulley system also adapts well where the skylight is flush with the ceiling and shelves cannot be hung, or where other access is too difficult.) If a skylight is to serve as a growing area, venting is mandatory. You must particularly watch for heat buildup on unseasonably warm days. Because the skylight in the Demonstration Kitchen was installed on a high ceiling, it has an electric opener. If the sun does not beat down directly on the skylight, the area can also be designated for hanging fresh cut herbs to dry. Where there is full exposure to the sun, herbs can be placed in a paper bag to protect the flavor oils.

THE SPROUTING SHELF

Over the last few years many people have discovered that the kitchen, no matter what size, can be used to grow unlimited amounts of fresh vegetables called sprouts. Sprouts are produced from seeds or beans that have been moistened and allowed to germinate.

The process of sprouting involves the daily flushing of the seeds in special trays or bottles outfitted for this purpose. Although there is nothing wrong with the jar method, we have found over the years that tray sprouting produces a greater yield and enables you to sprout several different seeds at the same time. To make this easy task even more convenient, we installed a small sliding shelf directly below the vegetable preparation sink to hold the tray. This is an ideal location, since the sprouts require a dark place to germinate and grow, and their home under the sink facilitates daily rinsing.

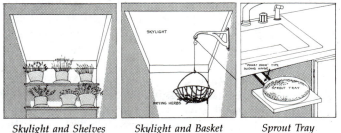

Skylight and Shelves   *Skylight and Basket*   *Sprout Tray*

THE COUNTERTOP HERB GARDEN

As mentioned earlier (see Chapter 4), full-spectrum lights, or "grow lights," are used for lighting under the cabinets in the Demonstration Kitchen. This is another area that can be used to grow herbs and the like on the countertop.

WINDOW GREENHOUSES

A miniature window greenhouse is another interesting way to make your kitchen more productive. It can hang on the outside of the house over a window in a reasonably sunny spot. A good greenhouse should allow for ventilation within it, but note that it will probably not give you the same amount of room ventilation as an ordinary window does. Skylight retailers are a good source of window greenhouses.

Part IV
PLANNING THE KITCHEN

One of the easiest ways for nonprofessionals to design is to lay out plans right in the space to be utilized. If this is not possible use another space with similar dimensions.

Once you have a sense of how the room works, map its dimensions on graph paper and make a stack of copies. (Reproducible graph paper is supplied at the end of this chapter.) Make note, particularly in existing situations, of the position and size of windows, doors, recesses, protrusions, and such service points as water, gas, or electrical outlets. Indicate, too, appliances, cabinets, and such that will be retained.

The next step is to experiment with several different arrangements. Initially, think of "production line" efficiency. First, storage as you enter with groceries (refrigerator, pantry, and adjacent counter space); next, moving the food to preparation areas, water for cooking, and preparation utensils (sink, drawers, cabinets, counters); then, the cooking (stove top, oven, pots, and so on) and serving centers (dish storage). This sequence must relate to kitchen entrance and exit. After you work this out, start to fit in variables—for example, where to put a second sink, how to reroute traffic, where to put counters of different heights, and the like.

A popular way to plan is to cut out small pieces of paper to scale to represent counters, refrigerator, stove, and so on. (Templates of these can be found at the end of this chapter.) Play with the elements in different positions. Fantasize working in the kitchen. "Let your fingers do the walking" through different tasks on the paper to see how the work flows.

Once you find a few layouts that seem feasible, go back to the room and block out the areas on the floor with masking tape. Or, move furniture, cardboard boxes, and the like into place to give you a sense of the space. An adjustable ironing board can be used to test counter heights. (This blocking out can also be done initially.) "Try to live with it as much as is practical," advises environmental designer Bruce Small. This is a helpful point of view for the overall layout as well as for small areas of the kitchen.

Make sure to review "The Standards" in this part before you do any serious designing. These conventions will help you maximize work flow, work triangles, and other aspects of kitchen design. But remember, they are not etched in Formica™. With the introduction of multi-oven, -sink, -workspace kitchens, they will need to be adapted to changing situations.

Study other people's kitchens for what works and what doesn't. Inspiration can be found in magazines and books. I particularly like Terence Conran's *The Kitchen Book*. Another useful publication is *Kitchen Planning Standards* from the University of Illinois.

Although it may seem at first that kitchen design is influenced only by layout and selection of appliances, there are two other factors you should consider right at the start. These are the overall space the kitchen should occupy and the relationship of the kitchen to the rest of the house. The first factor is usually decided mainly by what you can afford, but you should also take into account appliance and counter needs and the amount of storage and activity space your household requires. Deciding on the second factor—the location of the kitchen and how it interplays with the rest of the house—can be a lot trickier, since it influences not only traffic patterns and window and door placement but, more important, the social life of the occupants. Americans spend 50 percent of their waking time at home in their kitchens. Thus, overall style of the kitchen deserves serious attention: whether it will be open or closed to the rest of the house—the dining room, the living room, and perhaps even the den or porch.

THE OPEN/CLOSED KITCHEN

Many designs today have almost completely obliterated the line between kitchen and living space. In the Demonstration Kitchen I, too, wanted to open the kitchen to the living-dining area so that those who were doing the cooking were not separated from household activity and company.

I recognized, however, that in some cases it is preferable to shut the kitchen off from the rest of the house—for example, when preparing odoriferous food, or when some privacy is needed during food preparation while entertaining. The ability to close up the kitchen during cooking is a simple way to contain cooking fumes and the products of gas emission. Moreover, if you have a nearby smoke detector that tends to go off during intense cooking, you might appreciate being able to isolate the room. A closable kitchen is also advantageous for child, noise and fire control.

The wall between the living-dining space and the Demonstration Kitchen is rather small, most of it taken up by a swinging door and the end of a counter. If I removed both the door and the wall above the counter, I would be giving up all the features of a closed kitchen yet gaining very little exposure. So instead, I created a closable pass-through in the wall above the counter. When the door and pass-through are both open, it's almost as if the wall were gone. The pass-through conveniently opens onto the dining area. The stainless steel shelf that serves as its sill makes it very easy to pass food and dishes back and forth—a considerable step saver. The pass-through also creates a nice architectural detail. We now have the best of both worlds: a closed kitchen when we need it and an open space that integrates the kitchen and cook into the rest of the household.

If you plan an open (but not closable) kitchen, you should thoroughly research the noise level of the dishwasher, garbage disposal, exhaust system, refrigerator, and floor and countertop materials you will use. Also pay attention to the sound-absorbing qualities of the room itself. The kitchen is the noisiest room in the house. (See Chapter 5.)

AN OUTSIDE ENTRANCE

If you are designing a kitchen for a house (as opposed to an apartment), another item of import is whether an outside entrance can be incorporated into the plan. It is a great convenience for access to garden and carport—for example, for bringing in food. Also, today, architects have noted, friends like to enter through the kitchen rather than the formal front door.

Many homes are alternately designed with a small room between the kitchen and an exterior door that houses the laundry area, pantry, and other utility space. This is an extremely desirable entry to the kitchen. A large "slop sink" is very useful in this area, as are shelving, cabinets, and so forth, to hold cleaning materials out of children's reach and other odds and ends that would merely clutter up the kitchen. This is also a good place to feed pets. In inclement weather it doubles as a mud room.

THE STANDARDS

There is a large body of useful information available on *overall* kitchen design. Guidelines for the general layout of the kitchen with suitable "work stations" joined by "work triangles" are indeed helpful. I have few problems with these concepts, with two exceptions:

- "Standard counter height" by its nature does not take into account individual differences or the variability of kitchen tasks (see Chapter 1).

- The strict application of "work triangles" has become somewhat outmoded with the multiplication of kitchen appliances in many modern settings.

What follows is a summary of the traditional approaches that can be useful in planning any kitchen, in addition to some suggestions for change.

The Basic Shape

Plan your kitchen keeping in mind the principal activity that goes on there: meal preparation. Think of it as a workshop. If the sink, refrigerator, and cooking appliances are situated in sequence, and if you have adequate storage and work areas that are also conveniently located, the tasks can proceed efficiently.

If the design follows any one of the first three basic floor plans for kitchens ("U," "L," or "galley"), you are on the way to a good layout. The "one wall" is the least serviceable. But often, particularly when remodeling, you must make compromises (or innovative solutions). That's the fun. But remember, no matter how original the design, you must concentrate on how the work flows.

THE U-SHAPED KITCHEN

The U-shaped kitchen is a very efficient design, offering easy access between workstations and many options for storage and additional appliances. It effectively removes the kitchen from household traffic flow. But it may result in hard-to-reach storage areas in the two corners. The U is considered the ideal design in a large space, but in a small room, where the base of the U is under 5 feet, it can be too confining. It is also well suited to variations, such as an island or one arm of the U being turned into an angled peninsula. Note that the U can be interrupted by a door.

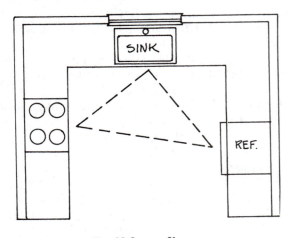

THE U-SHAPED KITCHEN

THE L-SHAPED KITCHEN

The L-shaped workspace is adaptable to almost any space and lends itself to an efficient work triangle. The L enables you to travel easily between the work areas that are situated close to the right angle, but there may be too great a distance between the L's extreme ends. This can be overcome by the addition of a peninsula or island. Difficult corner cabinet access is another drawback to the L. This design does tend to eliminate traffic through the work area. It is often used when an adjacent dining area is desired.

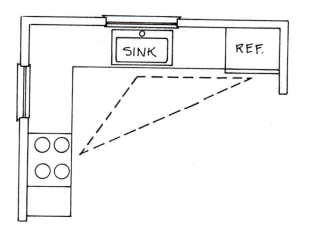

THE L-SHAPED KITCHEN

THE GALLEY KITCHEN

The galley—also called the corridor or two-wall design— allows convenient storage and countertop space and minimizes steps. It is most appropriate to long, narrow rooms; however, there must be at least 48 inches between opposing counters. If the corridor is wide enough (54 to 64 inches), the kitchen can be used simultaneously by two friendly cooks. One drawback of this mode is that unless you provide an alternate door, it may become a thoroughfare for room-to-room traffic. An eating area is often placed at one end.

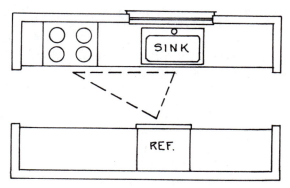

THE GALLEY KITCHEN

THE ONE-WALL KITCHEN

The one-wall kitchen, unless quite compact, is not very efficient, since it requires many steps to get from one area of activity to another. It is most common in small houses and apartments. If space leaves no choice, or this is an existing situation, adding a peninsula, an island, a large cart or work table can greatly improve the flow. This layout is certainly not suitable for large kitchens.

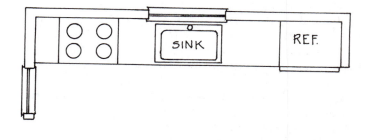

THE ONE-WALL KITCHEN

Work Triangles

Some kitchens are more functional than others. The reason usually is because they incorporate efficient *work triangles*. Work triangles are a well-developed aspect of kitchen *ergonomics* (the study of the relationship of people to machines in order to facilitate maximum work efficiency).

Traditionally, kitchens have been divided into three main centers of work: the sink, the range and the refrigerator. The principle of work triangles is that these three centers are located at approximately equidistant points of a triangle, connected by counters. The classic example is work surface—sink—work surface—range—work surface. According to the experts, no side of the triangle should be less than 4 feet or more than 7 feet, and the three sides should preferably total less than 22 feet. Respect for this concept will save time and steps. *Functional Kitchens* (Cornell University, Rev. Ed.), the publication that set many of these standards, states that a larger triangle, 23 to 26 feet, "may indicate the kitchen is too large for ordinary needs and would require excessive walking." The distances should be measured from the center front of each work area. Usually the triangles are smallest in galley and U-shaped kitchens. Traffic flow should not pass through the center of the triangle.

This triangle should be modified when necessary— to preserve a view, for example, or accommodate existing doorways. As new appliances are introduced— convection oven, grill, or a computer--changes may need to be made.

When it comes to work triangles mapping out the kitchen in place really pays off. By being able to "play" as if you were actually using the space you can get a sense how efficient, tiring, or cramped the plan really is. Does the flow from refrigerator and pantry proceed smoothly to preparation areas, sink and cooker? Is the garbage/recycling area near the point where waste will be generated? Does cooking move easily into the dining area? The difference between the amateur and the professional is that the latter can figure this on paper (or in his or her head).

Work Centers

The concept of *work centers* provides another useful technique for organizing kitchens. Work centers merely formalize the "Rule of First Use": The best organization is achieved when items are situated near the place of first use. Thus, soap is near the sink, pots near the cooker, and so on.

I have already mentioned the three traditionally recognized work centers: the range, the sink, and the refrigerator. But a counter used for food preparation is also a work center. Pantry storage and a desk area are often considered work centers as well. Moreover, there can be centers dedicated to growing food, processing food, composting of food wastes, and to recycling. Many designers add a dining center to this list since the kitchen should be designed in relation to the place where the food will eventually be served.

When you can move easily from one work center to another, cooking is more pleasurable. Simultaneous access to more than one work area can save steps (no running back and forth between preparation site and refrigerator to retrieve or replace food, for example) and lets you monitor one task (sautéing onions, for instance) while performing another (chopping vegetables).

The Sink Work Center(s)

The sink (or sinks) and surrounding cabinets comprise the most heavily used work center and should be centrally located. The sink and the stove should be placed so you can move between them with ease; if a lot of meal preparation is to be done using fresh food, however, the relationship between the sink and the refrigerator may be equally critical. Note that sinks are often placed in front of a window, which is nice but not based on any immutable design principle.

Ideally there should be 24 to 36 inches of counter on both sides of the sink. Where this is not possible, the larger counter space should be where food is prepared and dirty dishes stacked, with at least 18 inches for draining dishes on the other side. The sequence in which you work most comfortably and the location of the other work centers will determine whether the area to the left or right of the sink deserves the longer counter span. If you wish to have two people working at adjacent counters, you must allow 9 to 15 inches between the sink and the corner in an L- or U-shaped floor plan. Alternately, a special corner sink, or a conventional sink set diagonally in the corner, can work very well in the L or U layout.

It is very important that the sink be installed toward the front of the counter, since this shortens the reach, making it much more comfortable to work. The sink cabinet should be 6 inches wider than the sink; in no case should the sink's front rim, or barrier, be more than 3 inches wide. (See also Chapter 3.)

The dishwasher must be placed next to the sink. Try to choose the side most convenient to the dish cabinet, also taking into consideration any other appliances that might interfere. If a dishwasher is not part of your present plan, block out a 24-inch space or cabinet adjacent to the sink that could accommodate the unit later and put in shelves that can be easily removed. (Even if you never plan to install a dishwasher, the next occupant may be grateful.) Make sure that on opening, the dishwasher door will not interfere with other doors—either adjacent, in corners or opposite. In corner locations sometimes dishwasher door operation is impaired by adjacent handles. Don't situate the dishwasher face-to-face with the oven or refrigerator where both doors opened simultaneously can block traffic. Another common error is to position the dishwasher adjacent to a corner-angled sink or at right angles to the sink. A 20-inch loading area must be allowed next to the open door.

A portable dishwasher, though it ties up the sink during use, offers additional (and movable) workspace.

The Refrigerator Work Center

Situate the refrigerator in relationship to the kitchen entry to facilitate unloading of groceries. Also take into account relation to cooking and dining. Do not place the refrigerator where it will divide a counter into short sections. Allow at least 15 to 18 inches counter space next to the latch side of the door so that food can be moved in and out efficiently. For side-by-side refrigerators, the refrigerator door should open to allow access to the counter; corresponding space in relation to the freezer door is desirable, though less important. As mentioned, you will also want to position the refrigerator and adjacent counter so that it interrelates with the sink, where much food preparation takes place. In any case, the refrigerator should be convenient to a food preparation site. (See also Chapter 10.)

THE RANGE/OVEN WORK CENTER

Ranges

If possible, the range (or cooker as I often refer to it) should be close to the eating area for convenient service. It should relate to a preparation site as well, but must be out of the traffic flow. The cooktop should never be below a window, where a breeze might extinguish the flame or cause curtains to catch fire. (You may know not to hang curtains, but the next occupant might not.) There should be ample room to the left and right for pot handles to extend and 21 inches or more of heat-resistant counter on at least one side for setting pots down. More space is helpful if you follow what Nikki and I call the "Master Rule of Cooking." This rule states that if you measure out and assemble ingredients and utensils before cooking, the cooking event will be eased immeasurably.

Provide for storage of pots and pans nearby, as well as adequate ventilation for both the oven and range.

Ovens

An oven situated below or directly above the cooktop is never very comfortable to use. This is why a separate wall oven is so attractive. There is no big advantage to placing the oven near the eating area, but like the refrigerator, it should not divide a counter in two impractical expanses.

A well placed wall oven is safer and more inviting to use, especially if it's installed so that its floor is 1 to 7 inches below your bent-elbow height—or so that the most used racks are between 28 and 40 inches from the floor. According to *Functional Kitchens*, "the 1-inch distance favors less bending to inspect and turn broiling food in an electric oven; the 7-inch distance favors lifting."

There should be 21 to 24 inches of heat-resistant counter space next to the oven to put things down on. If you wish to utilize the flat surface above a wall oven for this purpose (as was done in the Demonstration Kitchen, see illustration, Chapter 12), rather than building a cabinet over it, choose a position that allows approximately eye-level (or lower) placement of items on its top. Of course, a double oven will have to be installed so that all shelves are within reach (which means a few will probably provide optimum comfort).

Avoid placing the oven near the refrigerator or having the refrigerator open onto the oven or range. If you really have no other choice, insulate *well* between them. (See Chapter 10.)

THE FOOD PREPARATION CENTER(S)

At least one site, and preferably two or three sites, should be available for preparing food. They should contain frequently used utensils, small appliances (the food processor, blender, and so on), as well as nonperishable staples. The food preparation work center is best located between the refrigerator and sink or between the sink and stove. The former (sink-refrigerator) saves steps if you work with a lot of fresh food. (Those who rely on reheating prepared foods may find a counter between the refrigerator and stove is more functional.) The minimum recommended unbroken span is 36 to 42 inches.

THE FOOD PRESERVATION CENTER (PANTRY)

It goes without saying that a kitchen needs space to store foods. The pantry, like the refrigerator, should be situated in a spot convenient to the kitchen entrance. It is nice to have as much storage as possible near the food preparation area, but that is not always feasible. I encourage the use of "cool spot pantries" for storage as a way of cutting refrigeration costs. (See Chapter 10.)

THE FOOD-GROWING CENTERS

The kitchen can be a food production location as well as a cooking arena. This activity can be as modest as sprouting or as elaborate as a greenhouse, and there are many levels in-between. (See "The Skylight," and "The Sprouting Shelf," and "Growing Under Full-Spectrum Lights," Chapter 16.)

THE FOOD WASTE CENTER

The smart kitchen integrates the recycling of food wastes. It's only right that we give back to the earth something of what we've taken. (See Chapter 15.)

THE GARBAGE AND RECYCLING CENTER

We must manage the growing level of waste that we produce. As a substantial amount of this waste is generated in the kitchen; building a convenient recyling center here makes the task that much easier. (See Chapter 15.)

THE DESK (AND COMPUTER) CENTER

A desk or counter space reserved for telephone, cookbooks, computer, and so on, is helpful in the kitchen. This area often becomes the "message center" for families; conveniently located notepads are essential and a message board adds a nice touch.

STANDARD DIMENSIONS

In laying out the kitchen, don't forget to allow space for its occupants. An average person requires about 30 inches of counter space to work in. If someone wishes to pass by, 16 to 18 inches will allow them to edge through; 26 to 30 inches provides more comfortable walking space.

Counter Heights

The standard counter height is 36 inches, although for the ideal work surface 3 inches below bent-elbow height is preferable for most tasks, and 6 to 7 inches below bent-elbow height is more suited to tasks for which you exert force (such as kneading bread and chopping). For maximum comfort, the sink rim could be a little higher than other counters to prevent uncomfortable bending when reaching into the bottom of the bowl. On the other hand, it should not be so high that the person washing dishes must work with raised shoulders.

Since "average" heights can cause great discomfort to many people, the Demonstration Kitchen contains an experimental adjustable counter. (For this and similar ideas, see Chapter 1.)

Cabinet Dimensions

	OVERHEAD CABINETS
Depth:	12'' to 18'' (usually 12'')
Height:	30'' to 33'' for basic storage, 12'' to 18'' over standard stove or refrigerator
Width:	9'' to 48'' (stock is available in 3'' increments)
Position:	15'' above counter (except when counter is narrower than normal), 24'' above range and sink
	BASE CABINETS
Depth:	12'' to 36''—average 24'' 30'' may mean less reliance on overhead storage
Height:	34½'' (plus countertop)
Door clearance and access space:	36''
	WALL OVEN CABINETS
Width:	24'' to 27''
Height:	84''

Reaching Dimensions

Studies at Cornell University have determined that the maximum overhead fingertip reach for women 5'3''–5'7'' tall is 80 inches. When the reach is over a 25-inch counter it is lowered to 69 inches. Maximum comfortable side to side reach is 48 inches and the low fingertip level is 24 to 31 inches from the floor.

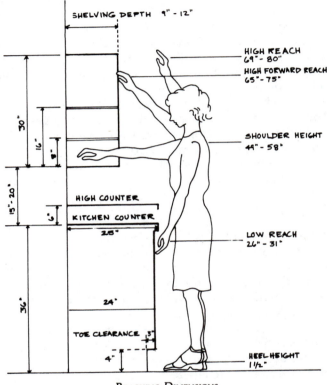

REACHING DIMENSIONS

Critical Dimensions

The following is a summary of minimum critical dimensions compiled from the Farmers Home Administration (FHA), the American Society of Heating, Refrigeration and Air Conditioning Engineers (ASHRAE) standards, and other sources. These will be helpful in the design process.

1. Total shelf area	50 ft² with not less than 20 ft² in wall or base
2. Total countertop area	11 ft.², 4' lineal at each work area of base, wall and counter, except 8' at sink
3. Total drawer area	11 ft.² minimum
4. Wall shelving	79 ¹⁄₂₄'' maximum height
5. Countertop height	38'' maximum, 30'' minimum 32'' mixing, 39'' sink (dish washing, etc.), 36'' general
6. Distance between countertop	24'' over range, sink and wall cabinets; 15'' elsewhere
7. Depth of shelving	4''–18'' wall, 12''–24'' base, 15''–26'' countertop
8. Backsplash	4'' minimum
9. Range	21'' counterspace on either side
10. Opposing counters	48'' apart
11. Cabinet door clearance	36''
12. Workspace for one	30''
13. Minimum width of passage	30'' for parallel high wall, 21'' for one low wall, 18'' for two low walls

Appliances

These common figures are provided to enable initial kitchen planning. Check manufacturers' specifications for exact measurements. Unless otherwise specified, all appliances are designed to fit a 24-inch-deep, 36-inch-high cabinet.

DISHWASHER

Width:	24″
Door clearance:	42″
Loading access space (adjacent):	20″

REFRIGERATOR

Width:	28″ to 36″
Height:	58″ to 68″
Depth:	30″ to 32″
Door clearance and access space:	36″

RANGE

Width:	30″ to 46″
Depth:	24″
Depth (with open door):	42″
Height:	36″ (plus back control panel, approx. 5″)
Door clearance and access space:	38″

COOKTOP

Width:	30″ to 46″

Wall Oven

Width:	22″ to 26″
Height:	25″ to 50″
Depth:	22″ to 25″
Door clearance and access space:	36″

SINK

Single Bowl

Width:	15″ to 43″
Depth:	5″ to 12″

Double Bowl

Width:	22″ to 43″
Depth:	6″ to 10″

FOR THE ELDERLY OR PHYSICALLY DISABLED

Many people have physical limitations that make bending, stooping, reaching, grasping or lifting difficult. Although the Demonstration Kitchen was not designed specifically for their special needs, this concern was kept in mind. Good design takes into account all residents and even considers future needs and residents.) The following is a summary of the features built into the project that make the kitchen a more comfortable environment for everyone:

- **Seating**. Places where people can sit and work in a chair or wheelchair are very helpful. The sink design used in the Demonstration Kitchen allows seating there and should be considered in every kitchen, since it costs little and can add substantially to everyone's comfort. (For those with impaired mobility the sink should be located in a corner between the stove and refrigerator, and should have two bowls ideally 6 inches and 3 inches deep. For seating safety the sink should be insulated underneath or made of a non-heat conductive material. Pipes, too, should be insulated. A single lever faucet is best with a long spray hose so water can be brought to the stove. Note that wheelchairs require a clearance of approximately 29 inches high and 27 inches wide. They also take up an area of about 5 square feet in turning and require doorways at least 32 inches wide.)
- The **adjustable counter** also makes the kitchen more accessible to seated workers.
- An **induction cooktop**. Diminishes the possibility of burns.
- **Wall oven**. Offers more placement versatility.
- **Open shelving**. Shelves within the shoulder-knee radius are most easily reached.
- **Light switches and other controls** convenient for those in wheelchairs. The sliding dimmer switches and fan control used over the Ideal Cooker cannot be reached by hand from a wheelchair, but since they slide up and down, they can be controlled with a stick or cane.
- A **jar opener** for hard-to-open jars. These devices mount under cabinets or on the wall and provide an "extra hand" when needed.
- **Easily accessed garbage**.
- **Refrigerator with bottom freezer**. (Side by side is also good.)
- **Bottom cabinet drawers and open storage spaces** instead of cupboards. (Shallow shelves are best.)

For more information on designing kitchens for the disabled see the following:

Terence Conran, *The Kitchen Book* (Crown, 1977), p. 118–119.

Suzanne Lunt, *A Handbook for the Disabled* (New York: Charles Scribner & Son, 1982).

Gwenn Conacher, *Kitchen Sense for Disabled People*, (Croom Helm Ltd./Routlege, Chapman and Hall, 1986).

31 RULES OF KITCHEN DESIGN FOR THE '90s

From the National Kitchen & Bath Association

1. A clear walkway at least 32" wide must be provided at all entrances to the kitchen.
2. No entry or appliance door may interfere with work center appliances and/or counter space.
3. Work aisles must be at least 42" wide, and passage ways mustbe at least 36" wide for a one-cook kitchen.
4. In small kitchens (150 sq. ft. or less), at least 144" of wall cabinet frontage (12" deep x 30" high) must be installed over counter tops. In larger kitchens (over 150 sq. ft.), 186" of wall cabinets are required. Diagonal or pie cut wall cabinets count as a total of 24". Difficult to reach cabinets above the hood, oven or refrigerator do not count unless specialized storage devices are installed within the case to improve accessibility.
5. At least 60" of wall cabinet frontage (12" deep by 30" high) must be included within 72" of the primary sink centerline.
6. In small kitchens, at least 156" of base cabinet frontage (cabinets must be at least 21" deep) and in larger kitchens 192" are required. Pie cut/lazy susan cabinets count as a total of 30". The first 24" of a blind corner box do not count
7. In small kitchens at least 120" of drawer frontage or roll out shelf frontage must be planned. Kitchens over 150 sq. ft. require at least 165" of drawer/shelf frontage. (Measure cabinet width to determine frontage.)
8. At least five storage items must be included in the kitchen to improve the accessibility and function of the plan. These items can include, but are not limited to: wall cabinets with adjustable shelves, interior vertical dividers, pull out drawers, swing-out pantries, or drawer/roll-out space greater than the minimum 135".
9. At least one functional corner storage unit must be included. (Rule does not apply to a kitchen without corner cabinet arrangements.)
10. Between 15" and 18" of clearance must exist between the countertop and the bottom of wall cabinets.
11. In small kitchens, at least 132" of usable countertop frontage (16" depth) is required. Larger kitchens must have 198" or more. Counter must be 16" deep to be counted; corner space does not count.
12. No two primary work centers (the primary sink, refrigerator, preparation center, cooktop/range center) can be separated by a full height, full depth tall tower, such as an oven cabinet, pantry cabinet or refrigerator.
13. There must be at least 24" of counter space to one side of the sink and 18" on the other side. (Measure only countertop frontage, do not count corner space.) The 18" and 24" counter space sections may be a continuous surface, or the total of two angled countertop sections. If a second sink is part of the plan, at least 3" of counter space must be on one side and 18" on the other side.
14. At least 3" of counter space must be allowed from the edge of the sink to the inside corner of the countertop if more than 21" of counter space is available on the return. Or, at least 18" of counter space from the edge of the sink to the inside corner of the countertop if the return counter space is blocked by a full height, full depth cabinet or any appliance which is deeper than the countertop.
15. At least two waste receptacles must be included in the plan, one for garbage and one for recyclables; or other recycling facilities should be planned.
16. The dishwasher must be positioned within 36" of one sink. Sufficient space (21" of standing room) must be allowed for the dishwasher and adjacent counters, other appliances and cabinets.
17. At least 36" of continuous countertop is needed for the preparation center and must be located close to a water source.
18. The design should allow for at least 15" of counter space on the latch side of a refrigerator (or either side of a side-by-side refrigerator), or at least 15" of landing space which is no more than 48" across from the refrigerator. (Measure the 48" walkway from the countertop adjacent to the refrigerator to the island countertop directly opposite.)
19. For an open ended kitchen configuration, at least 9" of counter space is required on one side of the cooktop/range top and 15" on the other. For an enclosed configuration, at least 3" of clearance space must be planned at an end wall protected by flame retardant surfacing material and 15" must be allowed on the other side of the appliance.
20. The cooking surface cannot be placed below an operable window unless the window is 3" or more behind the appliance and/or more than 24" above it.
21. There must be at least 15" of landing space next to or above the oven if the appliance door opens into a primary family traffic pattern. 15" of landing space, which is no more than 48" across from the oven, is acceptable if the appliance does not open into traffic area.
22. At least 15" of landing space must be planned above, below, or adjacent to the microwave oven.
23. The shelf on which the microwave is placed is to be between counter and eye level (36" to 54" off the floor).
24. All cooking surface appliances are required to have a ventilation system with a fan rated at 150 CFM minimum.
25. At least 24" of clearance is needed between the cooking surface and a protected surface above. Or, at least 30" of clearance is needed between the cooking surface and an unprotected surface above.
26. The work triangle should total less than 26'. The triangle is defined as the shortest walking distance between the refrigerator, primary cooking surface and primary food preparation sink. No single leg of the triangle should be shorter than 4' nor longer than 9'.
27. No major household traffic patterns should cross through the work triangle.
28. A minimum of 12" x 24" counter/table space should be planned for each seated diner.
29. At least 36" of walkway space from a counter/table to any wall or obstacle behind it is required if the area is to be used to pass behind a seated diner. Or, at least 24" of space from the counter/table to any wall or obstacle behind it is needed if the area will not be used as a walk space.
30. At least 10 percent of the total square footage of the total living space which includes the kitchen should be appropriated for windows/skylights.
31. Ground fault circuit interrupters must be specified on all receptacles that are within 6' of a water source. A fire extinguisher should be located near the cooktop. Smoke alarms should be included near the kitchen.

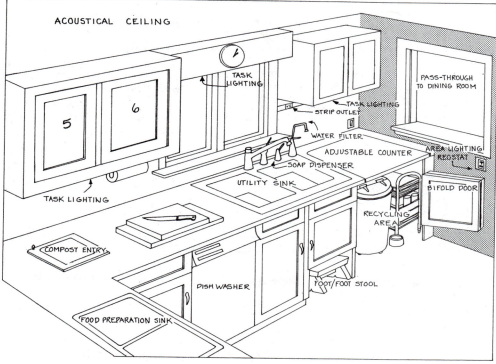

Demonstration Kitchen: Utility Sink Area

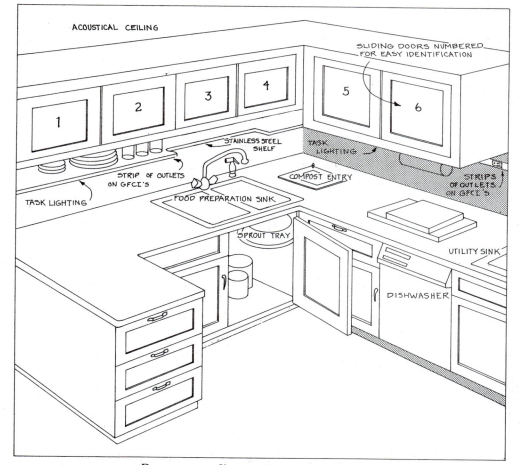

Demonstration Kitchen: Food Preparation Area

APPLIANCES AND CABINET TEMPLATE
SCALE ¼" = 1'-0"

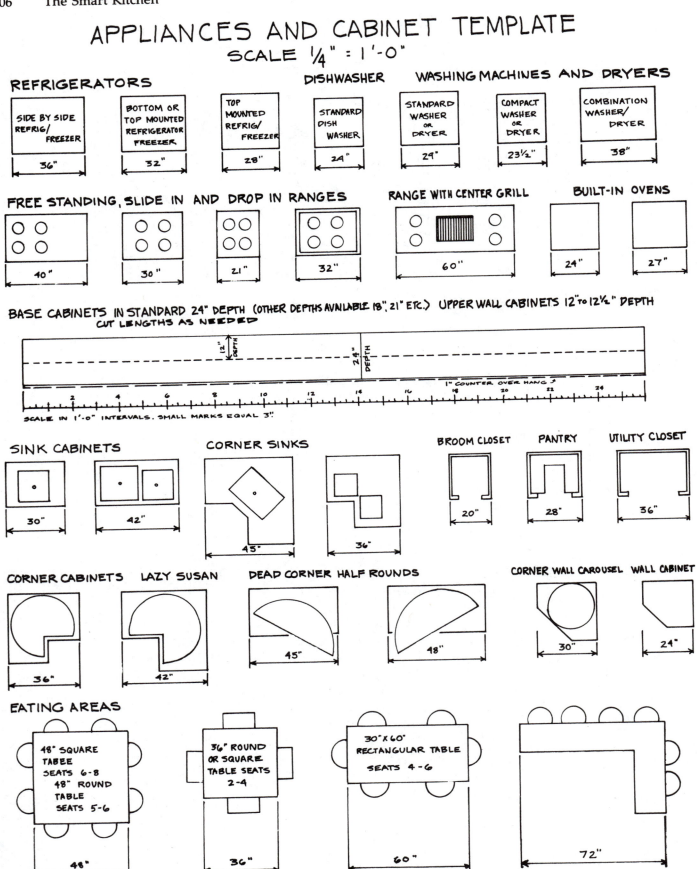

REFRIGERATORS
- SIDE BY SIDE REFRIG/FREEZER — 36"
- BOTTOM OR TOP MOUNTED REFRIGERATOR FREEZER — 32"
- TOP MOUNTED REFRIG/FREEZER — 28"

DISHWASHER
- STANDARD DISH WASHER — 24"

WASHING MACHINES AND DRYERS
- STANDARD WASHER OR DRYER — 29"
- COMPACT WASHER OR DRYER — 23½"
- COMBINATION WASHER/DRYER — 38"

FREE STANDING, SLIDE IN AND DROP IN RANGES
40"   30"   21"   32"

RANGE WITH CENTER GRILL
60"

BUILT-IN OVENS
24"   27"

BASE CABINETS IN STANDARD 24" DEPTH (OTHER DEPTHS AVAILABLE 18", 21" ETC.)   UPPER WALL CABINETS 12" to 12½" DEPTH
CUT LENGTHS AS NEEDED

12" DEPTH   24" DEPTH   1" COUNTER OVER HANG

2 4 6 8 10 12 14 16 18 20 22 24

SCALE IN 1'-0" INTERVALS. SMALL MARKS EQUAL 3".

SINK CABINETS
30"   42"

CORNER SINKS
45"   36"

BROOM CLOSET
20"

PANTRY
28"

UTILITY CLOSET
36"

CORNER CABINETS
36"

LAZY SUSAN
42"

DEAD CORNER HALF ROUNDS
45"   48"

CORNER WALL CAROUSEL
30"

WALL CABINET
24"

EATING AREAS
- 48" SQUARE TABLE SEATS 6-8 / 48" ROUND TABLE SEATS 5-6 — 48"
- 36" ROUND OR SQUARE TABLE SEATS 2-4 — 36"
- 30"x60" RECTANGULAR TABLE SEATS 4-6 — 60"
- 72"

SMART KITCHEN MAINTENANCE

Site	What to Do	When
Circuit breaker box	Check that breakers are marked to correspond to rooms or appliances they service. (To check, turn on all appliances and lights, then switch off breakers one at a time.)	When you first move in (or now if you've never done it).
Countertops	Wash down with light sanitizing solution.	Once a week or after meat preparation.
Dishwasher	Clean spray arm of clinging food and holes of food particles.	Once a week.
	Check filter screen (over drain at bottom, underneath spray arm) for trapped seeds, bones, or food. (You may have to remove spray arm to get to screen.) A clogged filter prevents efficient washing and proper filling and draining.	
	Set water heater (supply) at 110° to 120°F. (Raise if dishes don't come clean.)	Before first use or if you suspect water is too hot or too cold.
Exhaust system	Clean filter and hood.	Monthly.
Fire Extinguisher	To inspect: Check indicator on pressure gauge to be sure that extinguisher is charged. Be sure lock pin is firmly in place and intact. Check discharge nozzle to be sure it's not clogged. Keep extinguisher clean and check for dents, scratches, and corrostion. *Do not test by partially discharging extinguisher. Loss of pressure will occur.*	At least once a month (more often if exposed to weather).
	Discard contents and have professional refill unit.	At least once every 6 years.
First aid kit	Replenish stock.	As needed.
	Check expiration date and condition of contents.	Once a year.
Freezer	Defrost (manual-defrost models) Remove drain cover and clean defrost drain with a bottle brush. Replace the cover.	When ice is ¼ unit thick.
	Wash inside with solution of baking soda and water, using a soft cloth or sponge.	*Manual:* after defrosting. *Automatic:* every 6 months.
	Wash door gasket with mild soap and warm water. Rinse and dry.	Every 6 months.
	Vacuum condenser (if exposed).	Once a year.
GFCIs	Run test according to manufacturer's instructions.	Once a month or as directed.
Microwave oven	Wipe all spills and food splatters with warm water and a soft cloth (use mild detergent if needed). Dry. *Do not let soil build up around door seal.*	Immediately.
	Clean air vents with a damp cloth.	Once a week.
	Have service center check for proper operation and adequacy of door seals and interlocks.	Every 6 months or when concern dictates.
Range	Remove grease filter on underside of hood; scrub with scrub brush and sudsy water and rinse (or run through dishwasher). Dry thoroughly before repositioning.	Once a month.
	On gas ranges, clean dust and debris from area around pilot light and air vents.	Once a month.
	On electric ranges, clean reflector pan under burner elements.	Once a week.

Refrigerator	Clean condenser coils (on back or underneath) with crevice or brush attachment on vacuum cleaner.	Once a month.
	To empty and clean drain pan, slide from holder and wash in detergent and warm water. Let dry and replace. (Do not wash in dishwasher—it may warp.)	Every 6 months in cold weather; once a month in hot weather.
	Clear the drain hole (on bottom deck of refrigerator) with screwdriver or piece of wire. Force water with baster.	Every 6 months.
	Defrost freezer section (in manual or partially automatic defrost models).	When ice is thicker than ¼ inch.
	Turn off heater switch (also called power saver, power economizer, or energy saver).	When the weather is dry.
	Turn on heater switch.	When weather is humid.
	Clean door gaskets with mild soap and warm water, rinse, and dry. Wipe with a light film of petroleum jelly.	Every 6 months.
	Replace door gasket. (To test rubber seal, close the door on a crisp new dollar bill in several different locations. If the dollar bill can be pulled out easily, the seal probably needs to be replaced. To test magnetic gasket, place flashlight inside, point at seal and turn kitchen light out.)	Every 6 years or when it wears out
	Check temperature inside refrigerator with household thermometer. (Refrigerator section should be 37°F, freezer section 0°F.)	Once a year.
Smoke detector	Test or check according to manufacturer's directions.	As directed.
Water filter (point-of-service, activated carbon unit)	Replace carbon cartridge.	Every 20 gal. or once every 3 weeks, unless manufacturer says otherwise.
Water filter (large units)	Replace carbon cartridge.	When flow becomes restricted.
Water heater	Drain off a pailful of water to draw off sediment from bottom of tank. (Open draincock at bottom of tank.)	Once a month.
	Manually open safety valve (temperature-pressure relief valve) at top of tank on hot-water line to test operation; wear gloves and use a bucket to catch the water that will come out. Be sure the valve returns to its original position.	Twice a year.
	Electric heater: Drain tank completely to flush out scale, rust, and sediment. (Attach garden hose from opened drain cock to yard or cellar drain.) Remove heating elements, soak them in vinegar solution (1 cup vinegar to each gallon of water), and scrape off mineral deposits. *Be sure to shut off power to heater at the fuse box or circuit breaker before you begin.*	Once a Year.
	Gas heater: Shut off, then check exhaust vent and air shutter openings for dirt and obstructions. Inspect burner unit for dust and dirt. Clean burner of lint and dirt, and vacuum air passages to burner.	Twice a Year.
Well	To analyze water for bacterial contamination, take water sample in sterilized bottle to your local or state public health office. (Keep sample in cooler and deliver within 24 hours.)	Once a year.
	To analyze water for chemical and mineral contamination, take sample in morning, when concentrations are the highest. Most common testing: lead, cadmium, copper, formaldehyde, phenolics, xylenes, refinery hydrocarbons, chlorinated phenolics, and hydrogen sulfide. (See "Selected Resources" or check local health department for labs.)	If taste or color change.

Adapted from "An All-House Maintenance Manual," *New Shelter*, April 1983.

Selected Resources

Part I. Human Comfort and Safety

Chapter 1. Kitchen Counters

AN ADJUSTABLE COUNTER

Bearings

Thomson Industries, Inc.*
Shore Rd. and Chanel Dr.
Port Washington, NY 11050
Product: SPB16OPN Linear Bearing
Pillow Blocks

Support Rails

Thomson Industries, Inc.*
Shore Rd. and Chanel Dr.
Port Washington, NY 11050
Product: SR-16

Actuator

C and H Sales Company
PO Box 5356
Pasadena, CA 91117

**Thompson Saginaw Ball and Screw
Company Inc.***
628 N Hamilton
Saginaw, MI 48605
Product: Standard 110VAC Performance
Pak Actuator 5703551

Hydraulic Lift Tables

**Business and Institutional Furniture
Corp.**
611 N Broadway
Milwaukee, WI 53202
Product: Catalog

Safe Stepstool

Demco
Box 7488
Madison, WI 53707
Product: Kick-Step Stool

SELECTING COUNTERTOP MATERIAL

Tung Oil Finish

Mohawk Finishing Products, Inc.*
Route 30
Amsterdam, NY 12010

Woodpecker's Tools, Inc.
614 Agua Fria St.
Sante Fe, NM 87501

Nontoxic Finishes

Baubiologie Hardware
PO Box 3217
Prescott, AZ 86302

Eco Source
PO Box 1656
Sebastopol, CA 95473

The Natural Choice
Eco Design Company
1365 Rufina Circle
Sante Fe, NM 87501

Slate

Hilltop Slate Corporation
PO Box 201
Middle Granville, NY 12849

Vermont Structural Slate Company
Box 98
Fair Haven, VT 05743

Countertop Inserts

AMA Company
17138 Von Karmen Ave.
Irvine, CA 92714

Vance Industries
7401 W Wilson Ave.
Chicago, IL 60656
Product: Surface Saver

Countertop Maintenance

Kitchen Tune-Ups
131 North Roosevelt
Aberdeen, SD 57401
800-333-6385 (for local agent)
Product: Countertop restoration

Vermont Country Store
PO Box 3000
Manchester Ctr. VT 05255
Product: Formica™ Polish

Chapter 2. Cabinets

Cabinet Aids

Amerock Corp.
PO Box 7018

Rockford, IL 61101
Product: Cabinet Hardware Catalog

Hafele America Company
203 Feld
PO Box 1590
High Point, NC 27261
Product: Lockable cabinet
compartment 545.48.248

Hafele Canada Inc.
6345 Netherhart Rd.
Mississauga, Canada L5T 1B8
Product: see above

Hafele Canada Inc.
Eastern Branch
8604 Boulevarde Pie IX
Montreal, Canada H1Z 4G2
Product: see above

Ilco Unican
7301 Decaire
Montreal, Canada H4P 2G7
Product: Simplex childproof locks

Kitchen Considerations
21801 Industrial Blvd.
Rodgers, MI 55374
Product: Catalog

Perfectly Safe
7245 Whipple Ave. NW
North Canton, OH 44720
Product: Cabinet safety devices

Safety Zone
PO Box 182247
Chattanooga, TN 37422
Product: Cabinet safety devices

Scan-Plast Industries, Inc.
1 Industrial Dr.
Rutherford, NJ 07070
Product: Elfa wire products catalog

Simplex Access Controls
2941 Indiana Ave.
Winston Salem, NC 27115
Product: Simplex childproof locks

Plastic Shelves

Rohm and Haas*
Independence Mall W.
Philadelphia, PA 19105

Cabinet Resurfacers

Brookside Veneers (wood)
215 Forrest St.
Metuchen, NJ 08840

Dial One Delux Cabinet Works
(plastic, wood)
4605 SW Beaverton Hillsdale Hwy.
Portland, OR 97221

Dura-Oak Cabinet Front Systems
(wood)
863 Texas Ave.
Shreveport, LA 71101

Flexible Materials Inc. (wood)
11209 Electron Dr.
Louisville, KY 40299

Facelifters (plastic,wood)
800 Snediker Ave.
Brooklyn, NY 11207

Jasper Plastics (urethane or styrene)
Kimball Industrial Park
W 12th Ave.
Jasper, IN 47546

Kitchen Saver (plastic)
606 Island Ave.
McKees Rocks, PA 15136

Long Island Laminates (plastic)
35 Engineers Rd.
Hauppauge, NY 11788

Yankee Wood (urethane or styrene)
195 Industrial Park Dr.
Northampton, MA 01060

Non-Toxic Cabinet Materials

Medite Corp.
Box 4040
Medland, OR 97501
Product: Medex Fiberboard

AFM Enterprises
1140 Stacy Ct.
Riverside, CA 92507
Product: 3 in 1 Adhesive

RWP Company
10601 N.W. H.K. Dodgen Loop 366
Temple,TX 76502
Product: Lokweld 10 Glue

Formaldehyde Sealants

AFM Enterprises, Inc.
1140 Stacy Ct.
Riverside, CA 92507

Allergy & Health Emporium
5635 E Mockingbird La.
Dallas, TX 75106

Allergy Store
PO Box 2555
Sebastopol, CA 95473

Nigra Enterprises
5699 Kanan Rd., No. 123
Agoura Hills, CA 91301

Woodpecker's Tools, Inc.
614 Agua Fria St.
Sante Fe, NM 87501

Non-toxic Paints and Finishes For Cabinets (and Interiors)

AFM Enterprises
1140 Stacy Ct.
Riverside, CA 92507

Auro Sinan Company
PO Box 857
Davis, CA 95617

Best Paint Company
PO Box 3922
5205 Ballard Ave. NW
Seattle, WA 98124

Biofa Paints
PO Box 190
Alton, NH 03809

Bonakemi
14805 East Moncreiff Pl.
Aurora, CO 80011

Color Your World
10 Carson St.
Toronto, Canada M8W 3R5

Coronado Paints
308 Old Country Rd.
Edgewater, FL 21321

Ecos Paint
PO Box 375
Saint Johnsbury, VT 05819

Glidden Paint
925 Euclid Ave.
Cleveland, OH 44115

Murco
300 NE 21st St.
Fort Worth, TX 76106

W.F. Taylor
13660 Excelsior Dr.
Santa Fe Springs, CA 90670

Woodfinisher's Pride
9311 Monroe Rd., Suite J
Charlotte, NC 28270

Formaldehyde-Free/Low VOC Cabinets

Neff Kitchens
Stratum Storage Systems
6 Melanie Dr.
Brampton, Canada L6T 4K9

Steel Cabinets

Areslux USA
8229 NW 66th St.
Miami, FL 33166

Davis Products Company
111 Beeson St.
PO Box 360
Dowagiac, MI 49047

Emerald Custom Kitchens
PO Box 2237
314 N. Maple St.
Enfield, CT 06082

Fillip Metal Cabinet Company
701 N Albany St.
Chicago, IL 60612

King Mini Kitchens
76-02 Woodhaven Blvd.
Glendale, NY 11385

Marvel Division
PO Box 997
Richmond, IN 47375

Marvel Metal Products Company
3843 W 43rd St.
Chicago, IL 60632

St. Charles
1400 Greenbriar Pkwy. # 200
Chesapeake, VA 23320

Trade Associations

*Directory of Certified Cabinet
   Manufacturers
Recommended Construction and
   Performance Standards for Kitchen
   and Vanity Cabinets* ($1)
Kitchen Cabinet Manufacturers Assoc.
1899 Preston White Rd.
Reston, VA 22091

Canadian Kitchen Cabinet Assoc.
27 Goulburn Ave.
Ottawa, Canada KIN8C7

Chapter 3. Sinks

Double Bowl

Moen Group*
377 Woodland Ave.
Elyria, OH 44036
Product: Lancelot sink LSR3344-4

Preparation Sink

Luwa Corporation*
PO Box 16348
Charlotte, NC 28216
Product: Belaform 18/10 stainless
   steel sink

Rising Faucet

Moen Group*
377 Woodland Ave.
Elyria, OH 44036
Product: Riser faucet LSR3224WF

Bar-Type Faucet

Grohe America, Inc.*
900 Lively Blvd.
Wooddale, IL 60191
Product: Classic line 31.739 faucet
with hose

Faucet Hose

International Plumbing AG
8090 Hihn Rd.
Ben Lomond, CA 95005
Product: Extra long sink hose

Sink Stool

Charette
PO Box 4010
Woburn, MA 01880
Product: Cambridge adjustable stool

Water Conservation

One Song Enterprises
PO Box 1180
Willoughby, OH 44094
Product: Flip control aerator

Water Safety

The Memry Corp.
83 Keeler Ave.
Norwalk, CT 06854
Product: Faucet Anti-Scald Device

Chapter 4. Lighting and Thermal Comfort

Window Insulation

Real Goods
966 Mazzoni St.
Ukiah, CA 95482
Product: Catalog

Appropriate Technology Corporation
PO Box 975
Brattleboro, VT 05301
Product: Window quilt, showcase,
comforter

First Law Products, Inc.
PO Box 888
69 Island St.
Keene, NH 03431
Product: Insulshutter

Thermal Technology Corporation
600 Alter St.
Broomfield, CO 80020
Product: Insulating curtain wall,
SuperShade, Thermocell

Energy Saving Bulbs

DuroTest Corporation*
9 Law Dr.
Fairfield, NJ 07006
Product: Watt Saver™ bulbs

Energy Answers
PO Box 24
Lake Bluff, IL 60064
Product: Catalog

North American Philips Corp.
Philips Square, CN 6800
Somerset, NJ 08873

P'lovers
1525 Birmingham St.
Halifax, Canada B3J 2J6

Real Goods
966 Mazzoni St.
Ukiah, CA 95482
Product: Catalog

Fluorescent Bulbs

Daycoa
50 Walnut Rd.
Medway, OH

DuroTest Corporation*
9 Law Dr.
Fairfield, NJ 07006
Product: Vita-Lite, DuroLite
plant light

Environmental Systems, Inc.
204 Pitney Rd.
Lancaster, PA 17601
Product: Ott-Lite

Fluorescent Fixtures

Power Products Company
Cayuga and Ramona Sts.
Philadelphia, PA 19120
Product: Under-cabinet light model
UC15 or UCWG15

Lighting Controls

Lutron Electronics Company, Inc.*
205 Suter Rd.
Coopersburg, PA 18036
Product: Linear dimmers

Skylight

Paeco, Inc.*
1 Executive Dr.
PO Box 968
Toms River, NJ 08753
Product: Skyliner VG4630 and electric
operator

Automatic Skylight Opener

Braemen Company
PO Box 70
Salem, MA 01970
Product: Thermofor

Publications

Lighting Your Life ($1)
American Home Lighting Institute
435 N Michigan Ave.
Chicago, IL 60611

Chapter 5. Acoustics and Noise Reduction

Acoustic Wallcovering

Laminating Services, Inc.
PO Box 40232
Louisville, KY 40218
Product: Sempatap™

Acoustic Panels

L. E. Carpenter and Company
170 N Main St.
Wharton, NJ 07885
Product: Vicracoustic™ Panels

Publications

Noise Control ($1)
Small Homes Research Council
1 E St. and Mary's Rd.
Champaign, IL 61820

Chapter 6. Flooring

Floor Covering

Carlisle Tire and Rubber Company
PO Box 99
Carlisle, PA 17013
Product: Rubber tiles from recycled
tires

Flexco
Box 553
Tuscumbia, AL 35674
Product: Rubber flooring from
recycled tires

Forbo Industries, Inc.
PO Box 667
Hazelton, PA 18201
Product: Natural linoleum

IPO Cork
Kennesaw, GA 30144
Product: Cork tiles

Laminating Services
PO Box 40232
Louisville, KY 40218
Product: Sempafloor

Mars, Inc.
PO Box 916
Braintree, MA 02184
Product: Rubber tiles from
recycled pvc

Nairn Floors International
560 Weber St. N.

Waterloo, Canada N2L 5C6
Product: Natural linoleum

Floor Skids
Abbeon Cal Inc.
123 Gray Ave.
Santa Barbara, CA 93101
Product: Anti-fatigue mats, cushion tiles

Hardwood Flooring

Missouri Hardwood Flooring Co.*
Birch Tree, MO 6543
Product: Clear red oak

Remilled Flooring

Albany Woodworks
PO Box 729
Albany, LA 70711

Atlantic Wood Flooring
1206 Laskin Rd.
Virginia Beach, VA 23451

Coastal Millworks
1335 Marietta Blvd. N.W.
Atlanta, GA 30318

Castle Burlingame
10 Stone St.
North Plainfield, NJ 07060

Centre Mills Antique Wood
PO Box 16
Aspers, PA 17304

Chestnut Specialist
38 Harwinton Ave.
Plymouth, CT 06782

**Conklin's Authentic Antique
  Barnwood**
RD 1, Box 70
Susquehanna, PA 18847

Duluth Timber Company
3310 Minnesota Ave.
Duluth, MN 55802

The Great Barn Room & Furniture Co.
152 Old Clinton Rd.
Westbrook, CT 06498

J.L. Powell & Company
600 South Madison St.
Whiteville, NC 28472

The Joinery Company
Box 518
Tarboro, NC 27886

K-Wood & Logs
PO Box 22
Fawn Grove, PA 17321

Mayse Woodworking Company
319 Richardson Rd.
Lansdale, PA 19446

Mountain Lumber Company
PO Box 289A, Rte. 606
Ruckersville, VA 22968

North Fields Restorations
PO Box 741
Rowley, MA 01969

Old Home Building & Restoration
PO Box 384
West Suffield, CT 06093

Pappas Antiques
PO Box 335
Woodbury, CT 06798

Sea Star Trading Company
Perpetua Hardwoods
PO Box 513
1218 NW Grove
Newport, OR 97365

Sylvan Brandt, Inc.
651 East Main St.
Lititz, PA 17543

Tiresias, Inc.
Dukes Ave.
Orangeburg, SC 29115

Vintage Lumber Company
9507 Woodsboro Rd.
Frederick, MD 21701

What It's Worth
PO Box 162135
Austin, TX 78716

Woodhouse
PO Box 7336
Rocky Mt., NC 27804

The Woods Company
2357 Boteler Rd.
Brownsville, MD 21715

The Wood Cellar
Atlantic Wood Corporation
1206 Laskin Rd., Ste. 202,
Virginia Beach, VA 23451

Floor Finish†

Eco Source
PO Box 1656
Sebastopol, CA 95473
† See also listings under Chapter 2
  "Non-Toxic Paints & Finishes for
  Cabinets (and Interiors)"

Chapter 7. Small Wonders in the Kitchen

The Food Processor

Cuisinarts, Inc.*
5 Wisconsin Ave.
Norwich, CT 06360
Product: Model CLC7 Superpro
            food processor

Oster*
5055 North Lydell Ave.
Milwaukee, WI 53217
Product: PulseMatic 16-speed blender

The Mini-Vacuum

Black & Decker*
6 Armstrong Rd.
Chelton, CT 06484
Product: Dustbuster 9330

Computer Software

Digital Systems Research
10085 Scripps Ranch Ct.
San Diego, CA 92131
Product: Healthy Cooking

Eatec
2904 San Pablo Ave.
Berekely, CA 94702
Product: Eatec I-V

ESHA Research
PO Box 13028
Salem, OR 97309
Lake Zurich, IL 60047
Product: Nutrition Pro

Hopkins Technology
421 Hazel La.
Hopkins, MN 55343
Product: Food Analyst Plus

N-Squared Computing
First DataBank Division
Hearst Corp.
11 Bayhill Rd.
San Bruno, CA 94066
Product: Food/Analyst Plus

Nutridata Software Corp.
PO Box 769
Wappingers Falls, NY 12590
Product: Cooking Companion

Computer Bulletin Boards with Nutrition/Health Conferences

Compuserve
PO Box 20212
Columbus, OH 43220

The Well
7150 Bridgeway #A200
Sausalito, CA 94965

Ergonomic Chair

Sears Roebuck and Company*
Sears Tower
Chicago, IL 60684
Product: Ergonomic chair 3AX77916

Chapter 8. Safety

Fire Extinguishers

The Safety Zone
PO Box 182247
Chattanooga, TN 37422
Product: Fire blanket

Sears, Roebuck and Company*
Sears Tower
Chicago, IL 60684
Product: Fire extinguisher 9K58044

Environmental Smoke Alarms

EcoWorks
2326 Pickwick Rd.
Baltimore, MD 21207
Product: Smoke Alarms

Nuclear Free America
325 East 25th St.
Baltimore, MD 21218
Product: Smoke Alarms

Electric Shock

Square D Company*
Home Automation
1601 Mercer Rd.
Lexington, KY 40511
Product: Ground fault circuit interrupters

Multiple Outlet Strips

The Wiremold Company*
PO Box 10639
West Hartford, CT 06110
Product: Stainless steel Plugmold 2000

Clock

Bulova Watch Company, Inc.*
26-15 Brooklyn-Queens Expressway
Woodside, NY 11377
Product: Water's Edge clock,
　　　　style C4802

Part II: Appliances and Energy Efficiency

Chapter 9. Refrigeration

Refrigerator

Amana Refrigeration, Inc.*
Amana, IA 52204
Product: Refrigerator/freezer BC20E

Dometic
2320 Industrial Pkwy.
PO Box 490
Elkhart, IN 46515
Product: Ammonia/gas refrigerators
　　　　and freezers

Lehman's
Box 41
Kidron, OH 44636
Product: Servel gas refrigerator

Low Keep Refrigeration
24651 Second Ave.
Otsego, MI 49078
Product: Energy-efficient refrigerator

Norcold
600 Kuther Rd.
Sidney, OH 45365
Product: Gas absorption refrigerators

Sunfrost
PO Box 1111
Arcata, CA 95521
Product: Energy-efficient refrigerators

Whirlpool Corp.**
Administrative Center
Benton Harbor, MI 49002
Product: Kenmore, KitchenAid,
　　　　Whirlpool Super Energy
　　　　Efficient Refrigerators (SERP)

Refrigerator Thermometer

Brookstone*
565 Vose Farm Rd.
Peterborough, NH 03458
Product: Digital refrigerator thermometer

Refrigerator Curtain

The Conserve Group
PO Box 1560
Bethlehem, PA 18016
Product: Chill Shield

Refrigerator Energy Measuring Device

Brookstone*
565 Vose Farm Rd.
Peterborough, NH 03458
Product: Energy Teller

REFRIGERATOR MAINTENANCE

Condenser Coil Brushes

Fuller Brush
One Fuller Way
Great Bend, KS 67530

Real Goods
966 Mazzoni St.
Ukiah, CA 95482-3471

Vermont Country Store
PO Box 3000
Manchester Ctr., VT 05255

Condenser Coil Vacuum Attachment

Energy Answers
PO Box 24
Lake Bluff, IL 60044

Leichtung Improvements Catalog
4944 Commerce Pkwy.
Cleveland, OH 44128

Vermont Country Store
PO Box 3000
Manchester Ctr., VT 05255

The Crawlspace Pantry

Brookstone*
565 Vose Farm Rd.
Peterborough, NH 03458
Product: Sweat Stop

Abbeon Cal, Inc.
123 Gray Ave.
Santa Barbara, CA 93101
Product: Remote-reading thermometer
　　　　and hygrometer

Edmunds Scientific Company
101 E Gloucester Pike
Barrington, NJ 08007
Product: Remote-reading thermometer
　　　　and hygrometer

Publications

*The Most Energy-Efficient
Appliances* ($5)
**American Council for an
Energy-Efficient Economy**
2140 Shattuck Ave.
Berkeley, CA 94704

*Consumer Selection Guide to Refrig-
erators and Freezers* ($1.50)
*Directory of Certified Refrigerators
and Freezers* ($1)
**Association of Home Appliance
Manufacturers**
20 N Wacker Dr.
Chicago, IL 60606

Chapter 10. Dishwashing

Water Conserving Dishwashers

AEG
Andi-CO Appliances, Inc.
65 Campus Plaza
Edison, NY 08837

ASEA Brown Boveri Company
ABB Appliances, Inc.
903 N. Bowser #200
Richardson, TX 75081

Miele Appliances, Inc.
22 D Worlds Fair Dr.
Somerset, NJ 08873

Bosch
PO Box 4601
North Suburban, IL 60197

Regency VSA
PO Box 3341
Tustin, CA 92681

Sears, Roebuck and Company*
Sears Tower
Chicago, IL 60684
Product: Kenmore Three-Level with
　　　　Power Miser, #7034

Chapter 11. Cooking

Metallic Laminate

Ralph Wilson Plastics Company
600 General Bruce Dr.
Temple, TX 76501

Gas Cooktop

Dacor
950 South Raymond Ave
Pasadena, CA 91109
Product: Gas cooktop GGC 303

Modern Maid*
403 N Main St.
Topton, PA 19562
Product: Cooktop with ComboGrille
GT483

Oven

Dacor
950 South Raymond Ave
Pasadena, CA 91109
Product: Electric/convection oven
W305

Induction Cooktop

Sanyo Electric, Inc.*
200 Riser Rd.
Little Ferry, NJ 07643
Product: Portable induction cooker
1C54

Toaster/Oven

Black & Decker, Inc.*
6 Armstrong Rd.
Shelton, CT 06484
Product: Toast-R-Oven T93B

Professional/Home Ranges

Viking Range Corporation
PO Box 8012
Greenwood, MI 38930
Product: Professional Range

Wolf Range Company
19600 S Alameda
Compton, CA 90224
Product: Gourmet Gas Range (A)(AS)

Cooktop Reflector Pans

Range Kleen
PO Drawer 696
Lima, OH 45802

Pot Rack

Taylor and Ng*
2600 Maxwell Way
Fairfield, CA 94533
Product: Track Rack system

Cookware

American International Trading*
PO Box 400
Glassboro, NJ 08028

Utensils

Colonial Gardens Kitchens
PO Box 66
Hanover, PA 17333

Williams Sonoma
PO Box 7456
San Francisco, CA 94120

Smoke/Gas Detector

B.D.C. Electronics
PO Box 4996
Midlands, TX 79704
Product: Ultralert

Publications

Woodheat
Gilford Publishing
PO Box 2008
Laconia, NH 03247

Part III. Air and Water Quality, Waste Disposal, and Food Production

Chapter 12. Ventilation

Custom Exhaust Hoods

Artisan Metalworks
232 Madison Ave.
Wycoff, NJ 07481

Exhaust Systems

Broan Mfg. Company
926 W. State St.
Hartford, WI 53027
Product: Silhouette 1530

NuTone Division*
Scovill
Madison and Red Bank Rd.s
Cincinnati, OH 45227
Product: Exhaust fans

Vent-A-Hood
PO Box 426
1000 N Greenville Ave.
Richardson, TX 75080
Product: Vented hood

Flakt Ventilation
PO Box 5591300
Holmsund, Sweden
Product: Bahco kitchen hood heat
exchanger

RB Kanalflakt Inc.
1121 Lewis Ave.
Sarasota, FL 34237
Product: Metsovent

Fan Control

Lutron Electronics Company, Inc.*
205 Suter Rd.
Coopersburg, PA 18036
Product: Fan speed control

Air Cleaning Devices

Air Conditioning Engineers*
PO Box 616
Decatur, IL 6252-0616
Product: Air De-Pollution Unit 200LMF

Allergy & Health Emporium
5635 E Mockingbird La.
Dallas, TX 75106

N.E.E.D.S.
527 Charles #12A
Syracuse, NY 13209

Nigra Enterprises
5699 Kanan Rd., # 123
Agoura Hills, CA 91301

Air Cleaning Plant System

Bio Safe Inc.
Georgetown, TX 78627
Product: Bio Safe Carbon Plant Filter

Publications

*Certified Home Ventilating Products
  Directory*
Home Ventilating Institute
Division of AMCA
30 W University Dr.
Arlington Heights, IL 60004

*Heat Recovery Ventilation for
  Housing* ($2.25)
Superintendent of Documents
Government Printing Office
Washington, DC 20402

Trade Associations

Home Ventilation Institute
30 W University Dr.
Arlington Heights, IL 60004

**Heating Refrigerator and Air Condi-
  tioning Institute of Canada**
5468 Dundas St. W #226
Islington, Canada M9B 6E3

Chapter 13. Water Purity, Conservation, and Heating

Water Purifiers

Allergy & Health Emporium
5635 E Mockingbird La.
Dallas, TX 75106

Allergy Store
PO Box 2555
Sebastopol, CA 95473

Amway*
7575 E Fulton Rd.
Aba, MI 49355
Product: Water treatment system

Atlantic Ultraviolet
250 N. Fehr Way
Bay Shore, NY 11706
Product: Sanitron

FREE Market
1001 Connecticut Ave. NW #638
Washington, DC 20036

NEEDS
527 Charles #12A
Syracuse, NY 13209

Nigra Enterprises
5699 Kanan Rd., # 123
Agoura Hills, CA 91301

Water Testing

National Testing Labs
6151 Wilson Mills Rd.
Cleveland, OH 44143

Suburban Water Testing Labs
4600 Kutztown Rd.
Temple, PA 19560

Water-Test Corporation
33 S. Commercial St.
Manchester, NH 03108

Information

Water Quality Association
Naperville Rd.
Lisle, IL 60532

WATER CONSERVATION

Publications

*Grey Water Use In The Landscape:
How to Use Gray Water to Save Your
Landscape During Droughts* ($6)
Edible Productions
PO Box 1841
Santa Rosa, CA 95402

*How to Get Water Smart: Products
and Practices for Saving Money in the
90's* ($11.45)
Terra Firma
PO Box 91315
Santa Barbara, CA 93910

Thermostatically Controlled Mixing Valves

International Plumbing AG
8090 Hihn Rd.
Ben Lomond, CA 95005

The Spot Tankless Water Heater
Acutemp Corp.
2250 Belmont St.
Ann Arbor, MI 48105

Controlled Energy Corporation
Box 19
Fiddler's Green
Waitsfield, VT 05673

Chronomite Labs
21011 S. Figueroa St.
Carson City, CA 90745

Publication

*The Water Heater Workbook/A Hands-
On Guide to Water Heaters* ($11.25)
Larry and Suzanne Weingarten
Elemental Enterprises
PO Box 929
Monterey, CA 93942

Chapter 14. Recycling Kitchen Wastes

COMPOSTING

Recessed Countertop Container

Franke/Kitchen Division
212 Church Rd.
North Wales, PA 19454
Product: Waste Bin AE

Undersink Containers

Hafele America Company
203 Feld
PO Box 1590
High Point, NC 27261
Product: Big Box Trash Can

Hafele Canada Inc.
6345 Netherhart Rd.
Mississauga, Canada L5T 1B8

Hafele Canada Inc.
Eastern Branch
8604 Boulevarde Pie IX
Montreal, Canada H1Z 4G2

Melpa Inc.
PO Box 1469
High Point, N.C. 27260
Product: Built-in waste bin

Melpa Canada
121 Ganton Dr.
Richmand Hill
Mills, Canada L4B 3N4

Rubbermaid™
Wooster, OH 44691
Product: Under the Sink Recycling
Container

Compost/Food Storing Sink

Blanco America Inc.
1001 Lower Landing Rd.
Blackwood, NJ 08012
Product: Blancostyle Sink with Box Set

Compost/Food Grinder

Carbco Industries
240 Michigan St.
Lockport, NY 14094
Product: Kitch'n Komposter

Composting Devices

Alsto's Handy Helpers
PO Box 1267
Galesburg, IL 61401
Product: The Green Cone, Soilsaver,
Rotating Composter

Brookstone
5 Vose Farm Rd.
Peterborough, NH 03458
Product: The Earth Machine

Nova Sylva
C.P. 1624, 1587 rue Denault
Sherbrooke, Canada J1H 5M4
Product: The Earth Machine

RECYCLING

Under-Counter Recycling Containers

Amerock Corp.
PO Box 7018
Rockford, IL 61101

Feeny Manufacturing Company
PO Box 191
Muncie, IN 47308

Hafele America Company
203 Feld
PO Box 1590
High Point, NC 27261

Hafele Canada Inc.
6345 Netherhart Rd.
Mississauga, Canada L5T 1B8

Hafele Canada Inc.
Eastern Branch
8604 Boulevarde Pie IX
Montreal, Canada H1Z 4G2

Melpa Inc.
PO Box 1469
High Point, NC 27260

Melpa Canada
121 Ganton Dr.
Richmand Hill
Ontario, Canada L4B 3N4

Mill's Pride
423 Hopewell Dr.
Waverly, OH 45690

Rev-A-Shelf
2409 Plantside Dr.
Jeffersontown, KY 40299

Recycling Equipment

Haute House
1428 Danby Rd.
Ithaca, NY 14850
Product: Freestanding Recycling Center

Minneapolis Abrasives, Inc.
5639 Garfield Ave. S.,
Minn., MN 55419
Product: Dial Recycling Chute

Nova Sylva
1587 Denault St.
Sherbrooke, Canada J1H 2R1
Product: Murf Recycling Container

Lehman's
4779 Kidron Rd.
Kidron, OH 44636
Product: Can Crusher

Fidelity Products
Box 155
Minn., NM 55440
Product: Stackable Recycling Bins

Rubbermaid™
Wooster, OH 44691
Product: Stackable Recycling Centers,
    Refuse Containers

Newspaper Sorters

Buckhorn Canada
2775 Slough St.
Mississauga, Canada L4T 1G2
Product: Stak n' Tie

The Paragon
89 Tom Harvey Rd.
Westerly, RI 02891
Product: Newspaper Rack

Rubbermaid™
Wooster, OH 44691
Product: Newspaper Recyclers

Publications

Worms Eat My Garbage ($11.45)
Flowerfield Enterprises
10322 Shaver Rd.
Kalamazoo, MI 49002

Backyard Composting, Harmonius
Technologies, (Harmonius Press, 1992)

Beautiful, Easy, Lawns and Landscapes,
Larry Sombke, (Globe Pequot, 1994)
Chapter 4, "Clean Easy Compost"

Chapter 15. Food Production

The Skylight

Paeco*
1 Executive Dr.
Toms River, NJ 08753

Full-Spectrum Bulbs

DuroTest Corporation*
2321 Kennedy Blvd.
North Bergen, NJ 07047
Product: Vita-Lite

Sprouting Equipment

The Sprout Man
40 Rail Rd. St.
Great Barrington, MA 01230

Walnut Acres
Penns Creek, PA 17862
Product: Catalog

Part IV. Planning the Kitchen

General

Consumers Digest, "How to Save
Thousands on a New Kitchen or
Bath," August, 1992.

The Kitchen Book, Terence Conran
(Crown, 1977)

The Motion-Minded Kitchen, Sam
Clark (Houghton Mifflin, 1983)

Terence Conran's Kitchen Book,
(Overlook Press, 1993)

Trade Associations

**Association of Home Appliance
  Manufacturers**
20 N Wacker Dr.
Chicago, IL 60606

Gas Appliance Manufacturers Assoc.
PO Box 9245
Arlington, VA 22290

Canadian Kitchen Cabinet Assoc.
27 Goulbum Ave.
Ottawa, Canada K1N 8C7

**L'Association des Fabricants et
  Distributeurs de L'Industrie de La
  Cuisine du Quebec**
2814 Lere Ave.
Quebec, Canada G1L 3N9

National Kitchen & Bath Assoc.
124 Main St.
Hackettown, NJ 07840

National Kitchen Cabinet Assoc.
PO Box 6830
Falls Church, VA 22046

Artisans

Ken St. John
9 Reynolds La.
Woodstock, NY 12498
Specialty: Decorative stainless steel

SPECIAL NEEDS

Catalogs

The Dwyer Difference
Dwyer Product Corp.
Michigan City, IN 46360

Maneuverability
4015 Ave. U
Brooklyn, NY 11234

Cabinets for Wheelchair Users

Merillat Industries, Inc.
Adrian, MI 49221

Ergonomic/Universal Design Cabinets

Lifespec Cabinet Systems
428 North Lamar Blvd.
Oxford, MS 38655

Information

International Center for the Disabled
340 E 24th St.
New York, NY 10010

Resource Center for Accessible Living
Architectural Modification Consultation
602 Albany Ave.
Kingston, NY 12401

Publications

Home in a Wheelchair
Paralyzed Veterans of America
4330 East West Highway
Washington, DC 20014

Designs for Independent Living
AIS - Whirlpool Corp.
Administrative Center
Benton Harbor, MI 49022

Adaptable Housing ($3)
U.S. Dept. of Housing and Urban
  Development
HUD User
PO Box 6091
Rockville, MD 20850

ENVIRONMENTAL CONCERNS

Used Building Materials, Cabinets, Appliances, Etc.

American Salvage, Inc.
7001 NW 27th Ave.
Miami, FL 33147

Architectural Antiquities
Harborside, ME 04642

Artefacts Architectural Antiques
17 King St.
St. Jacobs, Canada N0B 2N0

The Bank Architectural Antiques
1824 Felicity St.
New Orleans, LA 70133

Bauer Brothers Salvage
174 East Arlington, St.
Paul, MN 55117

Colonial Antiques
5000 West 96th St.
Indianapolis, IN 46268

The Emporium
1800 Westheimer
Houston, TX 77098

Governor's Antiques & Architectural Materials
6240 Meadowbridge Rd.
Mechanicsville, VA 23111

Joe Ley Antiques, Inc.
615 East Market St.
Louisville, KY 40202

Ohmega Salvage
2407 San Pablo Ave.
Berkeley, CA 94702

Olde Theatre Architectural Company
Broadway St.
Kansas City, MO 64108

Pelnik Wrecking Company
8 Calvin St.
Yorkville, NY 13495

Restoration Treasures
PO Box 724
Cooperstown, NY 13326

The Re-Store
60 Usher St.
Brantford, Canada M3R 1C3

ReUze Building Centre
380 Birchmount Rd., Unit 3
Scarborough, Canada, M1K 1M6

Salvage One Architectural Artifacts
1524 South Sangamon St.
Chicago, IL 60608

Swan Creek Architectural Centre
333 North Main St.
Lambertville, NJ 08530,

United House Wrecking
535 Hope St.
Stanford, CT 06906

Urban Ore
Building Materials Exchange
1333 Sixth St.
Berkeley, CA 94710

Wastebusters
1390 Richmond Terrace
Staten Island, NY 10310

Wrecking Bar of Atlanta
292 Moreland Ave.
Atlanta, GA 30307

Designers

John Bower
7471 N Shiloh Rd.
Unionville, IN 47468

The Croxton Collaborative
1122 Madison Ave.
New York, NY 10028

Oliver Drerup
Drerup Armstrong Ltd.
PO Box 130
Carp, Canada K0A 1LO

John Friedman
PO Box 1148
Woodstock, NY 12498

David Goldbeck
Smart Kitchen Associates
PO Box 87
Woodstock, NY 12498
(914) 679-5573

Clint Good
PO Box 143
Lincoln, VA 22078

Audrey Hoodkiss
Ecology by Design
1341 Ocean Ave. # 73
Santa Monica, CA 90401

International Institute for Baubiologie™ and Ecology
Box 387
Clearwater, FL 34615

Henry Jacoby
314 Aspetuck Village
Huntington, CT 06484

Gail Lindsey
Design Harmony
614 N. Main St.
Wake Forest, NC 27587

Ed Lowans Jr.
Environmental Construction Network
3463 Yonge St.
Toronto, Canada M4N 2N3

The Masters Corporation
12 Burtis Ave.
New Canaan, CT 06840

William McDonough Architects
116 E. 27th St.
New York, NY 10016

Mary Oetzel
3202 W. Anderson La.
Austin, TX 78757

Susan Orena
Kitchens by Herzenberg
261 Little River Rd.
Westfield, MA 01085

Victoria Schomer
PO Box 2836
Mill Valley, CA 94942

Bruce Small
Sunnyhill Farm
RR #1
Goodwood, Canada L0C 1A0

Preston Sturgis Associates
1827 Powers Ferry Rd., Bldg. 11
Marietta, GA 30067

Carol Venolla
PO Box 694
39000 S Hwy. 1
Gualala, CA 95445

Rodney Wright & Associates
Rt 4, Box 175 A
Osseo, WI 54758

PUBLICATIONS

Consumer Guide to Home Energy Savings, Alex Wilson and John Morrill (American Association for an Energy Efficient Economy) ACEEE, 2124 Kittredge St. #95, Berekely, CA 94704 $6.95 ppd.

Healthier Home Plans, (Columbia Design Group, 1994) Columbia Design Group, PO Box 16554, Portland, OR 97216, $19.95 ppd.

Healing Environments, Carol Venolia (Celestial Arts, 1988)

Healthy House Building, John Bower (Healthy House Institute, 1993) Healthy House Institute, 7471 N. Shiloh Rd., Unionville, IN 47468, $21.95 ppd.

The Green Pages: The Contract Interior Designer's Guide to Environmentally Responsible Products and Services, Andrew Fuston and Kim Plaskon Nadel (1993) The Green Pages, 74 Trinity Place, New York, NY 10006, $39.00 ppd.

Healthy Houses, Clint Wood and Debra Lynn Dadd (Guarantee Press) Guarantee Press, 4720 Montgomery Ln, Bethesda, MD 20814, $22.95ppd.

The Natural House Book, David Pearson (Fireside Books, 1989)

Your Home, Your Health and Well Being, David Rosseau, W. J. Rea M.D., and Jean Enwright (Hartley and Marks, Vancouver, BC, 1988)

PERIODICALS

Building with Nature
PO Box 369
Gualala, CA 95445

Environmental Building News
RR 1, Box 161
Brattleboro, VT 05301

Interior Concerns Newsletter
PO Box 2386
Mill Valley, CA 94942

Note: To help make the Demonstration Kitchen project a reality, I solicited assistance from industry. Certain companies, marked with an asterisk (*) above, were asked to donate specific equipment or materials to the project that represented a superior design, or that would enhance wholefoods cooking, save energy, or make the kitchen safer or more comfortable. This was the first time I had utilized such resources, and I am very grateful to the kitchen's sponsors for their support. I want to make it clear, though, that all of these items were carefully selected beforehand for their suitability, not because of any business association with the manufacturer. As a matter of fact, when companies with equipment I thought exemplary did not accede to my request, I purchased the item. This procedure is quite different from many design projects we often see, which are — without any disclosure — underwritten by manufacturers to promote their products.

**For readers' information, in March 1994 I was engaged by the Whirlpool Corporation to be a spokesperson for the SERP refrigerator. (The SERP refrigerator had already been included in the galleys of the Second Edition of *The Smart Kitchen* based on merit alone.)

The SERP refrigerator gets its name from the Super Efficient Refrigerator Program. This program, created by a consortium of 24 public and private utilities, offered a $30 million prize to any appliance manufacturer who would produce a refrigerator both free of CFCs and 25 percent more efficient than Federal standards. The prize money will help make the SERP more affordable. This strategy was developed because it is less expensive and more advantageous to the utilities to reduce the demand for electricity than it was to build new power plants.

The "golden carrot," as the prize came to be known, was won by the Whirlpool Corporation. In April 1994, Whirlpool began marketing the SERP refrigerators under the KitchenAid, Whirlpool, and Kenmore labels. SERP refrigerators are currently available only in states serviced by the sponsoring utilities: parts of Arizona, California, Connecticut, Maine, Maryland, Massachusetts, Minnesota, New Jersey, New York, Oregon, and Wisconsin.

BIBLIOGRAPHY

PART I. HUMAN COMFORT AND SAFETY

Chapter 1. Kitchen Counters

Afflerbach, Raymond W. *Kitchen Specialist Training Manual.* Hacketstown, NJ: American Institute of Kitchen Dealers, 1975.

Cheever, Ellen and Associates. "Lifestyle Changes in the 1980s Will Affect Kitchen and Bath Design." *Kitchen & Bath Business,* January 1985.

Clark, Sam. *The Motion-Minded Kitchen.* Boston: Houghton Mifflin Co., 1983.

Conran, Terence. *The Kitchen Book.* New York: Crown Publishers Inc., 1977.

Cornell University Housing Research Center. *The Cornell Kitchen.* Ithaca, NY: New York State College of Home Economics, 1952.

Crowther, Richard L. "Ecology and Architecture." *Environ,* no. 7, 1988.

Habeeb, Virginia T., and Ralph Treves. Remodeling Your Kitchen and Building Your Own Cabinets. New York: Popular Science Books/Harper & Row, 1974.

Homemakers' Guide to Stainless Steel. American Iron and Steel Institute, Committee of Stainless Steel Producers, April 1979.

Jones, Judith Lea, and Jon P. Weimer. *Food Safety: Homemakers' Attitudes and Practices.* National Economic Analysis Division, Economic Research Service, U.S. Department of Agriculture. Agricultural Economic Report 360. (January 1977).

Kitchen Planning Standards, C5.32. University of Illinois, Small Homes Council—Building Research Council, 1981.

Krengel, James W. "Design Adaptable Kitchens for Clients' Changing Families." *Kitchen & Bath Business,* September 1988.

Martin, Linda. "For Countertops: Old, New and Newly Fashionable Materials." *The New York Times,* January 5, 1985.

Nutrition Week. "Bacteria Laden Meat: Who Is to Blame?" Community Nutrition Institute, April 9, 1987.

Nutrition Week. "Letters to the Editor." Community Nutrition Institute, May 22, 1987.

Russel, James E. *Advanced Kitchens.* Passaic, NJ: Creative Homeowner Press, 1981.

Snow, Jane Moss. *Kitchens.* Washington, DC: National Association of Home Builders of the U.S., 1987.

Steidl, Rose E. *Functional Kitchens.* Ithaca, NY: Cooperative Extension of the Northeast States, 1980.

Chapter 2. Cabinets

Afflerbach, Raymond W., *Kitchen Specialist Training Manual.* Hacketstown, NJ: American Institute of Kitchen Dealers, 1975.

Beltsville Energy Saving Kitchen: Design No. 3. U.S. Department of Agriculture, Leaflet No. 518, 1963.

Bliss, Steve. "Breathing Free, Part I." *Solar Age,* November 1984.

————. "Breathing Free, Part II. *Solar Age,* December 1984.

Brobeck, Stephen, and Anne C. Averyt. *The Product Safety Book.* New York: E. P. Dutton, Inc., 1983.

Clark, Sam. *The Motion-Minded Kitchen.* Boston: Houghton Mifflin Co., 1983.

Conran, Terence. *The Kitchen Book.* New York: Crown Publishers Inc., 1977.

Cornell University Housing Research Center. *The Cornell Kitchen.* Ithaca, NY: New York State College of Home Economics, 1953.

Dadd, Debra Lynn. *Nontoxic and Natural.* Boston: Houghton Mifflin Co., 1984.

————. *The Nontoxic Home.* Boston: Houghton Mifflin Co., 1986.

du Pont, Peter and John Morrill. *Residential Indoor Air Quality and Energy Efficiency.* Washington, DC: American Council for An Energy Efficient Economy and National Rural Electric Cooperative Association, 1988 (unpublished draft).

Feiffer, Guy O., and Casimer M. Nikel, eds. *The Household Environment and Chronic Illness.* Springfield, IL: Charles C. Thomas, 1980.

Foerstner, Abigail. "How to Buy Kitchen Cabinets." *The Family Handyman,* July/August 1985.

"Formaldehyde." *CIP Bulletin.* St. Louis, MO: Center for the Biology of Natural Systems, May 1980.

Habeeb, Virginia T., and Ralph Treves. *Remodeling Your Kitchen and Building Your Own Cabinets.* New York: Popular Science Books/Harper & Row, 1974.

Holm, Peter, with Jennifer Serrano. "Recipe for a Healthful Kitchen." *East West,* March 1987.

Jayess, R. "Designing Your Kitchen." *Lifestyle,* October 9, 1983.

Kitchen Planning Standards, C5.32. University of Illinois, Small Homes Council—Building Research Council, 1981.

"Particleboard Emission Standards." *Progressive Builder,* April 1985.

"Questions and Answers about Formaldehyde." *Your House and Your Health*. Plymouth Meeting, PA: National Indoor Environmental Institute, 1983.

"Questions and Answers on Pressed Wood Products." Washington, DC: U.S. Consumer Product Safety Commission.

Randegger, Ed and Zee. "A New Look at Formaldehyde and Health." *Environ*, no. 5, Fall/Winter 1986/87.

Randegger, Suzanne. "Formaldehyde and Health." *Environ*, no. 5, Fall-Winter 1986/87.

"Reducing Formaldehyde Levels." *Environ*, no. 5, Fall/Winter 1986/87.

Russel, James E. *Advanced Kitchens*. Passaic, NJ: Creative Homeowner Press, 1981.

Shabecoff, Philip. "Formaldehyde Found a Cancer Hazard." *The New York Times*, April 17, 1987.

Small, Bruce M. "Studies on Indoor Air Quality in Canadian Homes." Goodwood, Ontario (Canada): Bruce M. Small and Associates, Ltd., 1985.

Snow, Jane Moss. *Kitchens*. Washington, DC: National Association of Home Builders of the U.S., 1987.

Sondrostrom, Neil. "How to Work with a Kitchen Cabinetmaker." *Family Handyman*, July/August 1983.

"Status of the UFFI Ban." Washington, DC: U.S. Consumer Product Safety Commission, 1983.

Steidl, Rose E. *Functional Kitchens*. Ithaca, NY: Cooperative Extension of the Northeast States, 1980.

U.S. Consumer Product Safety Commission. *Questions and Answers on Pressed Wood Products*. Washington, DC: GPO, 1984.

―――. *Status of the UFFI Ban*. Washington, DC: GPO, July 22, 1983.

U.S. Department of Agriculture. *Easy-to-Build Kitchen Cabinets*. Home and Garden Bulletin, no. 18. Washington, DC: GPO, March 1952, January 1958.

Zamm, Alfred V., M.D., with Robert Gannon. *Why Your House May Endanger Your Health*. New York: Simon and Shuster, 1980.

Chapter 3. Sinks

Boffey, Philip. "After Years of Cleanup, Lead Poisoning Persists as a Threat to Health." *The New York Times*, September 1, 1988.

Cheever, Ellen. "Lifestyle Changes in the 1980s Will Effect Kitchen and Bath Design." *Kitchen & Bath Business*, January 1985.

Cornell University Housing Research Center. *The Cornell Kitchen*. Ithaca, NY: New York State College of Home Economics, 1952.

Conran, Terence. *The Kitchen Book*. New York: Crown Publishers Inc., 1977.

Consumer Guide, editors of. *Whole Kitchen Catalogue*. New York: A Fireside Book/Simon and Shuster, 1978.

Farallones Institute. *The Integral Urban House*. San Francisco: Sierra Club Books, 1979.

Habeeb, Virginia T., and Ralph Treves. *Remodeling Your Kitchen and Building Your Own Cabinets*. New York: Popular Science Books/Harper & Row, 1974.

"New Data Show Continued Risk of Lead Poisoning." *The New York Times*, July 19, 1988.

Shabecoff, Philip. "Coping with Lead in Drinking Water." *The New York Times*, November 13, 1986.

Sullivan, Walter. "Acidity Termed a Lead Hazard in Jersey Water." *The New York Times*, May 19, 1987.

Chapter 4. Lighting and Thermal Comfort

Beral, Valerie, et al. "Malignant Melanoma and Exposure to Fluorescent Lighting at Work." *The Lancet*, August 7, 1982.

Brody, Jane E. "From Fertility to Mood, Sunlight Found to Affect Human Biology." *The New York Times*, June 23, 1981.

"Color Power." *Building Profit*, Winter 1986/87.

Conran, Terence. *The Kitchen Book*. New York: Crown Publishers Inc., 1977.

Design for Energy Conservation with Skylights. Chicago: Architectural Aluminum Manufacturers Association, 1981.

Effective U-Values for Skylights. Chicago: Architectural Aluminum Manufacturers Association, 1980.

Farallones Institute. *The Integral Urban House*. San Francisco: Sierra Club Books, 1979.

Harding, Tim, ed. *Tools for the Soft Path*. San Francisco: Friends of the Earth, 1979.

Kotzsch, Ronald E. "Bringing the Sun Indoors. *East West*, March 1989.

Leckie, Jim. *Other Homes and Garbage*. San Francisco: Sierra Club Books 1975.

McGuiness, P. J., et al. "The Effects of Illuminance on Tasks Performed in Domestic Kitchens." *Lighting Research and Technology* (United Kingdom) 15, no 1, 1983.

Ott, John N. *Health and Light*. Old Greenwich, CT.: Devin-Adair Co., 1973.

"Overcoming the Winter Blahs." *University of California, Berkeley Wellness Letter*. November 1985.

Ponte, Lowell. "How Artificial Light Effects Your Health." *Reader's Digest*, February 1981.

Rossbach, Sarah. "Interior Design with Feng Shui." *East West*, December 1987.

Sorcar, Prafulla C. *Energy Saving Lighting Systems*. New York: Van Nostrand Reinhold Co., 1982.

"35th Annual Electric Utility Industry Forecast." *Electrical World*, 198, no. 9. Sept. 1984.

Weiss, Peter. "Lighting the Way Towards More Efficient Lighting." *Home Energy*, January/February 1989.

Window Insulation—How to Sort Through the Options. Washington, DC: U.S. Department of Energy. National Center for Appropriate Technology.

Chapter 5. Acoustics and Noise Reduction

Berendt, Raymond D. and Edith L.R. Corliss. *Quieting: A Practical Guide*. Washington, DC: National Bureau of Standards, 1976.

Conran, Terence. *The Kitchen Book*. New York: Crown Publishers Inc., 1977.

Certified Home Ventilating Products Directory. Rolling Meadows, IL: Home Ventilating Institute, 1988.

Council Notes: Noise Control, F5.0. University of Illinois, Small Homes Council—Building Research Council, 1983.

Chapter 6. Flooring

Burns, Max. "Finishing Touches." *Harrowsmith*, May/June 1989.

Buyer's Guide. Memphis, TN: National Oak Flooring Manufacturers Association, n.d.

Carley, Rachel. "Decorating the Stylish Floor: Many New Options." *The New York Times*, January 15, 1987.

Conran, Terence. *The Kitchen Book*. New York: Crown Publishers Inc., 1977.

Dadd, Debra Lynn. *Nontoxic and Natural*. Boston: Houghton Mifflin Co., 1984.

"Questions and Answers about Formaldehyde." *Your House and Your Health*. Plymouth Meeting, PA: National Indoor Environmental Institute, 1983.

The Sunnyhill Research Centre Newsletter (Goodwood, Ontario), Fall 1987.

Wood Floor Care Guide. Memphis, TN: National Oak Flooring Manufacturers Association, n.d.

Zamm, Alfred V., M.D., with Robert Gannon. *Why Your House May Endanger Your Health*. New York: Simon and Shuster, 1980.

Chapter 7. Small Wonders in the Kitchen

"Computer in the Kitchen." *Nutrition Notes*. Washington, DC: National Dairy Council, 1981.

Journal of Dietetic Software, Spring 1985.

Journal of Nutrition Education (Society for Nutrition Education), June 1984.

Matzkin, Jonathan. "Nutrition Databases: Changing Your Diet to Improve Your Health," *PC Magazine*, January 31, 1989.

Trivette, Donald B. "Eating Healthy to Stay Fit: Two Programs Help You Keep Track of Your Daily Diet." *PC Magazine*, September 22, 1988.

Chapter 8. Safety

Brobeck, Stephen, and Anne C. Averyt. *The Product Safety Book*. New York: E. P. Dutton, Inc., 1983.

"Burns Associated with the Kitchen." *Burn Care and Rehabilitation*, March/April 1989.

Fields, Terri. "Kitchen Safety: The Most Important Recipe." *Weight Watchers*, April 1982.

Fire in Your Home. Quincy, MA: National Fire Protection Association, 1978.

"Fire Safety in the Home." *The Building Services Contractor*, n.d.

"Home Electricity Risks." *The New York Times*, May 8, 1985.

How Safe Is Your Kitchen? Tampa, FL: Shriners Burns Institute, n.d.

Locked Up/Poisons Prevent Tragedy. Poison Prevention Week Council, n.p. June 1984.

National Electric Code. Sec. 210–8. (a)(5). Ground-fault Circuit-Interrupter for Personnel.

Smith, Dennis. *Dennis Smith's Fire Safety Book*. New York: Bantam Books, 1983.

Stewart, Arlene. *Childproofing Your Home*. Reading, PA: Addison-Wesley Publishing Co., 1984.

"2.3 Million Poisonings Estimated In '83." *FDA Consumer*, March 1985.

U.S. Consumer Product Safety Commission. *CPSC Guide to Electrical Safety*. Washington, DC: GPO, 1983.

———. *Product Safety Fact Sheet*, no. 9. "Kitchen Ranges." Washington, DC: GPO, 1979.

———. *Product Safety Fact Sheet*, no. 16. "Extension Cords and Wall Outlets." Washington, DC: GPO, 1982.

PART II. APPLIANCES AND ENERGY EFFICIENCY

CHAPTER 9. REFRIGERATION

Agricultural Marketing Research Institute. *Storing Vegetables and Fruits in Basements, Cellars, Outbuildings, and Pits*. Home and Garden Bulletin no. 119. Washington, DC: GPO, 1973.

"Appliances No One Wants." *The New York Times*, October 1, 1988.

Atwan, Robert, Donald McQuade, and John W. Wright. *Edsels, Luckies, and Frigidaires*. New York: Dell Publishing Co., Inc., 1979.

Axell, Elyse. "Efficient Refrigerators: The Japanese Challenge." *Tools for the Soft Path* (Friends of the Earth), 1982.

Brown, Lester, et al. *State of the World 1988*. New York: W.W. Norton, 1988.

"City to Halt Appliance Pickup." *The* (Kingston) *Daily Freeman*, September 1988.

A Compendium of Utility-Sponsored Energy Efficiency Rebate Programs. Washington, DC: Consumer Energy Council of America Research Foundation and American Council for an Energy-Efficient Economy, 1987.

Cowan, Thomas. *Beyond the Kitchen*. Philadelphia: Running Press/A Quartro Book, 1985.

D'Alessandro, Bill. "Appliances for Cool Savings." *Solar Age*, December 1983.

Dudek, Daniel J. "Industry Needs Incentives Not to Pollute." *The New York Times*, November 16, 1986.

"Electronics Gain Acceptance." *Kitchen & Bath Business*, January 1985.

Erickson, Robert C. "Household Appliance Efficiency Improvements." La Jolla, CA: Science Applications, Inc., n.d.

Federal Engineering Administration. *Study of Energy Saving Options for Refrigerators and Water Heaters, Vol. I* (Chart Ref. pp.122–23), Arthur D. Little, Inc., May 1977.

Flavin, Christopher and Alan B. Durning. "Don't Dim the Lights on the Energy Revolution." *Across the Board*, May 1988.

" 'Freezer' in Single-Door Refrigerator Has Limited Function." *MACAP Consumer Bulletin*. Chicago: The Major Appliance Consumer Action Panel, no. 6, February 1984.

Geller, E. Scott, ed. *Preserving the Environment: New Strategies for Behavior Change*. New York: Pergamon Press, 1982.

Geller, Howard S. "Efficient Residential Appliances and Space Conditioning Equipment: Current Savings Potential, Cost Effectiveness and Research Needs." Paper presented at the 1984 ACEEE Summer Study on Energy Efficient Buildings.

———. *Energy Efficient Appliance*. Washington, DC: American Council for an Energy-Efficient Economy, June 1983.

———. *Energy Efficient Appliance, 1986 Update*. Paper presented at the ACEEE Summer Study on Energy Efficiency in Buildings, Santa Cruz, CA, August 1986.

———. "National Appliance Efficiency Standards: Utility and Consumer Impacts." Paper prepared for the Third National Conference on Utility DSM Programs, Houston, TX, June 16–18, 1987.

———. "Progress in the Energy Efficiency of Residential Appliances and Space Conditioning Equipment." *Energy Sources: Conservation and Renewables*. American Institute of Physics, 1985.

Goldstein, David B. "Refrigerator Reform: Guidelines for Energy Gluttons." *Technology Review*, February/March 1983.

Goldstein, David B., and Arthur H. Rosenfeld. *Energy Conservation in Home Appliances through Comparison Shopping: Facts and Fact Sheets*. Berkeley, CA: University of California, 1978.

Hafemeister, D., Henry Kelly, and Barbari Levi. "Energy Sources: Conservation and Renewables." *AIP Conference Proceedings*. Washington, DC: American Institute of Physics, 1985.

Hobbs, Peter S. "How to 'Extra Insulate' Your Freezer." Ramona, CA: self-published, 1981.

Keough, Bill. "Improving the Icebox." *New Shelter*, January 1981.

Kirk and Othmer, eds. *Encyclopedia of Chemical Technology, Vol. II*. New York: John Wiley & Son, 1984.

Kukula, Kathy. "Keeping the Fridge Cool." *New Shelter*, April 1984.

Markey, Edward J. "To the Editor." *The New York Times*, July 24, 1988.

The Most Energy-Efficient Appliances. Washington, DC: American Council for an Energy-Efficient Economy, 1988.

"National Appliance Energy Conservation Act of 1987." P.L. 100–12, March 17, 1987 (42 USC 6291).

"Refrigerator/Freezers." *Consumer Reports*, February 1980.

"Refrigerators." *Consumer Reports*, March 1988.

"Refrigerators Energy Efficiency and Consumption Trends." Chicago: Association of Home Appliance Manufacturers, July 18, 1988.

Rosenfeld, Arthur H., Ph.D. "Energy Conservation, Competition and National Security." *Strategic Planning and Energy Management Journal* 8, no. 1, 1988, pp. 5–30.

Rothchild, John. *Stop Burning Your Money*. New York: Random House, 1981.

Schlussler, Larry, Ph.D. *Sun Frost*™. Arcata, CA: Sales Brochure, n.d.

"The Search for Ozone-Friendly Refrigerants." *Discover*, July 1988.

Shabecoff, Philip. "Suit Is Filed to Bar Possible Harm to Earth's Protective Ozone Layer." *The New York Times*, November 28, 1984.

Silvers, Donald. "Refrigerator Should Be on Top and Freezer on the Bottom." *Kitchen & Bath Business*, January 1988.

Villelli, Richard. Bonners Ferry, ID: personal communication, September 21, 1988, and January 16, 1989.

Williams, H., Gautam S. Dutt, and Howard S. Geller. "Future Energy Savings in U.S. Housing." *American Review of Energy* 8, 1983.

Yepsen, Roger B., Jr., and the editors of Rodale Press. *Home Food Systems*. Emmaus, PA: Rodale Press Inc., 1981.

Your Personal Guide to Buying an Energy-Efficient Refrigerator. New York: Consolidated Edison, 1986.

Chapter 10. Dishwashing

Farallones Institute. *The Integral Urban House*. San Francisco: Sierra Club Books, 1979.

Geller, Howard S. "Progress in the Energy Efficiency of Residential Appliances and Space Conditioning Equipment." *Energy Sources: Conservation and Renewables*. American Institute of Physics, 1985.

Gillespie, Mary. "Are You a 'Water Waster'? Take a Lesson from Your Dishwasher. *Home Appliance NewsLine*, September 1988.

———. "Will the Drought Break the Pre-Rinsing Habit?" *Home Appliance NewsLine*, September 1988.

"Heat Up Dishwashing Performance." *Changing Times*, November 1988.

The Most Energy-Efficient Appliances. Washington, DC: American Council for an Energy-Efficient Economy, 1988.

Rothchild, John. *Stop Burning Your Money*. New York: Random House, 1981.

Saving Energy with Your Dishwasher. Chicago: Association of Home Appliance Manufacturers, April 1982.

Chapter 11. Cooking

AGA. Sales Brochure. Stowe, VT.

Amana Model RS415T Use and Care Manual. Amana, IA: Amana Refrigeration, Inc., 1987.

"Ask the Experts." *Tufts University Diet & Nutrition Letter*. 3, no. 3, May 1985.

Bacm, Richard. *The Forgotten Art of Building and Using a Brick Bake Oven*. Dublin, CT: Yankee, Inc., 1979.

Becker, Robert O., M.D., and Gary Selden. *The Body Electric*. New York: Quill/WIlliam Morrow & Co., 1985.

Bingham, Joan, and Dolores Riccio. "Use Your Range for All It's Worth." *The Energy Crunch Cookbook*. Radnor, PA: Chilton Book Co., 1979.

Bliss, Steve. "Breathing Free, Part II." *Solar Age*, December 1984.

Brobeck, Stephen, and Anne C. Averyt. *The Product Safety Book*. New York: E. P. Dutton, Inc., 1983.

Britain, Valorie A. "Microwave Oven Labeling." *FDA Consumer*, July-August 1975.

Brown, Peggy. "A Stove for Serious Cooks." *Newsday*, May 8, 1986.

Burns Associated with Microwave Ovens. Shriners Burns Institute, 1988, 1989.

Cheever, Ellen. "Consider Safety and Ventilation When Installing a Commercial Range At Home." *Kitchen & Bath Business*, February 1984.

Clark, John W. "Letters to the Editor." *New Shelter*, December 1984.

Code of Federal Regulations, Title 21, Sec. 1002.30, 1002.31, 1002.40, 1002.41, 1030.10.

Conran, Terence. *The Kitchen Book*. New York: Crown Publishers Inc., 1977.

Dadd, Debra Lynn. *The Nontoxic Home*. Boston: Houghton Mifflin Co., 1986.

Deacon, Richard. *Richard Deacon's Microwave Cookbook*. Los Angeles: HP Books. 1977.

"Do Microwaves Cause Cancer?" *Science*, November 1984.

du Pont, Peter and John Morrill. *Residential Indoor Air Quality and Energy Efficiency*. Washington, DC: American Council for An Energy Efficient Economy and National Rural Electric Cooperative Association, 1988 (unpublished draft).

Erlander, Stig R., Ph.D. "Microwaves: Cancer Producing Ovens?" *A Diet to End Diseases*, vol. 1, no. 11, 1981.

Fechter, J. V., and L. G. Porter. *Kitchen Range Consumption*. Washington, DC: U.S. Department of Energy, Office of Conservation, June 1978, (issued March 1979).

Feiffer, Guy O., and Casimer M. Nikel, eds. *The Household Environment and Chronic Illness*. Springfield, IL: Charles C. Thomas, 1980.

Freedom of Information Act Request F88-29162. "All Reports on Microwave Ovens." Rockville, MD: FDA, 1988.

Freedom of Information Act Request S-901088. "Microwave Malfunctions, Complaints and Injuries from Microwaves." Washington, DC: U.S. Consumer Product Safety Commission, 1989.

Gas Ranges. Arlington, VA: Gas Appliance Manufacturers Association, n.d.

Geller, Howard S. "Progress in the Energy Efficiency of Residential Appliances and Space Conditioning Equipment." *Energy Sources: Conservation and Renewables*. American Institute of Physics, 1985.

Grant, E. H. "Biological Effects of Radiowaves and Microwaves." *Phys. Technol.* 11., 1980.

Henkenius, Merle. "Install a Separate Circuit for Your Microwave." *Workbench*, 44:328, September/October 1988.

Herman, William A., and Donald M. Witters, Jr. *Inexpensive Microwave Survey Instruments: An Evaluation*. HEW Publication (FDA) 80–8102, November 1989.

"How Much Electricity Do Microwave Ovens Save?" *Energy Auditor and Retrofitter*, November/December 1987.

"How Safe Is the Four-Minute Baked Potato?" *Current Health*, January 1985.

How to Cook without Sweating It. SCE&G Energy Information Center, n.d.

How to Get the Best from Your Microwave Oven. Louisville, KY: General Electric, Model JE1425G.

How to Get the Best from Your Microwave Oven. Louisville, KY: Hotpoint, Model RE1450.

"Indoor Air Pollution." *Consumer Reports*, October 1985.

Indoor Air Pollution: A Serious Health Hazard. Plymouth Meeting, PA: National Indoor Environmental Institute, 1983.

Informational Requirements for Cookbooks and User and Service Manuals. Silver Spring, MD: FDA, 1988.

Jacobs, Brian W. "The Politics of Radiation When Public Health and the Nuclear Industry Collide." *Greenpeace*, July/August 1988.

Kafka, Barbara. *Microwave Gourmet*. New York: William Morrow & Co., 1987.

Kent, Rosemary. "A Status-Symbol Stove for the U.S." *New York Times*, January 23, 1986.

Kreschodek, Margie. *Guaranteed Fool-Proof Microwave Cookbook*. New York: Bantam Books, 1987.

Kummer, Corby. "Fast Fish." *Atlantic*, December 1987.

Leviton, Richard. "Rating the Cooking Fuels." *East West*, June 1987.

Lorenz, K., and W. Dilsaver. "Microwave Heating of Food Materials at Various Altitudes." *Journal of Food Science* 41 (1976).

"Make Sure LP-Gas Appliances Are Properly Adjusted by Installer." *Consumer Bulletin*. Chicago: The Major Appliance Consumer Action Panel, no. 9, December 1985.

Maley, Matthew P., "Burns from Microwave Ovens" (letter). *The Lancet*, May 17, 1987.

Maley, Matthew P. "Microwave Oven Associated Burns." *Rekindle*, December 1986.

"Mastering Meat and Poultry in the Microwave." *USDA News Feature*. Washington, DC: USDA, October 26, 1987.

Microwave Burn Prevention. Tampa, FL: Shriners Burns Institute, 1988.

Microwave Emission in Excess of the Standard as a Result of Improper Repair Procedure. Rockville, MD: HEW Doc. 3198-MA, n.d.

The Microwave Oven. Chicago: Association of Home Appliance Manufacturers, 1979.

Microwave Oven Radiation. Rockville, MD: HHS publication no. (FDA) 80-8120.

Microwave Oven User's Guide. Newton, IA: The Maytag Company, form no. 225FE.

"Microwave Ovens." *Consumer Reports*, March 1981.

"Microwave Ovens." *Consumer Reports*, January 1988.

"Microwaves and Radiowaves." *CIP Bulletin*. St. Louis, MO: Center for the Biology of Natural Systems, 1970.

The Microwave Tidal Wave. Camden, NJ: Campbell Microwave Institute, n.d.

"Microwaves: A New Approach to Cooking." *Consumer Close-ups*. New York: Cooperative Extension, 1973.

"Microwaving Your Vitamins." *University of California, Berkeley Wellness Newsletter* 2, issue 8, May 1986.

"The New Wave in Microwave Ovens." *Consumer Reports*, November 1985.

Panasonic Operating Instructions. Secaucus, NJ: Matsushita Electric Industrial Co., Ltd., 1986, Model NN-7606.

Potential Chemical Interaction on Safety Interlock Switches. Silver Spring, MD: Department of Health and Human Services, FDA, January 25, 1988.

"Radiation Control for Health and Safety Act of 1968." Public Law 90–602. 90th Congress, HR 10790, October 18, 1968.

Raloff, Janet. "Cleaner Cooking with Gas." *Science News* 125, January 14, 1984.

Rawlings, Roger. "Waste Watchers." *New Shelter*, January 1981.

Repke, Sarah E. "Energy Costs in the Kitchen." *Good Housekeeping* 190, no. 3, March 1980.

The Safe Food Book. Washington, DC: USDA, Food Safety and Inspection Service, Home and Garden Bulletin no. 241 (sightly revised June 1985).

Safeway's Nutrition Awareness Program. "The Wave of the Future Is Basic Microwaving." Oakland, CA: Safeway Stores, Inc., 1983.

Sass, Lorna. "Cooking on an Open Hearth: An Echo of the 18th Century." *The New York Times*, March 5, 1980.

Spengler, John D., and Ken Sexton. "Indoor Air Pollution: A Public Health Perspective." *Science*, July 1983.

Shute, Nancy. "The Other Kind of Radiation." *American Health*, July/August 1986.

Small, Bruce M. "Studies on Indoor Air Quality in Canadian Homes." Goodwood, Ontario (Canada): Bruce M. Small and Associates, Ltd., 1985.

Smay, V. Elaine. "Now: Non-polluting Gas Ranges." *Popular Science*, September 1984.

Spengler, John D., and Ken Sexton. "Indoor Air Pollution: A Public Health Perspective." *Science*, July 1983.

"Stay Away from Home Canning Equipment for Microwave Ovens." Missouri Cooperative Extension Service News Release, June 9, 1988.

Steneck, Nicholas H., et al. "The Origins of U.S. Safety Standards for Microwave Radiation." *Science*, June 1980.

U.S. Department of Agriculture. *Beltsville Energy-Saving Kitchen*, Leaflet nos. 418, 463, 518. Washington, DC: GPO, August 1957, April 1961, and February 1963.

Use and Care Guide. Benton Harbor, MI: Whirlpool Corporation, Model MW8500XS, 1987.

Use and Care Manual. Topton, PA: Caloric Corporation, Microwave Oven MPS218.

Venola, Carol. *Healing Environments*. Berkeley, CA: Celestial Arts, 1988.

Verdon, Rene and Jacqueline Mallorca. *Convection Cuisine*. New York: Hearst Books, 1988.

Vogel, Carol. "The Commercial Kitchen at Home: Pros and Cons." *The New York Times*, December 2, 1982.

Voss, G. "Prof Raises Call for Safety Checks of Microwave Ovens in Resale Market." *Appliance Service News*, December 1979.

Wells, Patricia. "Energy Cut in Kitchen of Future." *The New York Times*, February 13, 1980.

"When It Comes to Microwave Ovens Everybody's the Cook." Camden, NJ: Campbell Microwave Institute. n.d.

Zamm, Alfred V., M.D., with Robert Gannon. *Why Your House May Endanger Your Health*. New York: Simon and Shuster, 1980.

PART III. AIR AND WATER QUALITY, WASTE DISPOSAL AND FOOD PRODUCTION

CHAPTER 12. VENTILATION

Bales, Erv, and Heinz Trechsel. "Experts Mull Moisture Problems." *Solar Age: Progressive Builder*, April 1985.

Bliss, Steve. "Breathing Free, Part I." *Solar Age*, November 1984.

———. "Breathing Free, Part II." *Solar Age*, December 1984.

Certified Home Ventilating Products Directory. Rolling Meadows, IL: Home Ventilating Institute, 1988.

Clapp, David E. and Charles E. Neelley. "A Program for Rating the Loudness of Consumer Fan Products." *Noise Control Engineering*, July/August 1978.

Donahue, Russ. "History of Ventilation." Speech notes. Richardson, TX: Vent-A-Hood, n.d.

du Pont, Peter and John Morrill. *Residential Indoor Air Quality and Energy Efficiency*. Washington, DC: American Council for An Energy Efficient Economy and National Rural Electric Cooperative Association, 1988 (unpublished draft).

"Formaldehyde." *CIP Bulletin*. St. Louis, MO: Center for the Biology of Natural Systems, May 1980.

Freundlich, Naomi J. "Purify Air the Space-Station Way: With Plants." *Popular Science*, August 1986.

"Heat-Recovery Ventilators." *Consumer Reports*, October 1985.

Home Ventilating Guide. Rolling Meadows, IL: Home Ventilating Institute, 1980.

"Indoor Air Pollution." *Consumer Reports*, October 1985.

"Indoor Air Pollution: An Issue Backgrounder." *Solar Age*, December, 1983.

"Indoor Air Pollution: A Serious Health Hazard." Plymouth Meeting, PA: National Indoor Environmental Institute, 1983.

Karg, Richard. "Tips and Cautions about Air Exchangers." *Solar Age*, October 1984.

Kull, Kathie. "Fresh Air Indoors." *Practical Homeowner*, September 1988.

Lipp, Louie. "Save Energy in Your School Kitchen." *American School and University*, July 1978.

Lohmeier, Lynne,Ph.D. "Indoor Pollution Alert." *East West*, March 1987.

Nero, Anthony V., Jr. "Clean Indoor Air." *New Shelter*, February 1985.

————. "Controlling Indoor Air Pollution." *Scientific American* 258, no. 5, May 1988.

"Particleboard Emission Standards." *Progressive Builder*, April 1985.

"The Perils of Indoor Air Pollution." *Current Health*, January 1986.

Randegger, Suzanne and Ed. "A Breath of Fresh Air." *Homebuilding & Remodeling Resource*, November/December 1988.

Shabecoff, Philip. "Formaldehyde Found a Cancer Hazard." *The New York Times*, April 17, 1987.

————. "U.S. Calls 11 Toxic Air Pollutants Bigger Threat Indoors Than Out." *The New York Times*, June 11, 1985.

————. "The In-House Air Pollution Threat." *The New York Times*, July 14, l985.

Shurcliff, William A. *Air-to-Air Heat Exchangers for Houses*. Andover, MA: Brick House Publishing Company, 1982.

Small, Bruce M. "Studies on Indoor Air Quality in Canadian Homes." Goodwood, Ontario (Canada): Bruce M. Small and Associates, Ltd., 1985.

Spengler, John D., and Steven D. Colome. "The In's and Out's of Air Pollution." *Technology Review*, August/September 1982.

Spengler, John D., and Ken Sexton. "Indoor Air Pollution: A Public Health Perspective." *Science*, July 1983.

"A Test of Small Air Cleaners." *New Shelter*, July/August 1982.

Vapor Removal from Cooking Equipment. Quincy, MA: National Fire Protection Association.

Wallace, Lance, et al. "Personal Exposures, Outdoor Concentrations, and Breath Levels of Toxic Air Pollutants Measured for 425 Persons in Urban, Suburban and Rural Areas." Paper presented to the Air Pollution Control Association, San Francisco, CA, June 25, 1984.

Wilford, John Noble. "The Common House Plant Does Its Bit for Cleaner Air." *The New York Times*, July 26, 1988.

Zamm, Alfred V., M.D., with Robert Gannon. *Why Your House May Endanger Your Health*. New York: Simon and Shuster, 1980.

Chapter 13. Water Purity, Conservation, and Heating

"Both Indoor and Outdoor Water Conservation Is Vital during Nationwide Drought." Chicago: Plumbing Heating Cooling Information Bureau, June 1988.

"Chlorinated Water a Potential Carcinogen." *Nutrition Week* (Washington, DC: Community Nutrition Institute), July 28, 1988.

"Clean Water at Your Tap." *New Shelter*, October 1983.

Coffel, Steve. "But Not a Drop to Drink." *New Age Journal*, January/February 1989.

Council Notes: Water Conservation, C1.6. University of Illinois, Small Homes Council—Building Research Council, 1977.

"Endless Hot Water." *Energy Auditor & Retrofitter*, January/February 1986.

Federal Engineering Administration. *Study of Energy Saving Options for Refrigerators and Water Heaters, Vol. I* (Chart Ref., pp. 122–23). Arthur D. Little, Inc., May 1977.

Geller, E. Scott, ed. *Preserving the Environment: New Strategies for Behavior Change*. New York: Pergamon Press, 1982.

Geller, Howard S. *Energy Efficient Appliance: 1986 Update*. Paper presented at the ACEEE Summer Study on Energy Efficiency in Buildings, Santa Cruz, CA, August 1986.

————. "Progress in the Energy Efficiency of Residential Appliances and Space Conditioning Equipment." *Energy Sources: Conservation and Renewables*. n.p. American Institute of Physics, 1985.

"Good Product Review." *Solar Age*, June 1983.

Gottlieb, Robert. *A Life of Its Own: The Politics and Power of Water*. San Diego, CA: Harcourt Brace Javonovich, 1988.

King, Jonathan. *The Poisoning of America's Drinking Water—How Government and Industry Allowed It to Happen, and What You Can Do to Insure a Safe Supply in the Home*. Emmaus, PA: Rodale Press, 1985.

Kukula, Kathy. "Hot Water on Demand." *Popular Science*, February 1982.

LaRue,James and Alan Wasco. "Lead in Drinking Water." Cleveland: *Housemending Notebook*, 1987.

Meier, Alan. "Degradation of Water Heater Performance." *Energy Auditor & Retrofitter*, January/February 1987.

————. "Saving Water Heating Energy." *Energy Auditor & Retrofitter*, January/February 1985.

Murray, Allison. "As 40% of U.S. Counties Go Dry, Laws Call for Water-Saving Products." *Kitchen & Bath Business*, August 1988.

————. "Water Treatment Market Hits $3.5 Billion Mark." *Kitchen & Bath Business*, August 1988.

Powell, Evan. "Tankless Water Heaters." *Popular Science*, February 1982.

Rose, Harry, and Amy Pinkerton. *The Energy Crisis, Conservation and Solar*. Ann Arbor, MI: Ann Arbor Science, 1981.

Shabecoff, Philip. "Permanent Global Water Shortage Foreseen." *The New York Times*, September 22, 1985.

————. "Regulation Called a Boon for Clean Water, But Pollution Remains a Threat." *The New York Times*, May 13, 1985.

"Selection of Home Drinking Water Units for Phase 3 of EPA/GSRI Contract Study #68-01-4766," n.p., October 1981.

U.S. Department of Housing and Urban Development. *Hot Water from the Sun*. Rockville, MD: National Solar Heating and Cooling Information Center, 1980.

————. *Solar Factsheet*. Rockville, MD: National Solar Heating and Cooling Information Center, 1980.

Water: It's What We Make It. Lisle, IL: Water Quality Association, 1988.

Wing, Charlie. *House Warming*. Boston: Little, Brown and Company, 1983.

Chapter 14. Recycling Kitchen Wastes

Jabs, Carolyn. "Composting in an Apartment." *The New York Times*, June 24, 1979.

Partsch, Bill. "Kitchens Need Fresh Design Ideas to Deal with Rotten Trash Ideas." *Kitchen & Bath Business*, November 1988.

Rawlings, Roger. "Independent Kitchens: The Jantzen Example." *New Shelter*, January 1981.

Householder's Recycling Guide: A Game Plan. New York State Department of Environmental Conservation, 1988.

Temporary Storage Of Organic Kitchen Wastes. Berkeley, CA: University of California Press, 1974.

Williams III, Gurney. "Kitchens That Recycle." *Practical Homeowner*, March 1989.

Yepsen, Roger B., Jr., and the editors of Rodale Press. *Home Food Systems*. Emmaus, PA: Rodale Press Inc., 1981.

Chapter 15. Food Production

MacManiman, Gen. *Dry It—You'll Like It*. Fall City, WA: Living Food Dehydrators, n.d.

Part IV: Planning the Kitchen

Afflerbach, Raymond W. *Kitchen Specialist Training Manual*. Hacketstown, NJ: American Institute of Kitchen Dealers, 1975.

Clark, Sam. *The Motion-Minded Kitchen*. Boston: Houghton Mifflin Co., 1983.

Conacher, Gwenn. *Kitchen Sense for Disabled People*. New York: Croom Helm Ltd./Routledge, Chapman and Hall, 1986.

Conran, Terence. *The Kitchen Book*. New York: Crown Publishers Inc., 1977.

Cornell University Housing Research Center. *The Cornell Kitchen*. Ithaca, NY: New York State College of Home Economics, 1953.

Cowan, Thomas. *Beyond the Kitchen: A Dreamer's Guide*. Philadelphia: Running Press, 1985.

Habeeb, Virginia T., and Ralph Treves. *Remodeling Your Kitchen and Building Your Own Cabinets*. New York: Popular Science Books/Harper & Row, 1974.

Jayess, R. "Designing Your Kitchen." *Lifestyle*, October 9, 1983.

Kitchen Planning Standards, C5.32. University of Illinois, Small Homes Council—Building Research Council, 1981.

Klein, Carol E., "12 Ways to Design for the Mobility Impaired." *Kitchen & Bath Business*, August 1988.

Lunt, Suzanne. *A Handbook for the Disabled*. New York: Charles Scribner & Son, 1982.

Russel, James E. *Advanced Kitchens*. Passaic, NJ: Creative Homeowner Press, 1981.

Snow, Jane Moss. *Kitchens*. Washington, DC: National Association of Home Builders of the U.S., 1987.

Steidl, Rose E. *Functional Kitchens*. Ithaca, NY: Cooperative Extension of the Northeast States, 1980.

Welsch, Roger L. "Unused Front Doors: Why Guests Head For The Kitchen." *The New York Times*, January 31, 1980.

Wilson, Beverly. "Plan a Smart Kitchen." *New Shelter*, April 1984.

General Reference

"An All-House Maintenance Manual." *New Shelter*, April 1983.

Beard, James, et al. *The Cook's Catalogue*. New York: Avon Books, 1975.

Brand, Stewart, ed. *The Whole Earth Catalog*. New York: Random House, 1980.

Celehar, Jane H. *Kitchens and Gadgets 1920 to 1950*. Des Moines, IA: Wallace-Homestead, 1982.

Chiogioli, Melvin H., and Eleanor N. Oura. *Energy Conservation in Commercial and Residential Buildings*. New York: Marcel Dekker, Inc., 1982.

Consumer Guide, editors of. *Whole Kitchen Catalogue*. New York: A Fireside Book/Simon and Shuster, 1978.

Consumer News. Pueblo, CO: Consumer Information Center, 1978.

Consumer Reports, editors of. *Money-Saving Guide to Energy in the Home*. Mount Vernon, NY: Consumers Union, 1978.

Consumer Reports 1983 Consumer Buying Guide. Mt. Vernon, NY: Consumers Union, 1982.

Consumers Research Handbook of Buying, Issue '78. Washington, NJ: Consumers' Research Inc., October 1977.

Crowther, Richard L. "Ecology and Architecture." *Environ*, no. 7, (1988).

Ditch, Steve. "Comment." *Kitchen & Bath Concepts*, January, 1988.

Energyworks, Inc. *Energy Efficient Products and Systems*. New York: John Wiley & Sons, 1983.

Fantel, Hans. "Electronic Comfort in 'House Future.'" *The New York Times*, August 25, 1983.

Giedion, Siegfried. *Mechanization Takes Command*. New York: Oxford University Press, 1948.

Farallones Institute. *The Integral Urban House*. San Francisco: Sierra Club Books, 1979.

Home Energy Products and Ideas. Laconia, NH: Gilford/Energy Publications, Inc., 1983.

"HM Readers Tell How They'd Improve Their Kitchens." *Home Mechanics*, February 1983.

Lifshey, Earl. *The Housewares Story*. Chicago: National Housewares Manufacturing Association, 1973.

McClintock, Mike. *The Home How-to Sourcebook*. New York: Charles Scribner's Sons, 1984.

Mees, Joan. "Revolution in the Kitchen." *Food Technology*, November 1984.

Messenger, Roger. *Residential Conservation Demonstration Program*. Florida Public Service Commission, 1984.

Objects For Preparing Food. Washington, DC and New York: Renwick Gallery and The Museum of Contemporary Crafts, 1972.

Papanek, Victor, and James Hennessey. *How Things Don't Work*. New York: Pantheon Books, 1977.

"Remodeling Ideas." *Better Homes and Gardens*, Fall 1983.

Robinson, Steven, and Fred S. Dubin. *The Energy-Efficient Home*. New York: Plume/New American Library, 1978.

Rodale's New Shelter, editors of. *Kitchens*. Emmaus: Rodale Press, 1986.

U.S. Department of Agriculture. *Food and Home Notes*. Washington, DC: GPO, 1974.

Ward, Joan S. "Critical Ergonomics Factors in Domestic Kitchen Design." *Ergonomics* (Department of Ergonomics and Cybernetics, University of Technology, England) 17, no. 2, 1974.

Weiss, Jeffrey. *Kitchen Antiques*. New York: Harper Colophon Books, 1980.

Welsch, Roger L. "Design Notebook." *The New York Times*, January 31, 1980.

Environmental Concerns

Dadd, Debra Lynn. *Nontoxic and Natural*. Boston: Houghton Mifflin Co., 1984.

———. *The Nontoxic Home*. Boston: Houghton Mifflin Co., 1986.

Feiffer, Guy O., and Casimer M. Nikel, eds. *The Household Environment and Chronic Illness*. Springfield, IL: Charles C. Thomas, 1980.

Holm, Peter, with Jennifer Serrano. "Recipe for a Healthful Kitchen." *East West*, March 1987.

Hughes, John R. "Allergy Free in Ottawa." *Fine Homebuilding*, January 1986.

Jones, Marjorie Hunt, R.N. *Allergy Self-Help Cookbook*. Emmaus, PA: Rodale Press, 1984.

Maciocha, Edward. "Baubiologie™ Germany's Surprising Natural-Home Movement." *East West*, March 1987.

Pell, Ed. "Our Industry Can't Duck Environmental Issues." *Kitchen & Bath Business*, November 1988.

Venolia, Carol. *Healing Environments*. Berkeley, CA: Celestial Arts, 1988.

Zamm, Alfred V., M.D., with Robert Gannon. *Why Your House May Endanger Your Health*. New York: Simon and Shuster, 1980.

INDEX

REUSE — The Next Step in Environmental Building

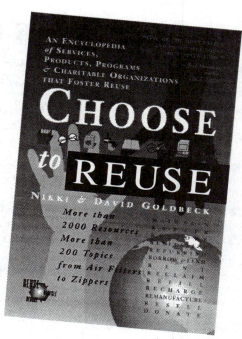

Reuse in building saves money, protects the environment by reducing construction debris and often yields rare and interesting building materials. Chemically sensitive individuals also appreciate the fact that used materials tend to outgas less.

Choose to Reuse is the first book to disclose the many ingenious but little-known ways to engage in reuse. Within the more than 200 topics and 2000 resources, there is a wealth of information that relates to green building and the home.

"[Using the resources in *Choose to Reuse*] ... we picked up a leaded glass window, a (new) brass faucet, a baluster and a post support, all at prices well below retail." — *This Old House Journal*

"Packed with information on how to reduce waste and conserve energy and resources." — *Country Living*

Sample Topics from *Choose to Reuse*

Air Filters	Fire Extinguishers	Light Bulbs
Appliances	Flooring	Lumber
Bathtubs	Furniture	Mattresses
Bedding	Garden Equipment	Mirrors
Building Materials	Hardware	Microwave Ovens
Carpets and Rugs	Home Furnishings	Paint
Caulking	Houses	Plumbing Supplies
Cleaning Supplies	Kitchen Cabinets	Refrigerators
Curtains and Drapes	Kitchen Counters	Roofing Materials
Doormats	Lamps and Lighting	Sandpaper
Fencing	Fixtures	Tools
	Lampshades	Water

What you can find in *Choose to Reuse*

More than 200 topics and 2000 resources ❏ Where to have just about anything fixed ❏ Sources of hard-to-find parts ❏ Where to rent things as an alternative to buying ❏ Sources of restoration and refurbishing ❏ Buying and selling in the used marketplace ❏ Sources of long-lasting goods ❏ Where to buy things made with reused materials ❏ Where to donate what you no long need (and get a tax deduction)

David Goldbeck has taught environmental design to professional and lay audiences in the U.S. and Canada, including such venues as the National Kitchen and Bath Association, the Austin Green Building Conference, Eco Expo, the International Kitchen & Bath Expo, Building the Sustainable Economy Conference, and at Ulster County Community College. He is President of Smart Kitchen Associates, a design and consulting firm.

★ All Ceres Press books are sold **satisfaction guaranteed** ★

BOOKS OF INTEREST

- **CHOOSE TO REUSE: An Encyclopedia of Services, Products, Programs & Charitable Organizations That Foster Reuse** by Nikki & David Goldbeck   *450 pages, illustrated*
  This revolutionary guide is the first to show the ingenious ways that individuals, businesses and charitable organizations profit from reuse — the second environmental "R." More than 200 topics and 2000 resources from Air Filters to Zippers. A Book-of-the-Month Club selection.

- **THE SMART KITCHEN: How to Create a Comfortable, Safe, Energy-Efficient and Environment-Friendly Workspace** by David Goldbeck   *134 pages, illustrations, tables*

- **CLEAN & GREEN: The Complete Guide to Nontoxic and Environmentally Safe Housekeeping** by Annie Berthold-Bond   *174 pages*
  A hands-on, practical guide by the "green Heloise," providing innovative ideas for cleaning literally everything from the kitchen sink to pesticide-coated food to the family car. Over 485 cleaning recipes based on harmless, non-polluting, renewable ingredients. Includes brand name recommendations for environmentally safe store-bought products.

- **AMERICAN WHOLEFOODS CUISINE: 1300 Meatless, Wholesome Recipes from Short Order to Gourmet** by Nikki & David Goldbeck   *580 pages, hardcover, illustrated*
  Called the new "Joy of Cooking" by more than ten authorities from *Food & Wine* to *Vegetarian Times*, this major cookbook will introduce you to a new American-oriented cuisine that "tastes great and happens to be healthy." 1300 recipes, plus 300 pages of valuable kitchen information. Over 150,000 in print.

- **THE GOOD BREAKFAST BOOK: Making Breakfast Special** by Nikki & David Goldbeck   *180 pages, illustrated*
  Over 375 breakfast recipes, from elegant brunches to quick workday and schoolday "getaways." Attention to high fiber, complex carbohydrates and fat control. Includes recipes suitable for vegans and those with wheat, dairy and egg sensitivities.

- **EARTHLY BODIES & HEAVENLY HAIR: Natural and Healthy Personal Care for Every Body** by Dina Falconi   *240 pages, illustrated*
  The new bible of herbal body care.

ORDER FORM
(please copy)

__ *American Wholefoods Cuisine* / Paper $16.95 / Hardcover $29.95	$ _____
__ *The Smart Kitchen* / Paper $17.95	$ _____
__ *Choose To Reuse* / Paper $11.95	$ _____
__ *The Good Breakfast Book* / Paper $9.95	$ _____
__ *Earthly Bodies & Heavenly Hair* / Paper $14.95	$ _____
__ *Clean and Green* / Paper $9.95	$ _____
TOTAL FOR BOOKS	$ _____

SHIPPING: First book $3.00 (Canada $4.00); additional books $1.00 each.
For gifts, compute separate postage for each address. $ _____

NEW YORK STATE SALES TAX (applies to books and shipping) $ _____

TOTAL* $ _____

Name _____

Address _____ Zip _____

Credit Card # _____ Exp. Date _____

☐ MC ☐ VISA _____ Phone _____

All orders must be accompanied by payment in U.S. funds or charged to MC/VISA. Sorry, no CODs.

CERES PRESS • PO Box 87 SK8 • Woodstock, NY 12498 • Phone & Fax (914) 679-5573 Tollfree(888)804-8848